THE MOVE
by J.M.MacLeod

To Ruby

With affection,

J. MacLeod

John 16:13

"truth"

TATE PUBLISHING
AND ENTERPRISES, LLC

Published by Tate Publishing & Enterprises, LLC
127 E. Trade Center Terrace | Mustang, Oklahoma 73064 USA
1.888.361.9473 | www.tatepublishing.com

Tate Publishing is committed to excellence in the publishing industry. The company reflects the philosophy established by the founders, based on Psalm 68:11,
"The Lord gave the word and great was the company of those who published it."

Published in the United States of America

ISBN: 978-1-62563-349-1
1. Religion / Cults
2. Psychology / Mental Illness
13.05.23

TABLE OF CONTENTS

———•⋅⋈⋅•———

PART ONE

PART TWO

· · ❈ · ·

PART THREE

· · ❈ · ·

AUTHOR'S FOREWORD

The McComb's horrific story is true.

The Charismatic Revival of the 1970's brought upheaval and challenge to Evangelical Christianity giving rise to neo-Pentecostal denominations, the Jesus Freak and the House Church movements as well as the burgeoning popularity of Faith & Prosperity teachers.

Encountering otherworldly phenomena, Jonathan and Betsy McComb (pseudonyms) became deeply involved with a radical, charismatic group calling itself The Move of God, a spin-off of William Branham's Latter Rain movement.

Sam Fife, a Baptist preacher, received what he termed the "Baptism in the Holy Ghost" and subsequently believed that he was commissioned as an apostle to restore spiritual gifts and the five-fold ministry (Ephesians 4:11-13) to the Church. His parishioners also received "the Baptism" along with special end-time revelations, thus launching "The Move".

Taking many of Branham's teachings as well as his own dreams, epiphanies and original insights, Fife established numerous fellowships throughout the United States and abroad that supported his flourishing five-fold ministry, swelling to over 10,000 adherents by the early 1970's.

Fife taught that his group, a.k.a. The Manifested Sons of God (derived from Rom. 8:21) would develop dynamic spiritual power by living on wilderness farms and that they would emerge at the end of the Great Tribulation to liberate the world from Satan's grip.

Chronology of The Move: the Church at Sapa has been altered slightly; dialogue is accurate in content, albeit truncated, and where fabricated, kept true to form. Fife's teachings in this book are paraphrased from The Move's literature.

Names have been changed with the exception of Sam Fife and a couple of other well-known personalities. Some characters are composites.

It is the author's purpose to warn the reader that things which appear to be spiritual and godly might be deceptive underneath if they do not wholly conform to the Bible. John the apostle warns us to "…believe not every spirit, but test the spirits to see if they are of God; for many deceivers are gone out into the world… I Jn. 4:1

To the McComb's, their encounter with the Move made Christianity seem more vital and Scriptural than the fundamental denominations in which they grew up. They didn't look close enough…

The McComb's have recovered from the trauma they suffered while in The Move; though healed, they still bear scars.

Here is their story…

PROLOGUE

But they understood not that saying…Mark 9:32

SUNDAY, FEBRUARY 20, 1972

Jonathan McComb yearned for everything to be the way it had been, but, unless he could honestly discredit what he had seen, heard and experienced, there was no going back.

Just down the hall from Jon's room, at the head of the stairs, was a locked door. Animal-like mutterings and wild chattering emitted from behind that door. Jon's wife of less than a year, Betsy, was the source of those sounds.

Downstairs, the home-style church assembled from various areas surrounding Stroudsburg, Pennsylvania.

The house-church elders insisted Betsy's condition was due to demonic possession. Doctors had said Betsy's condition was a clear-cut case of clinical psychosis.

Jon wrestled in indecision: who was right, the doctors, or these Bible-thumping proponents of primitive Christianity? Should Jon take his demented bride and flee this potentially heretical group, or tenaciously cling to them as the fullest expression of truth he'd ever encountered?

Certain his face would betray doubt, Jonathan had purposely stayed upstairs to avoid the growing assemblage of worshippers. The bed creaked as he rolled over. "Jesus, don't let me make a mistake. I must know who's right?"

Betsy and Jon had gained a reputation for hungering after truth in what the adherents called The Move of God; he didn't want to be seen as he was now, riddled with fear and dark doubts.

Raised in fundamentalist, main-line denominational churches, Jon and Betsy McComb had recently been captivated by a new and exciting interpretation of scripture since attending Move meetings. Just a week prior, Betsy and Jon had been among those in the meeting waiting for the anointing to fall on someone with a revelation, song, or tongue and interpretation. Now, a week later, Jon's dreams and life were in shards.

Betsy's voice, cackling with riotous laughter and prattling meaningless phrases reverberated through the door again.

Incongruously, gentle singing wafted upstairs as if bearing a special message for Jon:

> "We're flowing, flowing, flowing into God…
> It takes a breaking, it takes a melting,
> It takes a breaking, it takes a melting—flowing into God."

The chorus was repeated, as if especially inviting Jon to put away fear, come downstairs, lift his hands, accept the breaking taking place in his life and flow into God.

Jon buried his head in the pillow sobbing, "Please Jesus, I have to know the truth, don't let me be deceived. Should I take Betsy to the hospital, or subject her to more futile deliverance sessions?"

Deliverance sessions: people surrounding Betsy, holding her in a chair, shouting in her face, "Come out demon, in Jesus' name!"

Would Betsy ever recover if her condition wasn't demons, but psychosis?

But if she truly was in the grips of demonic powers, modern psychiatry would only prescribe counseling and medication that would cover the symptoms but couldn't touch the spiritual nature of the problem. Demons would always be lurking just below the surface, stirring up confusion, depression and madness, a fate as bad, if not worse, than having emotional scars from unnecessary exorcism.

Jon swung his feet over the side of the bed. He heard voices in his mind:

"The Move is genuine, New Testament Christianity."

"You're a fool to risk so much by trusting them."

Was he going insane, too?

In the few short weeks he'd been exposed to the Move, what did Jon really know about the people he was entreated to trust? Were they an authentic expression of Christianity—or a cult? Did they teach truth or oppose biblical teaching?

J.M. MACLEOD

Jon had been raised in a home that revered the Bible; in the midst of this storm, the Bible now loomed as the only rock to which he could cling. If he could discover any teaching or practice of the Move's that opposed God's Word he could, in good conscience, take Betsy to a hospital. On the other hand, if all conformed to Scripture...

Jon lay back down and stared at the cracked ceiling. How could he feel loyalty to this group and yet have misgivings at the same time? Where did the truth lay? Was truth to be found by reviewing the steps that brought them to this group?

How had this nightmare begun?

PART ONE

CHAPTER ONE

... for the times past of our lives... I Peter 4:3

SATURDAY, JUNE 5, 1971

"I do," Jon said, looking into the bright green eyes of his fiancée-turned-wife. He grinned as Betsy repeated, "I do," after Jon's brother-in-law pastor, Lionel Kyle. In an instant they changed from sweethearts to husband and wife, braving the future with optimism borne of brash naïveté.

Jon and Betsy met in a small Christian college, fell madly in love, and were married by June. Their only plans for the future were to go to Indiana where Jon had a temporary summer job as director of a Christian coffeehouse. Starry-eyed and confident, the newly-weds set forth.

Betsy's parents had offered no objections, for they—especially Betsy's Dad—believed that the chief purpose of life was to marry and have kids; then find out what life was all about. Nor did Jon's parents oppose the marriage; they hoped the responsibility of marriage would settle him down. Thus, with parental blessings, Jon and Betsy loaded their few possessions in Jon's vintage Rambler and headed west.

Syracuse, Indiana, on lake Wawasee, was a sleepy little town, served spiritually by one Roman Catholic and five Protestant churches. The five Protestant churches had jointly opened an evangelistic coffeehouse venture dubbed "The Sign of the Fish," to reach the area youth with the gospel as a counter-measure to the worldly pull of the Chicago Seven, hallucinogenic drugs and the sexual revolution. Jon, having previously been involved in a Campus Life coffeehouse, had been hired mid-way through the previous summer to manage the Sign of the Fish. The original director had been fired for not being an example of the believer in faith and purity. Thus it was that Jon returned in 1971 to continue the summer ministry—with a wife in tow.

Only a handful of the coffeehouse regulars returned as the summer started, and those who showed up were more interested in anti-establishment rhetoric, sex, drugs and rock 'n' roll than in talking about Jesus.

The young marriage was off to a rocky start as well. The honeymoon brought stark reality crashing in on the starry-eyed couple. Betsy was abandoned for hours on end in a dank, dark apartment with no TV, radio, friends or anything with which to divert herself.

Meanwhile, Jon ran into various roadblocks trying to get the coffeehouse up and running again. When he came home in the evening after a frustrating day, Betsy wanted all his attention, but he was too tired and frustrated to comply. Arguments and hurt feelings ensued. They both questioned what they'd gotten themselves into.

After a week of bickering, Jon wondered if Betsy might be heading for a psychotic breakdown. She'd had one before they'd met. In fact, when they met in college, Betsy was still recovering. A new wonder drug, lithium, had been tried with good results, and in Betsy's case, brought dramatic results. Her dad had told Jon, "You won't have any trouble as long as she takes her medicine." After praying about it, Jon felt assured that everything would be all right. But now, watching his pretty young bride reduced to emotional outbursts every night, he wondered.

One night Jon came home and found things had taken a turn for the weird. Betsy wanted to talk about a neighborhood Bible study she'd attended. She said, " ...So, Marge told me about a time when she and Grace actually demanded a demon to come out of one of their friends!"

"Demons!" Jon said. "Are they out of their minds? America doesn't have demons, at least none of any significance. Demons inhabit places where they're worshipped, like Africa, South America and India, not here."

"Well, I don't know," Betsy said, "… they seemed pretty confident."

"Well, demons have nothing to do with us," Jon said, remembering talks the two had had when Betsy confided fears that her breakdowns were caused by the Devil. "We're born-again Christians, and everybody knows Christians can't have demons. What you have is chemical, purely chemical, not demonic. As long as you take lithium, those problems are behind us."

Betsy cast her eyes around the room. "I hope you're right. Even so, spooky things have been happening all afternoon."

A chill ran down Jon's spine. "Spooky?"

"Footsteps on the stairway when there's no one there. Taps on the door, slurred voices coming from... from..."

Jon embraced his shivering wife. "It's just your imagination, that's all. Those kooks got you all stirred up." He wished he were as confident as he sounded. Their dark apartment did suddenly appear malevolent. He tried to shake it off by changing the topic. "Anyway, I found an apartment for us up in Syracuse."

"Really?" Hope shone from her eyes. "I hate this musty old place. It bothers me to be alone. I want to be where you are, working with hippies."

"Yeah, I'd like that too. And I wouldn't have that forty-mile drive every day. I'll put a down payment on it tomorrow."

And so they moved to Syracuse. With permission from the pastoral board, Jon changed the name of the coffeehouse from "Sign of the Fish" to "Ichthus" lest hippie astrologers get the wrong idea. But instead of the ideal lakefront café with dock and swimming area that they'd had the previous summer, the only place Jon found to relocate the ministry was an unused cinder-block garage. It wasn't a cool hang out like the other place, but it was the only site available.

Everything connected with the ministry was also at low ebb: Jon's weekly reports were in a downhill trend—less people dropping in, less money in the offering, less witnessing, and less usefulness for the director. Why was everything at a standstill? Hadn't they prayed, believing this was God's will?

Making matters worse, Betsy and Jon argued frequently. More often than not, Jon returned home to their unfurnished efficiency apartment after a day of uselessness to meet a disgruntled bride who expected more out of life than staring at bare walls.

One particular argument was about the new charismatic move sweeping through churches, including a nearby Christian coffeehouse in North Webster called "The Glory Barn." Jon was opposed to any and all such religious emotionalism.

Betsy took exception and was just as adamant, relating that a godly woman in her home church began speaking in tongues spontaneously during her prayer time. "I'm telling you, Jon, it wasn't wild; she just found herself praying in a strange language one day."

"This was your pastor's wife?" Jon fumed because Betsy wouldn't admit that the charismatic gifts were superfluous since the completion of the Bible. They pulled into a grocery store lot. Jon shut off the ignition.

It started raining.

"Yes, and a sweeter, more mature Christian you couldn't find. Besides, where does it say in the Bible that tongues were only for the first century?"

Jon had heard numerous expositors prove that tongues were no longer viable. Everybody knew that his denomination had the best Bible expositors, everybody except Betsy, that is. Jon grabbed a Bible from the glove box and flipped to I Corinthians, confident of finding the right verse.

Outside, it rained harder.

"Well, I'm waiting."

"It's here, it's here." Jon's frustration grew as he searched.

"Do you mean I Corinthians 13:8?"

Jon turned there, '...whether there be tongues, they shall cease...'. "Yeah, that's it!" He was embarrassed that she knew the verse, but, alright, that answered the challenge.

"Well, if that's true, knowledge has passed away as well. Doesn't the same verse say something about knowledge passing away too?"

Jon's knuckles grew white gripping the steering wheel. "Well, that's not what I was looking for, then. There must be another verse that makes it plainer."

Instead of letting up as they had expected, the rain turned into a downpour. The couple sat silently for several minutes. There was no chance of leaving the car without a severe drenching.

The windows steamed up; still the rain pelted down.

"Jon, listen to what the Bible says..." Betsy read chapters twelve, thirteen and fourteen as rain drummed on the convertible roof. When finished she asked, "Why would the Holy Spirit put so much instruction in the Bible about these gifts if they were to pass away within the next hundred years?"

"But that letter was to the corrupt church at Corinth," Jon shouted above the din on the roof. "They were perverts. That's the kind of church that goes for that emotional, exhibitionist stuff."

"Mrs. Moyer wasn't a pervert. Besides, all the apostles had Holy Spirit gifts, and they weren't perverts. It says ...forbid not to speak with tongues.... And I do know that she almost always had her prayers answered."

"Well, that proves nothing."

Jon knew the woman of which Betsy spoke. She was a capable pastor's wife, mother of nine children, one of whom was autistic, and her love and care both in and beyond her family was well known. Jon stewed; he'd lost the argument.

Then a sobering thought crossed his mind. Was he arguing against truth? He certainly didn't want to oppose truth. Was there a sensible approach to the gifts of the Holy Spirit, an approach that didn't lend itself to emotional exhibitionism? Did his denomination know everything? He must tread cautiously lest he resist the Holy Spirit. But, he didn't want to give in too easily, either.

"Well... maybe... in rare cases, God might still do these things. But the way most holy-roller groups carry on has little or no relationship to what you read," he said, though he'd never witnessed a Pentecostal or Charismatic service in his life.

"I agree, Jon. But you just can't condemn the whole experience. That's all I'm saying," Betsy gingerly reached over and touched his hand, hoping for a truce.

The rain stopped; sunlight sparkled through the droplets on the windows. They were free to get out and do their shopping.

But, something in Jon had changed.

Weeks later Betsy's mom sent an unexpected source of encouragement. Included in a care package of clothing was a small book, Prison to Praise by Merlin Carothers. Jon didn't really want to read it, but it promised temporary relief from brooding over the dismal state of the coffeehouse ministry. Betsy, due to another argument, had retired to the bedroom, weeping, making Jon feel more ogre-like than ever.

"Looks like another formula bad-guy-gets-saved story," Jon muttered. He grabbed a pillow, settled on the living room floor and began reading. He soon became engrossed in the drama of young, hard-core-sinner Merlin's life. Jon was surprised when Merlin became born-again toward the beginning of the book. "So, what's the rest of the book about?"

Merlin became a chaplain and wanted to help others find Christ's forgiveness. Jon identified with Merlin: both felt called to ministry, both desired to be strong in the faith, both wanted to glorify the Lord with their lives. But then, Merlin ran into problems; personal problems. A sense of failure and frustration, worthlessness and futility overshadowed him. Jon's identification with Merlin was growing. Merlin questioned whether God had really called him to ministry—the very point Jon was at.

All thought of time was forgotten. How did Merlin eventually overcome failure in his life and ministry? Jon read on.

Merlin and a friend were invited to a Christian retreat. Thinking he might find answers, Merlin decided to go. They realized too late that it was a Charismatic retreat. They decided to stay, after all, how much harm could a weekend surrounded by religious crazies do? During the teaching and testimonies Merlin felt a need for the Holy Spirit's power in his life and ministry. He had been born again, justified by Christ's blood, indwelt by the Holy Spirit, just as Jesus had promised, yet he wasn't experiencing the Spirit's power in his own life, much less counseling or preaching. He often doubted God would answer his prayers.

Several people gathered around him offering answers to his questions. Before long they laid hands on him and prayed—some in strange languages. Carothers was startled at hearing tongues for the first time, but the loving gentleness of the people persuaded him that he wasn't in any danger.

Jon laid the book down and stretched his arms overhead. "Hoo-boy! How's he going to get out of this wacky group unscathed?" When Jon resumed reading, his Baptist soul was jolted into full alert. Merlin claimed to have received the Baptism in the Holy Spirit! "I can't believe Merlin fell for that!" Jon skimmed ahead, expecting Merlin to expose the experience as false, or else, embrace some doctrine so bizarre that Jon could say, "Aha! He wasn't really saved!" But Merlin merely went on to describe the joy that transformed his life, and not his life only, but his ministry as well. He became effective, bringing people into the kingdom and teaching them to live victoriously.

"Gotta be an error here somewhere." Jon reread the book from the beginning, scrutinizing every detail, looking for something—anything—to disprove Merlin's testimony. When Jon again reached the part where Merlin received the Baptism of the Holy Spirit, he paused.

Jon was aware of the debate raging among noted theologians on both sides of the issue, but since losing the "tongues" argument in the grocery store parking lot, "expert" assertions didn't carry as much weight.

Jon felt a nagging emptiness in his own soul. In the depths of his being he wanted the Holy Spirit to fill him; he wanted to know that the God of the Bible was the same yesterday, today, and forever. In addition to being torn between the testimony in his hands and the doctrines he'd heard growing up, Jon had to admit that he was terrified to release complete control of his being to Jesus, even his tongue, if, indeed, the Spirit would give him a prayer language.

"If this is true, and it's still for today, don't you want it?"

Jon cocked his head. Was that the Lord... or his own thought?

Did the source matter? The question was valid.

Suddenly, nothing else mattered; if he could know God in a fuller way, experience His power in his life and ministry... A desire to know Jesus deeper welled up from within. "Jesus," Jon prayed "... I don't know if all this about being baptized in the Holy Spirit is still for today. Please protect me from deception; I'm not clever enough to sort out the arguments for and against. I don't know if You still do those things today—and if You don't, please protect me. But if the Baptism in the Holy Spirit is of You, and if it's still for today, I need the Holy Spirit's power in my life. Please, Lord, baptize me in Your Holy Spirit."

Jon half expected something dramatic: trumpets blaring, angels flitting about, maybe a voice from heaven ... What actually took place surprised him. He was swept up in a current of intense joy and a deeper love for Jesus, culminating in a fuller realization of how much Jesus loved him. Verses flooded his mind ...if a son asked for a fish, his father wouldn't substitute a serpent...

An intense awareness of Jesus' presence like he'd never known rose up and out of some inner recess, permeating his emotions and mind. Tears coursed down his cheeks and still this rapturous phenomenon continued. There was no question; Jesus was blessing him with the Holy Spirit. Throughout the experience, Jon was aware that, although this sensation didn't originate with him, he was in control of letting it flow or making it stop, as he willed.

"It's real," Jon sobbed aloud. "It's for today!" Long stifled emotions were expressed in waves of thanksgiving. "It's real, oh thank You, Jesus, it's real, it's still for today."

Betsy cautiously poked her head through a narrow opening in the doorway. "Jon, are you okay?"

Jon looked up.

Betsy had never seen Jon like this, rocking to and fro on the floor, tears streaming down his face, saying, "It's real, oh, it's for today, thank You, Jesus, I love You, Jesus."

Jon tried to explain, but all that came from his lips was, "Oh honey, it's real... it's for today!"

CHAPTER TWO

And these signs shall follow them that believe... Mark 16:17

Betsy wasn't sure how to handle the new Jon. They'd only been married a couple of months and she'd already learned that he could be moody. During those times Betsy was better off steering clear. But the new Jon was cheerful, optimistic, helpful—and hungry to read the Bible and pray.

At one point Jon thought Jesus wanted to give him the gift of tongues. The very idea was scary—yielding his tongue even to the Holy Spirit, but, he decided, if Jesus was the One doing it, it would be safe. So he sat, waiting for his tongue to start moving by itself. Nothing happened. A couple of unusual syllables came to mind, but the Spirit didn't take control of his tongue.

After three days of seventh heaven, however, Jon's joy subsided. Jon wondered if it was because he hadn't pursued speaking in tongues. A few days of living in the bright sunshine of spiritual blessing didn't negate the need to repudiate sin, and Jon was soon burdened again by some old habits. Within a week he was depressed again. After two weeks, all vestige of the spiritual blessing was gone; he barely remembered the touch he'd received from the Lord.

Betsy and Jon closed out the summer ministry on that sour note—with the added knowledge that Betsy was pregnant. They left Indiana and moved back to Pennsylvania, settling into a small apartment in Tannersville as discouraged newlyweds.

Jon found a factory job, but spiritually was in a slump. He didn't want to go to his parents' fundamentalist church. His new beliefs and experience, faded though it was, would make him a pariah. Jon was reluctant to try a Pentecostal assembly due to rumors about people speaking blasphemies in obscure languages or swinging from chandeliers. So he stayed away from all Christian fellowship.

Betsy, however, couldn't accept Jon's self-imposed isolation. One day she approached him about her attending a woman's Bible study and he reluctantly agreed. Betsy's delivery date was near, and Jon thought it would be good for her to socialize with people before giving birth when she would, of necessity, be more or less confined to their apartment.

So it was that Jon was alone in the apartment in early December listening to rock music, waiting for Betsy's return from the Bible study. His sullen mood matched the music. He anticipated Betsy precipitating a discussion about church attendance. She undoubtedly would have met some nice people that he would "just have to meet". He wasn't in the mood. Christmas, just a couple of weeks away, was going to be sparse, indeed they barely had enough money for food, rent and utilities. Jon got up and stretched his legs, wanting his wife to come home so he could lock the door and go to bed.

The album finished and another disc slipped over the spindle, pulsing out shadowy harmonics to a driving beat when Jon heard the crunch of tires in the driveway below.

"Hi Hon, I'm home," Betsy called cheerily as she came up the steps. "Guess what?" Without giving him a chance to guess, she continued, "I met a lady tonight who believes in being baptized in the Holy Spirit."

He feigned interest.

Betsy continued, "She goes to another Bible study group where everybody believes in the baptism of Holy Spirit. She attends your parents' church, but also worships with believers who know how to let the Holy Spirit give revelations. Jonathan, do you think we might go... together?"

"Aw Betsy, you don't know what you're getting into with those Pentecostal types. I mean, you have to be real careful about what they teach and do."

"I wish you'd come to church with me, any church. I thought that maybe you'd like a home-style church where they believe the way you do. You're so cynical, especially of late."

"Betsy, you just don't understand. Things aren't that easy. Everything is a struggle: the Christian life, reading the Bible, prayer, even sitting like a bump on a pew would be such a chore... I just want to be a normal person. I'm born again, that's enough. Let somebody else save the world. I just want to raise our family and be like everybody else."

The light in Betsy's eyes faded. "Life isn't hard for me. It's just like Jesus said it would be—easy, and His yoke is light. I don't understand why you treat life as such a battle all the time."

"Because, it is a battle. Oh, don't pay me any mind. I'm just depressed. Nothing I say makes sense. Look if it makes you feel better, you go to those Bible studies, but don't involve me, okay?"

"I'd really like you to come with me. I know just getting out of this apartment would be good for you. I'm sure you'd like the people. Mrs. Dymond said there are young couples like us that attend."

"Mrs. Dymond?"

"She's the lady who goes to your folks' church on Sunday and the home meeting Tuesday night. During the discussion she said something about healing and tongues, so I talked with her afterwards, asking her point blank what she knew about spiritual gifts. Jon, I believe the Lord led me to her. Please, let's go."

"No," Jon said firmly. "You go if you want, but don't involve me. And be careful about any weird stuff they might pull."

The following Tuesday night Jon skimmed a Vonnegut novel as a winter chill crept into their flat. He found concentration on Cat's Cradle difficult. Finally, the '67 Chevy BelAir pulled in. Betsy climbed the stairs, entered the room, wordlessly placed her Bible on the table and hung up her coat. "Jon, they are the deepest Christians I've ever met."

Jon cocked his head; his appetite was surprisingly whetted. "Really?"

"They have such a profound understanding of the Bible—they believe that denominationalism is wrong. And ... they're sure the Tribulation is about to begin."

Jon's ears perked up. "Do they think they know when the rapture will occur? After all, nobody is supposed to know that."

"They don't believe there's going to be a rapture and they can prove it from the Bible." Betsy sat on a footstool opposite her husband and continued, "There weren't many there, only six or seven—mostly all ladies, except for Mr. Dymond, Alice's husband. But he slept most of the time."

"But Betsy, the Bible clearly says there is a rapture."

"Maybe, but not before the Antichrist rises to power. They showed it to me in Second Thessalonians. You know, as they explained the end times, it does look like the Church will go through the Tribulation. And they showed me other verses."

Jon grabbed his Scofield Reference Bible and turned to II Thessalonians.

Let no man deceive you by any means; for that day will not come except there come the falling away first, and that man of sin be revealed, the son of perdition…

Hmmm, it does seem as if the Antichrist will come first, at least from this verse. That's discomforting."

Betsy continued, "Minnie—she's one of the elders—says that the falling away is the denominational church system—even Bible believing churches, because they deny the power of the Holy Spirit and put people to sleep with their Pre-Trib Rapture Theory. The Antichrist will catch them all asleep and brand them with "666" before they know what's happening."

"That's pretty heavy. Are you sure you understood?"

"They also showed me a lot of other errors we were taught."

"Wait just a minute. I've been taught the Bible all my life, and I know that of all denominations, ours are as close to the truth as any."

"Jon, you know yourself that their understanding of spiritual gifts and the Baptism of the Holy Spirit is wrong. Maybe there's more they got wrong. If you were to meet Minnie and Sonya, you'd see how wise they are. You can even feel the anointing, er, spiritual power, around them."

"Maybe I will go," Jon said. "After all, I teethed on the Bible growing up. I think I can give them a run for their money."

———··✄··———

Jon was jittery as Betsy guided him to the house-church that next Friday night. "They meet at a house because that's the scriptural example, in this case, Minnie Eastman's home," Betsy explained," … that way their tithe money goes for more important things than upkeep on a building that's used twice a week."

The more Betsy told him, the more Jon liked the way this group thought.

"Turn here," Betsy pointed to a small road. "It's the half double with the porch light on. I know you're going to like this."

"I hope you're right. Look," Jon said," … if something doesn't set right, we'll leave, okay?"

"Okay, but I know you're going to enjoy this."

Jon and Betsy stamped snow off their shoes and entered the old house. Enough folding chairs to accommodate twenty-five to thirty people filled the room. "I had no idea this many people were expected," Jon whispered as they edged their way to some unoccupied seats.

Betsy grinned. "Oh look, there's Mr. and Mrs. Dymond." Jon saw a dignified, elderly couple nodding at them; he smiled in return.

"So nice to see you again, Betsy," Mrs. Dymond said. "Is this your husband? Nice to meet you, Mr. McComb."

Betsy returned a greeting and chatted for a moment before taking a seat. More people filed into the room. The chairs were set in three semi-circular tiers, so that everyone could see everyone else. There was a podium set up in the middle-front, facing the chairs. A middle-aged woman, nearer sixty than fifty, bustled about in the adjoining room, making last minute adjustments to the refreshment table.

A younger woman in the front row strummed an Autoharp. There was something vaguely familiar about her—then Jon remembered. She had been one of his student teachers in high school. Small world!

People began energetically singing:

"Lift Jesus higher, Lift Jesus higher…"

Jon liked the bright, happy tune. He sang along, tapping his foot. Betsy glanced at him with an "I told you so" look. Other songs were sung with equal enthusiasm. Every now and then someone with a rapt look upon their face raised one or both hands. Compared with what Jon had expected, everything seemed rather tame.

Half an hour later the singing stopped; everyone sat in silence, as if waiting. Then a woman from across the room spoke: "Oh my children, do you not know the hour is late? You must learn to rise up and be sons of God. Realize who you are; you are my sons, called to set Creation free from the grip of Satan and sin. Behold, three trumpets have sounded. It is time to assemble in the holy place and seek Me there."

It dawned on Jon that this was what Paul referred to as a prophecy. Jon mulled the prophecy over. He recalled that there were seven trumpets mentioned in Revelation, and this prophecy had said something about the third trumpet. Jon flipped his Bible open and read silently from Revelation 8:

And the third angel sounded, and there fell a great star from heaven, burning as though it were a lamp. And it fell upon a third part of the rivers and the fountains of waters. And the name of the star is called Wormwood, and many men died of the waters because they were made bitter.

Was the prophecy saying that the Tribulation was already well under way—even up to the third trumpet? Jon looked up and was startled to see Minnie smiling at him.

"If you feel you have something to share," Minnie said, "…just go to the podium and share it."

Betsy had previously explained their format: that anyone who felt the "anointing", i.e. the leading of the Holy Spirit, was supposed to stand up and teach. Jon was flattered that they thought that he, a first-timer, might have something worthwhile to say. Maybe he was more spiritual than he thought…

Jon picked his way toward the podium. He had no idea what he was going to say, but the modus operandi of this group was to "let the Lord fill your mouth." He glanced at his expectant audience. The only one with a surprised expression was Betsy.

Jon read the passage aloud, then said, "I really don't know much about prophecy and all that stuff, but it seems to me that the Lord is saying that the Tribulation has started." That was it. He could think of nothing more to say, and so wended his way back to Betsy's side. Betsy took and squeezed his hand.

From the resulting silence, Jon couldn't tell if what he'd said was so weighty it stilled the meeting, or altogether foolish and everybody felt embarrassed for him.

Minnie broke the silence. "I believe the Lord was referring to the trumpets that were blown at the various festivals rather than one of the trumpets of Revelation. But we certainly are grateful for pointing out that scripture."

Jon felt he was about to be stoned, but all he encountered were friendly looks. Minnie's eyes were full of encouragement. Jon's heart went out to this room of gentle people then and there.

The meeting continued with some more songs, often followed by quiet worshipping in tongues and upraised hands; a few people gave testimony about the Lord speaking to them during the week or meeting a specific need; then Sonya gave a teaching about becoming the sons of God. Then the meeting was over.

Betsy and Jon were invited to partake of the refreshments. They chatted with various folks, and when it was discovered that Jon played guitar, Minnie and Sonya (the autoharpist) insisted he bring it sometime and play along. Jon reluctantly agreed, wondering how his rock 'n' roll style would fit in with their gentle praises.

Jon had many questions, but both elders, Minnie and Sonya, were pressed by other body members who sought prayer or counseling, so his questions had to wait. As it was, Betsy and Jon had a lot to chew on. Jon's blunder had been quickly forgotten as Sonya taught about the Manifestation of the Sons of God from Romans chapter Eight.

Sparse snowflakes drifted down from the sky as Jon and Betsy drove home in meditative silence. Jon was impressed. Betsy beamed.

The following Tuesday Jon occupied himself by changing strings on his twelve-string guitar while awaiting Betsy's return from the women's meeting. Since the Body had expressed interest, Jon renewed playing his guitar. He was still fine-tuning the new strings when Betsy arrived home.

Jon looked up expectantly. "Hi. How'd things go?"

Betsy had an enigmatic expression. "Well," she grinned sheepishly, "… I was prayed for to receive the Baptism of the Holy Spirit."

"And?"

She put her coat away and sat beside Jon. "They wanted to know all about us: when we were born again; what churches we went to; what we believed, things like that. When they asked about whether we believed in "the Baptism", I told them what happened to you in Indiana."

"What'd they say?"

"They smiled when I told them how you sat on the floor crying over and over, 'it's real, it's real.'"

"Who was there?" Though he hardly knew them, Jon wanted to be highly regarded by these people. They were so friendly, and had such a vibrant faith. Jon had been to Faith at Works, Young Life, Campus Life, and Intervarsity, but these people were different. Jesus was all they lived for. Most Christians that Jon and Betsy knew put their Christianity on and off like a coat. These Body people, or, "the Move", as they sometimes referred to themselves, had re-awakened a stirring in Jon for a deeper, committed life. He didn't even know if their interpretation of scripture was accurate, or their prophecies authentic, but, he reasoned, these questions would be settled in due time.

Betsy answered, "let me see… there was Minnie, Sonya, a woman named Millie Jackson I hadn't met before, and another Minnie, and a middle-aged couple from New Jersey named Larry and Mary. There were only a few."

"Not Alice Dymond?"

"Oh yes. Alice and Jack were there too. But let me get on with what I was telling you."

"Okay, I'm sorry. What happened?"

"Well, after I told them about your experience, Minnie asked if I'd ever been baptized in the Spirit. I told her how we prayed with Barney and Andrea when we first got home from Indiana, but that nothing happened."

"I didn't know you prayed with Barney and Andrea."

"Well, not Barney, just Andrea—when you and Barney went out for that long walk. Andie and I talked about the Baptism, then she prayed for me to receive it, laying her hands on my head and shoulders."

"I didn't know that."

"I didn't want you to know—because—nothing happened, well almost nothing."

"Almost?"

"A kind of spooky feeling came over us as we prayed. We were both frightened. Andrea explained that Satan was hindering me from receiving the Baptism. That really scared me. You know how I've always been afraid that Satan is going to appear to me."

"What did you do?"

"Andrea prayed and commanded a demon of fear to go away."

"And...?"

"The spookiness got stronger. We both got goose bumps." Betsy's eyes were downcast.

"I remember," Jon said, "… that you couldn't sleep that night? Oh Hon, you should have told me."

"I know, I know," she said. "I was just ashamed of not being as spiritual as you. You never told me what happened with Barney on that long walk."

"Oh, it's not important," Jon said. "I'll tell you some other time. Right now, tell me about tonight."

"Sonya and Minnie told me that a spirit of fear had indeed attacked to hinder me. Then Sonya asked if I'd like to be prayed for again. I was nervous, but they assured me that they knew what to do if demons—they call them 'the enemy'—attacked. They seemed so sure, that I agreed.

"First they bound enemy spirits from interfering. Then Sonya and Minnie, and one or two others, gathered around my chair and laid hands on my head and shoulders. Someone started speaking in tongues, others joined in. Then someone, I think it was Sonya, prayed out loud for Jesus to send His Holy Spirit upon me."

"Did you feel that joy well up from within?" Jon asked, recalling his own experience.

"Not exactly," Betsy said. "But I did speak in tongues. I said 'Santo, santo, santo' over and over." There was a hint of a smile at the corners of her mouth.

"Did anybody interpret?"

"Sonya told me that 'santo', in Spanish, means 'holy'. And I didn't know that, so I must have been baptized in the Holy Spirit, right?"

"I guess so," Jon said. "I expected tongues but got an emotional rush, I guess it can work the other way around too."

"Well, they took it as a sign that their prayers were answered," Betsy said. "Minnie said I should keep saying that word over and over until more words came. She called it 'praying in the spirit'."

"Santo, huh?" Jon toyed with the idea of repeating santo until he got a complete language too.

"Jon?" Betsy interrupted. "Did you pray with Barney to receive the gift of tongues?"

They prepared for bed. Jon glanced at the prominent bulge beneath Betsy's night-gown that was soon to be their first-born, trying to think of a way to evade the question. "Uh, yeah, we uh, prayed."

"And?"

"And, well... I don't know. Look, I have to get up early for work. I'll tell you another time," Jon put out the light and crawled into bed. He didn't sleep right away, remembering the disappointment he'd felt when Barney and he knelt by the roadside praying for Jon to receive a prayer language.

———•✄•·——

When Jon's coffeehouse job had ended in September Betsy and Jon returned to Pennsylvania, stopping briefly at her parents' farm in Sunbury. By coincidence, Barney and Andrea, friends from college, happened to be visiting their own parents in Sunbury. They decided to give Betsy's parents a call to see when Jon and Betsy were expected back. After a long day's drive, the last thing Jon wanted to do was sit up all night with some college acquaintances.

Betsy's brother, Ron, handed the phone to his sister. "It's for you."

Betsy chatted with Andrea for a few moments, then told Jon that they'd like to visit. Jon shook his head. Barney and Jon had been friendly rivals on campus, so Jon wasn't eager to see them. Betsy handed Jon the phone. "He insists."

Jon sighed and took the receiver. "Hello Barney, look, Betsy and I just got in from Indiana, and all we want to do is relax and see a movie in town tonight..."

"Praise the Lord Jonathan, I'm glad you're here," Barney began, not listening to Jon's lame excuse. "I've got something really terrific to share with you."

"Uh, like I said, not tonight. Maybe some other—."

"Jon, it's really important that I talk with you. Something dynamic happened to me this summer, glory to Jesus, and I've just got to tell you. I know what, Andrea and I will go to the movie too—what's playing?"

Jon glanced at the paper. "The Hellstrom Chronicle. Looks like an end-of-the-world-by-rampant-bugs scenario." Jon felt himself weakening.

"Praise the Lord. We'll meet you there, and afterward follow you back out to Betsy's folks, okay? This thing that happened to me—Hallelujah! You'll never believe it!"

Jon cupped his hand over the phone and whispered, "I think Barney got saved this summer. Maybe he was one of those people who thought they were saved, but weren't."

"Oh Jon," Betsy chided, "Barney's been a Christian as long as I have."

"Well, maybe he just thought he was. That happens a lot you know."

"Hello? Jon, are you still there?" the voice on the phone persisted.

"Uh, yeah, Barney, I'm here. We'll meet you at the theater about 7:15." Jon hated himself for caving in.

"Hallelujah! See you then."

Jon looked hopelessly at Betsy. "What else could I do?"

—··✗··—

Barney had an even bigger smile than Jon remembered, and Andrea had a certain sparkle about her, too. The four college friends sat around the table in the Rutlidge's spacious country kitchen. The movie had been a documentary on insects taking over the world. Even that dour topic didn't dent Barney's glee.

"So, what's so important?" Jon hadn't really wanted to ask, but knew Barney and Andrea wouldn't leave until the subject had been broached.

"Hallelujah!" Barney's smile intensified. "I got baptized in the Holy Spirit this summer!"

Jon's mouth dropped open; that old, familiar hunger stirred within. Barney told them about a Bible study that taught the Spirit-filled life. Jon recalled his own experience, and his desire for the gift of tongues.

"Barney, I've got to talk to you, alone. Let's go for a walk."

"Sure Jon."

The two stepped out into the crisp air. It was 1:A.M., not a soul stirred in the farming community. The sky scudded over with clouds threatening to drop their burden of rain; but there was enough ambient light by which to see. As they walked, Jon told him about the Indiana coffeehouse, his sense of failure, how, he too, had received the Baptism in the Holy Spirit, but somehow lost its effect, and he was back in the same old rut.

Barney quoted verses and tried to give wise counsel.

"Listen Barney," Jon interrupted, "… can't we just pray—now?"

Barney placed his hand on Jon's shoulder as they knelt side by side in front of some farmer's house. It was close to 2:A.M.

"Jesus," Barney began, " Now I know why I felt such urgency. Please Lord, fill Jon again with your Spirit—and Lord, please give him the gift of tongues so he can keep his anointing."

Jon then prayed, "Lord, I know you give good gifts to your people. Please refill me with your Spirit, and give me the gift of tongues."

Barney prayed in tongues, his right hand on Jon's shoulder, his left hand extended to the sky as if he were going to grasp the gift and pull it down for Jon.

Jon waited, wondering when his tongue was going to move. Nothing happened. In fact, Jon was emotionally dry. There was no sweet sense of Jesus' presence as he'd felt in Indiana. Barney kept praying, restless because nothing was happening and uncomfortable from kneeling on the gravel berm. He stood, his hand still upon Jon's shoulder, praying louder.

A dog began woofing. At any moment a light would come on and some irate farmer with a shotgun would charge out, wanting to know who was speaking in tongues in his yard at this ungodly hour.

Jon realized that it wasn't going to happen.

Barney was oblivious. He was so intent on Jon getting blessed that he was willing to stay there until dawn. For the last half-hour he'd besought heaven for Jon, faithfully pressing in. Jon, not wanting to let Barney down, tried to imitate the sounds Barney made. The result was a mishmash that sounded nothing like any language Jon had ever heard. Nevertheless, Barney was satisfied. He shouted triumphantly.

Suddenly Barney grew quiet. He stood with both hands straight up, his head thrown back, eyes gazing at the full moon overhead. "It's a sign!" he said.

"What do you mean?" Jon asked, goose bumps rising on his neck.

"The moon. When we came out, the whole sky was cloudy. But look—the entire sky is still cloudy except for right around the moon. Satan's darkness has been taken off your mind and God's light is shining through."

"Really?" Jon was uncertain how to handle this information. Would God change the weather just to give him a sign? Or... had Jon just spent the last couple of hours with a nut?

"But look Barney, are you sure it's a sign? Clouds are covering the moon again."

"That just means that Satan is going to try to rob you. But don't worry, God's light is more powerful than the Devil's darkness," Barney said. And as soon as he spoke, the clouds cleared away again.

They walked back with limited conversation, but upon arrival at the Rutlidge farm, Jon grabbed Barney's arm and pointed to the sky. Stars were visible. "Well, it looks like a sign to me too, Barney. The weather bureau predicted rain."

Barney and Andrea left within minutes. As Jon closed the door he heard a strange, rustling sound. Opening the door and looking out, he discovered it was raining.

Jon pondered these events of so many months ago as he drifted off to sleep. "Hmmm, Santos, santos, santos...."

CHAPTER THREE

...Have we not prophesied in Thy name? Matthew 7:22

JANUARY 7, 1972

After the meeting Betsy and Jon sat at the kitchen table pummeling Minnie with questions. There were so many new insights from the Bible they'd never seen or heard preached before. Since attending the first meeting, Jon had applied himself anew to the scriptures. Due to harsh weather, not many had shown up for tonight's meeting, but the few who had braved the elements enjoyed a sweet time of song and prayer. Betsy and Jon stayed after to ask questions. They particularly wanted to quiz Minnie about the Move's departures from denominational Christianity. They already knew the Move opposed the fundamentalist teaching against the Baptism and gifts of the Holy Spirit and the Pre-Trib Rapture. The Baptist tradition in which Jon had grown up appeared shallow in light of the Move's teachings. His own experience with the Baptism of the Holy Spirit backed up Minnie's teaching, only she went deeper, dazzling the newlyweds with profound spiritual insights.

"Just how did this body start, anyway?" Jon asked.

Minnie sat back and smiled. "Let me see, it was about a year ago, I suppose, yes, just about a year—maybe a little over a year, that I was invited to a Charismatic convention at Gray Ledges in New England. I went with some church people."

"Which church was that?" Betsy asked.

"South-Side Assemblies."

"A Pentecostal church?" Jon asked.

"That's right, but I don't go there any more," Minnie said. "Though, I dearly love and miss those people. Truth is, they wouldn't allow me back even if I wanted to go, they believe that anyone not believing in the Pre-Trib Rapture is demon possessed."

"Preposterous!" Jon interrupted. "Surely Pentecostals know that a born-again Christian can't have a demon."

"Don't be so sure," Minnie said. "But anyway, back to how the Lord started this body. The second night I was at the conference, this man, Sam Fife, preached; when he talked we all felt the presence of God. He explained how denominations are Satan's ploy to keep Christians from uniting into a mighty, holy army of soul-perfecting, sickness-healing, demon-chasing believers. He explained that one denomination believing this and another believing that causes arguments and resentment. Satan laughs because his kingdom remains unchallenged. Brother Sam told how God called him as a Southern Baptist pastor some ten years ago—baptizing him and most of his church in the Holy Ghost. God showed Sam that his mission was to call believers out of the denominational system and to re-establish church order as Jesus originally ordained it. Only then could the Church become perfect."

Minnie opened her Bible to Ephesians four and waited for her pupils to find it. "And He gave some apostles," she read aloud, " ...and some prophets, and some evangelists, and some pastors and teachers..." She looked up.

Jon asked, "What are you getting at?"

Minnie's eyes twinkled. "Where are apostles now?" she asked.

"In heaven, I suppose," Jon said.

"And prophets?"

"In heaven, too?"

"Not all of them," she tantalized.

Betsy and Jon glanced at each other sensing some great revelation was about to unfold.

"Look at verses 12 and 13," Minnie said. "… For the perfecting of the saints, for the work of the ministry, for the edifying of the body of Christ; till we all come in the unity of the faith, and of the knowledge of the Son of God unto a perfect man, unto the measure of the stature of the fullness of Christ... Let me ask you—are the saints perfect?"

"No, of course not," Betsy said. Jon nodded.

"Are believers united in the Faith?" Minnie asked.

"No," they said in unison.

"Have Christians attained the measure of the stature of the fullness of Christ?"

Bewildered, Jon said, "No, only Jesus Himself has that standard of perfection."

"Look again," Minnie said. "It does say 'till we all come', doesn't it?"

"So—o, that's why apostles and prophets and evangelists and pastors are still needed." Betsy mused. "Believers haven't come to perfection yet."

Minnie nodded.

"But, but that's not supposed to happen 'till we get to heaven." Jon said.

"Oh no!" said Minnie, jabbing the page with her forefinger. "… Jesus said, 'be perfect as your Father in heaven is perfect'—meaning in this life. He wouldn't need to command it for heaven, for there we'll have our glorified bodies. But we're off the track. Now, where was I? Oh yes…

"After Sam preached, he called people up to the platform for prayer. God was showing him who to ordain as elders from the various communities represented. These elders were to start local bodies in their hometowns.

"I was about to leave when my name was called over the loudspeaker. Why, I didn't even think anybody there knew me. I was just a name that the Lord had given Sam. Then he called Sonya; even though we were both from the Stroudsburg area, we'd never met before. Sam laid hands on us and prayed; then prophesied over us. Other apostles and prophets gathered around praying in the Spirit. Then and there we were ordained as elders of the Stroudsburg body."

Betsy and Jon stared wide-eyed. "That's awesome," Jon said.

Minnie's face glowed.

"Is Sam Fife an apostle?" Betsy asked.

"Yes, yes he is, child, Sam is a bona fide apostle."

Jon glanced at his watch. It was 1:A.M. As they stood to go, Minnie said, "You know, Jon, Tuesday's meetings aren't for women only. You're welcome to come too."

They thanked Minnie for sharing as they stepped out into a shower of sleet. Cautiously driving down the road Jon said, "Betsy, I never in my life expected to meet such spiritual people."

"Me either! You'd almost expect—ooh!"

"What's the matter?"

"Just the baby kicking."

Jon relaxed. Neither spoke much the rest of the way home.

By Tuesday Jon thought he might have discovered an error in the Move's teachings—not that he wanted to—he was seeing First-Century Christianity displayed before his very eyes, and it was so much more vibrant than the staid, denominational system in which he'd been raised. Nevertheless, truth must not be compromised.

The weather snapped bitterly cold; the mercury hovered near -10 F as Betsy and Jon were on the way to Minnie's, hoping that Minnie and Sonya would have a good answer to Jon's challenge.

The regulars were pleased to see them, and there were some present that Jon and Betsy didn't know. Most of these were from the New Jersey body just across the Delaware River. They had decided to meet with the Stroudsburg body since their own gatherings were sparsely attended.

The meeting progressed with various individuals relating blessings they'd received during the week, or leading a song, or giving an ecstatic utterance. Some people sang in tongues while others worshipped in English. The result was a blend of voices and instruments in a worshipful polyphony.

It bothered Jon that he still hadn't spoken in tongues. Sitting beside him, Betsy faithfully chanted, "Santos, santos, santos..." anxious for more of a spiritual vocabulary to develop.

Jon chimed in with English phrases that sounded like something from Psalms. An hour and a half later the meeting ended; Betsy and Jon lingered to pump the elders for more spiritual insights. There was a hubbub around the two elders in the meeting's aftermath, so Betsy and Jon waited until they had Minnie and Sonya to themselves. Even though the hour grew late, neither Minnie, Sonya seemed to want to retire.

When all others had gone, Jon asked, "I hope you don't mind my asking, and I really hope there's a good answer, but, I think I found an error in the Move's teaching."

Minnie and Sonya glanced at each other.

Jon continued, "In I Timothy, chapter two, uhh-hh, " his voice trembled, " ...verse twelve, '...but I permit not a woman to teach, nor to usurp authority over the man; but to be in silence.' Doesn't that, sort of, disqualify you both from being elders?"

Minnie said, "Look up II Corinthians 3:6, and read it."

Jon found it and read: "Who also made us able ministers of the new testament, not of the letter, but of the spirit; for the letter killeth, but the spirit giveth life." He looked up, eyebrows knitted.

"It's not what the Bible says in the letter of the word that counts, but the spiritual meaning behind the word," Sonya said.

Jon glanced at Betsy. She also struggled with the concept. "Exactly what does that have to do with women pastors?" Betsy asked.

"Here, let me show you," Minnie said. "Galatians 3:28." She paused while Jon flipped pages. "Down where it says: ' ...there is neither male nor female, for you are all one in

Christ Jesus.' Can you see that when we are born-again, God is no longer interested in our gender?"

"But...but then why does Paul make that distinction?" Jon asked.

"Paul wrote the letter of the word, the letter that kills, spiritually speaking. It's for that very reason that denominations are spiritually dead—they interpret everything by the letter, not the Spirit. It took the Baptism of the Holy Spirit and this Move of God to reveal the spiritual meaning behind the letter of the word—and that's why the Move is alive and denominations are dead. The Lord purposely hid it so only those hungry enough to pursue truth would find it," Minnie explained.

"Well, then, what's the spiritual meaning behind what Paul wrote?" Jon asked.

"It's getting late. There isn't time to give a full explanation," Sonya said, "...but, let me show you some fundamentals of interpretation. First: the Body of Christ is referred to as the Bride of Christ. Were you aware of that?"

Jon and Betsy nodded, if only obliquely aware of the significance to their question.

"Good," Sonya said. "Then I suppose you also know that Jesus is our heavenly bridegroom?"

Again they nodded.

"Okay, now, when someone is prophesying, or interpreting a tongue, is that the person speaking, or the Lord?"

"The Lord," Betsy said.

"Right. And how about when someone is anointed to give a teaching?" Sonya looked to Jon.

"The Lord," Jon replied.

"Then who is prophesying, the husband or the bride?"

"The husband, I guess," Jon said.

"Right! Now stay with me," Sonya said, "... the Lord has appointed a five-fold ministry to 'cover' or care for His bride and get her ready for Himself. These are apostles, prophets..."

"Evangelists, pastors and teachers," Jon broke in. "Minnie showed us Ephesians 4 last Friday."

"Oh good." Sonya was pleased. "You're further along than I thought. All right, these ministry gifts are His representatives to His bride—or in effect, the five-fold ministry is the husband, and the body is the bride. So when one of the five-fold ministry has a word, it's the husband, or 'the man' speaking. You see, Paul's word wasn't about male and female roles, that's the unspiritual, carnal interpretation. The spiritual understanding—for those who press into the deeper things of God—shows that only those ordained to the five-fold ministry should teach and exercise authority. The body can't properly govern herself without the five-fold ministry."

"I see," Jon said. "That explains a lot." Jon and Betsy were thrilled to be included among those discovering the deeper things of God.

Jon and Betsy found the ensuing meetings even more exciting. Minnie and Sonya took special time with them, showing them the ropes of discovering the "spirit of the word'" as well as dream and vision interpretation, although that seemed a trickier business. It wasn't long before Jon and Betsy began sharing during the 'Hatha' part of the meeting. (I Corinthians 14:23 each one hath a tongue, hath a revelation, hath a doctrine—'Hatha' meetings).

Despite attending the meetings and his renewed interest in the Bible, Jon still had doubts. He couldn't pinpoint anything specific, but the more he studied, the more his doubt increased. Even so, there was no question that he was growing closer to the Lord; involvement with the Move had rekindled his faith.

On a subsequent Tuesday Minnie announced to the dozen or so gathered that Brother Sam was coming for a week of meetings. There was an excited murmur from body members. All Jon and Betsy knew about Fife was that he traveled across the states and internationally teaching Move revelation to widely scattered bodies. From his Southern Baptist church a whole international movement had sprung up, spanning the USA, Canada, South America, Africa and Britain, claiming upwards of 10,000 adherents.

"You make it sound as if the apostle Paul was coming," Jon said.

"Brother, the Lord must have shown you that!" Minnie said.

Jon was pleased to have made such an anointed observation, and yet, despite the glorious news of the apostle's imminent visit, there was a gnawing doubt in the labyrinth of Jon's thoughts.

The following Friday found Betsy and Jon sitting with Sonya, Minnie, Jenny, and Millie Jackson. Outside a heavy snow was falling. The Jersey body, as well as many local members, hadn't come due to the inclement weather. But Betsy and Jon couldn't be kept away despite the eleven mile drive on slick roads. During the week Jon ignored

J.M. MACLEOD

his doubts and buried himself in Bible study, so that when Friday rolled around he was eager to give and receive revelation.

As they quietly waited for the Spirit to move, Jon's doubts again rose up. He struggled for several minutes; hadn't this group rekindled his desire for Christ more than any other church or Christian organization he'd been involved with? Didn't this Move answer questions that so many denominations either ignored or were afraid to ask? It all fit together so neatly; it had to be God. So why the nagging doubts?

Jon had to somehow quench the unease eating at him. He glanced at the others who'd braved the wintry weather: Minnie, to his left, sitting in her over-stuffed chair, her eyes closed, body rocking slightly to some internal song; Sonya sitting opposite, palms upwards, eyes closed, moving her lips in words that only the Savior heard. Others sat with heads bowed, except for Jenny who had a nervous condition and compulsively wrung her hands.

Nothing else happened. The Spirit wasn't moving.

Was God waiting for Jon to make his struggle known? Jon finally said, "I'd like prayer."

Questioning, but friendly faces looked up at him.

"I've been having doubts about whether the Move really is of God. I want to believe what's true, but I'm plagued by doubts."

Minnie and Sonya simultaneously rose from their seats. Jon knelt on the floor, and as he did, everyone gathered around, laying hands on his head and shoulders as they began praying.

Jon began to weep. He wasn't sad or upset, yet, for no apparent reason, tears coursed down his face.

Minnie placed both hands on Jon's head and authoritatively demanded, "Spirit of doubt, I bind you in the name of Jesus and command you to come out of him."

Jon kept sobbing, embarrassed to be so out of control. Somehow, he felt that the Lord was blessing him. He didn't think that a spirit of doubt needed to be cast out. Perhaps the evil spirit was external, but other than weeping, there was no response to Minnie's command.

Minnie removed her hands for an instant, but then immediately replaced them.

Then someone forced their way into Jon's arms. Opening his eyes he saw Betsy, staring wide-eyed at him, not wanting to be left out.

Minnie prophesied, "My son, I the Lord your God, have set my seal upon you. I have given you of my Holy Spirit. I have called you by My name to walk in My paths. You must set your face as a flint to seek Me and walk in My ways. I have called you to be an apostle, to proclaim My word, to teach My people, to live as an example. Follow Me only. Turn not to the right nor to the left; seek My face, and humble yourself, and I will reveal My ways to you. Thus says the Lord."

Jon was stunned, his face wet with tears. Had the Lord just spoken directly to him through prophecy—and calling him an apostle?

Minnie's eyes were wide with surprise. The prophecy had evidently been as unexpected to her as it had been to Jon.

"Minnie, did I hear right? Am I… an apostle?"

The elder hesitated, then said, "You're called to become one, but there were conditions—if you seek His face, in time, He'll make you an apostle. I will say this, you can be sure that that prophecy came from the Lord. He filled my mouth with words I would certainly never have dared say over anyone." Her eyes sparkled as she glanced at Sonya.

Sonya had been waiting for her opportunity. "I had a vision. Jon, you and Betsy were kneeling together, like you are now, only you were atop a golden altar. As you prayed, fire fell from heaven and consumed you both until there was nothing left on the golden altar."

"God has accepted your prayer and offering," Minnie interpreted.

Jon sat back, dazed. A prophecy, a vision, a destiny. Who was he that God should single him out for such honor? He embraced it with his whole heart; no more doubts. The Move was where he belonged.

Betsy squeezed her husband's hand, whispering, "What about me? Am I included?"

"Oh, I'm sure you are, " Jon said, "… whatever I'm called to, so are you. I felt those words in my spirit even as Minnie spoke them. I'm sure that that was the Lord."

The meeting dissolved as body members discussed the unexpected prophecy. In hushed tones Sonya asked Minnie, "Do you still have doubts about prophecy?"

"Not any more. I know that one came from the Lord."

Jon and Betsy left instead of staying for more questions and answers. Minnie embraced them at the door, whispering in Jon's ear, "Seek His face."

Jon turned and stepped out on the snow-covered walkway. "Thy face, Lord, will I seek."

CHAPTER FOUR

...have we not cast out demons in Thy name? Matthew 7:22

THURSDAY, JANUARY 27

Jon devoted himself to Bible study. There was much to learn if he was to be an apostle. He searched the scriptures for types and shadows—the spiritual meanings hidden inside the letter of the word. He had never read the Bible through, but now each evening he devoured huge portions.

One afternoon as Jon was reading Ezekiel he came across the passage when the prophet was instructed to take the choice pieces from the sacrifice and boil them until the scum rose to the top of the pot. The Lord pronounced a curse against Israel for not getting rid of the scum in the lives of those who should've been consecrated to Him. God declared that He'd judge the nation by keeping her filth and scum in her until He came in wrath and consumed everything. The first part of the chapter really caught Jon's attention. Jon saw himself—all the things still in his life that surely offended God. Had he known, the second half about Ezekiel's wife being taken away from the prophet was just as prophetic.

Jon knelt in earnest repentance and immediately felt impressed to get rid of his rock 'n' roll albums. His records were dear; they soothed him when troubled and excited him when bored, in short—he sought comfort from them instead of Jesus. They were idols! But, a lot of money was tied up in that collection... Should he give them to his younger brother, Danny? No, then the same worldly spirit would ensnare Danny. Was

Jon actually admitting there was a demon, an actual spirit of darkness, entwined in his life because of rock 'n' roll? Affirmation came from deep within. Was this the source of his moodiness? Would he get worse and worse like the scum in Ezekiel's pot?

Jon sorted his records, separating the obviously worldly from those he deemed okay. He couldn't sell them; nor could he give them away. They must be destroyed. He would pitch the offending records into the town dump. Jon returned a dozen records to the shelf, but as he did, a verse came to mind:

… because I have purged thee ,and thou wast not purged, that shalt not be purged from thy filthiness anymore—till I have caused my fury to rest on thee! (Ezekiel 24:13)

Repentance meant nothing unless it was thorough. Jon looked again at the dozen records he'd set aside and realized he couldn't retain anything of the world. He grabbed every record, put on his coat and headed out the door.

A bulldozer was covering trash as Jon arrived at the Tannersville dump. He picked his way across the rubbish mounds to a ledge above the bulldozer and heaved the records under the treads of the huge machine.

A wellspring of joy rose up within and he sang a Body song:

> "He's setting me free, with Holy Ghost power…"

Jon returned to his car free from an oppression he hadn't known he had been under. He couldn't wait to tell Betsy when she returned from shopping how the Lord had set him free.

"Praise the Lord!" she said. "I've been praying that you'd get rid of those foul things."

"I now know what you mean, Hon. When I watched the bulldozer crush them, a weight lifted off me. I don't even want to listen to rock anymore. I feel like… I've been delivered of a demon or something. I feel really clean inside."

"But Jon, we don't believe Christians can have demons—not inside."

"Hmmm, yeah, well whether it was inside or outside, it's gone now. You know, Baptists never taught us how to recognize, let alone deal with evil spirits; it's as if they're afraid of the topic. We're so blessed to find a real church that's not afraid to teach all the Bible."

The next night Jon shared his deliverance at the body meeting. Sonya and Minnie nodded approvingly. Jon wanted it understood that the demon couldn't have been inside him.

"Ahem," Minnie cleared her throat and said, "I've been delivered from demons—from inside! And not only once, but on a couple of occasions. The Bible doesn't say that a Christian can't have an evil spirit enter them," she said. "I know for a fact that they can, because I was delivered from demons of lust, religion, pride, and even cancer."

Jon glanced at Betsy who looked incredulous.

Minnie continued, "The cancer demon was the hardest to get rid of. Apostle Buddy Cobb delivered me of some at the Canton convention, then took me aside and told me that he sensed more spirits, but that I wasn't ready to be delivered of them yet. I needed to grow spiritually stronger to deal with them myself. Remember how Brother Sam had that dream about the huge snake that he and other children were to fight and conquer?" she asked.

Several heads nodded.

"Well, I got a word of knowledge—that in learning how to deal with the spirits inside me I'd become stronger and learn how to deal with spirits in others. So I fasted and prayed, and as I discovered one spirit or another, I commanded them to leave in Jesus' name, and they did. Then I noticed a lump in my abdomen. At first I didn't realize that this too, was spiritual warfare. I went to the doctor, who said I had a tumor the size of a grapefruit, and that it had spread to almost every part of my body.

"I came home so depressed, all I could do was cry. Then, after a while, when I was sitting on the sofa, the presence of the Holy Spirit surrounded me. He said, 'This too, is warfare.' I had a vision of this little, hideous, green gremlin running around inside me, touching here and there, making tumors grow. My spirit rose in anger and I began to come against that demon of cancer. I suddenly felt so sick I could hardly breathe—the demon was fighting back, trying to kill me. I not only needed deliverance, but physical healing, too. I prayed for strength to continue the fight until that devil was totally cast out. The fight went on for weeks; I saw no shrinkage of the tumor. My body got weaker; I was running out of time. The doctor gave me six months to live. I wondered if I was going to survive.

"One day I lost all resolve to fight; I wanted to die. I wearily sat on the couch and prayed, 'Lord, take my life, it's too much for me. Please, I'm tired of living, so ... take my life.'"

Everyone was on the edge of their seats.

With a twinkle in her eye Minnie looked around the room and said, "And, He did!"

"You died?" Jon blurted.

"No child, no," Minnie said. "He took what was left of my flesh man—all my will, my soulish desires, my self life, and put it to death. All those weeks of fighting that demon I never realized that he was clinging to the things I was holding on to. When the Lord showed me that, I realized I didn't really want to die; I just wanted to die to my flesh life. I immediately gave up everything I knew that displeased Him. Then I commanded that cancer demon out in Jesus' name. I didn't make it to the bathroom before I vomited out a huge ball of green slime. Instantly I felt better than I had in years. I probed my stomach; the tumor was gone! Well, I just had me a praise service right then and there.

"I went to the doctor and told him that Jesus had healed me. He couldn't believe it when he examined me. They had all kinds of x-rays and blood tests and the like that proved that I was dying of cancer, yet there I was in his office as healthy as if I'd never had cancer."

"Praise the Lord," several chorused. Betsy and Jon were enthralled but, Jon still questioned whether demons could inhabit believers. Minnie's testimony certainly gave the concept credence. Jon shuddered at the thought.

"I'd like to share something, and ask all of you to pray," said a voice alongside Jon. Betsy slowly stood. "As you know, I'm pregnant." Several smiled; she was well into her ninth month. "But many of you don't know that I have to take a drug called lithium. Since lithium is an experimental drug, they aren't sure of its effects on unborn or nursing babies. A couple of weeks ago," Betsy glanced nervously at Jon, "... Minnie and Sonya prayed for my healing. My psychiatrist says that without lithium I'll go crazy. I spent six weeks in a mental institution and only recovered when they gave me lithium. It snapped me right out of my delirium."

Everyone looked on sympathetically.

Betsy continued, "So, I claimed a healing in Jesus' name. I went home and threw away my pills as an act of faith. That was three weeks ago, and my mind has never felt stronger."

"Amen!" and "Well, Glory!" erupted from various parts of the room.

This was news to Jon. He caught her shy, nervous glance in his direction. Why hadn't she told him? Of course, he knew why. She doubted he'd go along. They'd often discussed her hatred of having to take lithium even before she was pregnant. It stigmatized her; making her feel "abnormal". Every time they talked about it, Jon reminded her of Dr. Hotchkiss' warnings. Now Betsy's stand of faith was a matter of public record; Jon was trapped. To disagree would be to manifest faithlessness. The last thing an up-and-coming apostle needed was to appear weak in the faith. Perhaps it was best he hadn't known about Betsy's decision and had been, therefore, unable to interfere.

"So," Betsy continued, "I ask for prayer support in claiming my healing." Betsy sat and returned Jon's gaze, nervously squeezing his hand. Jon winked at her and determined to fervently pray for her miracle. What a testimony her healing would be to their folks…

As usual, Betsy and Jon lingered after the meeting hoping to get just one more nugget of truth, another insight, another type and shadow. Minnie encouraged their ravenous curiosity, delighted to have such "spiritually hungry children". The three settled around the kitchen table to coffee and Bibles. Minnie asked, "Any more doubts, Jon?"

Jon grinned. "None."

"That's good. Brother Sam is coming next week. I want you to meet him, both of you." Minnie wanted to introduce them to Sam Fife as the Stroudsburg couple with the most potential.

"Minnie, am I really going to be an apostle? I mean, I didn't misunderstand, did I?" Jon blushed, realizing how proud his question sounded.

Minnie gently rebuked, "The Lord said that if you seek His face, and humble yourself, He'd reveal His ways to you."

Jon determined to not bring it up again. In a year or two, when he was walking in his calling, it would be known anyway.

Minnie changed the subject. "You had questions about my deliverance testimony tonight?"

"Oh, that. Well, Betsy and I aren't sure we understand how a believer can have a demon actually in them."

Minnie pursed her lips as she pondered. "Demons are engaged in many activities, and we must be alert to their attacks; Ephesians exhorts us to be ready."

Betsy opened her Bible.

"Paul is writing to Christians here, is he not?" Minnie asked.

Jon and Betsy nodded.

"And isn't he advising Christians about how to wrestle against the powers of spiritual darkness?"

Betsy and Jon pored over the passage. "Yes it seems so," Jon said, "...but it doesn't say Christians can be possessed, either."

"Doesn't the Bible say that darkness and light cannot abide together—or something like that?" Betsy said.

"If you mean I Corinthians 10, or II Corinthians 6, those are admonitions to avoid such situations, not statements that such conditions can't exist. In fact, Christians are Satan's primary targets. Brother Sam has a tape series that teaches about the six areas of Satan's attacks. I can loan it to you."

"Six areas of attack," Jon said, "... what are they?"

"Well, demons tempt, deceive, and vex, to get us out of the Spirit and in the flesh. Those are their outside activities—when demons hover in the air and bombard Christians with their thoughts so that they eventually become depressed—that's their entry point," Minnie tapped her chest, "... then they begin oppressing until ... they gain possession. And the Bible nowhere says that Christians, if they don't resist, but allow themselves to be driven to that extent or deceived, can't have demons in them."

"Sounds far-fetched," Jon said. He looked to Betsy for support. Betsy twisted her hands and glanced nervously about the room. Only then did Jon remember that talk about demons upset her.

Unaware of Betsy's fretfulness, Minnie continued, "I have a tape of a born-again and Spirit-filled young mother who needed deliverance. Would you like to hear it?"

"A testimony?" Jon asked, thinking it would be interesting to hear.

"No," Minnie said, "... I mean a tape of her deliverance."

"They actually taped the demons coming out?" Jon said as a chill ran down his neck.

"Not only coming out, but confessing the things they made her do."

"Oh, I don't I know if I'm ready to hear demons talking. We'd, uh, better wait on that one." Jon's concern wasn't only for Betsy; the thought of listening to demons—even on tape—was unnerving.

"Well, whenever you feel ready..." Minnie said, "... just ask for The Jane Tape."

Jon promised they would—in time. The after-meeting was over.

TUESDAY, FEBRUARY 1

"Jon... wake up honey. I think its time."

Jon peered groggily at the alarm clock and wondered why the numbers weren't what they should be.

Betsy was already out of bed. "Jon, do you hear me? I said it's time!"

"Time?"

"The baby?"

"Baby?" Jon bolted out of bed. "All-all-alright! Now, steady, be calm," he told himself. He scurried around the room, stubbing his toes, looking for his jeans and shirt, muttering to himself.

Betsy giggled. "Take it easy Hon, we've got lots of time. My contractions are twelve minutes apart."

"Are your bags packed? Where's my belt? Do we have to call the doctor? Who's excited? Why are you just sitting there? What's the hospital's number? Where is my belt? Shouldn't we be calling somebody?"

"It's on the chair under the coat. No, not yet—calling somebody—I mean. We should wait until the contractions are stronger and closer together."

Jon checked his watch. "11:37. When was your last contraction?"

"Right now," she said with a grimace.

Betsy was still in her nightgown. "Why aren't you dressed?"

"We have lots of time. I'm going to take a bath."

"It's going on midnight, we're about to have our first baby, and you want to take a bath? I mean, what if the hot water starts something?"

"Silly," she teased, "… it'll relax me so I'll be able to push when the real labor begins."

The rush of water in the tub drowned out whatever else she said. Jon shook his head and checked his watch again. Even as he was about to ask, she called out above the cascading waters, "Another one."

Eleven-forty-three; six minutes. "Better hurry; you're down to six minutes."

A short time later Betsy emerged and began dressing. "Mmmmph! Another one—stronger."

Eleven forty-eight. "Betsy, we're down to five minutes! You call the car, I'll get the hospital," Jon called over his shoulder as he descended the stairs two at a time remotely wondering why his coat felt so odd.

"Settle down, Hon," Betsy called. "The first one always takes a while. Why is your coat upside down?" she giggled as Jon charged outside.

CHAPTER FIVE

...and she brought forth a man-child... Revelations 12:5

FEBRUARY 2, 1972

The twenty-minute drive to the hospital was uneventful; Betsy's labor pains diminished. Had the cold air stalled the birth mechanism? Betsy was processed through the emergency room, and directed to the maternity floor.

The nurse on duty eyed Jon like a dorm mother glaring at a beau bringing his date back after curfew. She wordlessly pointed Jon down the long corridor to the expectant-father's waiting room, then ushered Betsy behind double doors. Jon went to the solarium and picked a chair from which he could monitor the comings and goings at the nurse's station. In his hand was Hind's Feet on High Places, by Hannah Hurnard, that Betsy had borrowed from a body member. Jon glanced mindlessly at his watch. He was not going to act the stereotypical first-time father pacing back and forth anxiously awaiting word of the blessed event. He'd sit calmly and read.

Forty-five minutes later the gruff nurse waddled down the corridor toward Jon. He tried to focus on the words on the page.

"Mr. McComb, you may see your wife now."

"It's done already?"

"Hardly! She's barely begun. She has some time to wait, and wants to see you."

"Oh," Jon mumbled, and followed her to the inner sanctum of the delivery room.

Betsy, face flushed, perspiration dotting her forehead, lay abed amid the antiseptic surroundings of the examining room. She opened her eyes and smiled wanly. "Hi, Hon."

"Hi, yourself," Jon said. "How're you doing?"

"Didn't they tell you?"

Jon shook his head and pulled a metal stool to her bedside. "Tell me."

"It was false labor."

"What does that mean? You're not going to give birth today?"

"Well, they've given me an injection to induce labor; they want me to stay. The doctor said I was close enough to term."

"How do you feel?"

"I want to sleep and sleep."

"Maybe I should go back to the solarium. I'm getting into that book you read."

"No. Don't go." She reached out. "I need you here. Uhhh." She grimaced as another spasm overtook her.

Jon held her hand. She groaned and shut her eyes.

"Labor pains?"

"Uh-huh. Ever since that shot, they really hurt."

The nurse poked her head through the privacy curtain asking, "How are we doing in here?"

"It's hurts more now," Betsy said.

"Well, what did you expect? You are having a baby, after all." The curtain flipped shut and she was gone.

"She's the meanest nurse…" Betsy said.

Jon believed her. He stayed with Betsy until the cramps made her cry out, and the "nazi nurse", as they called her, ordered Jon back to the solarium, convinced that he was the cause of Betsy "not bearing it like a woman."

Jon resigned himself to praying and reading as the nighttime hours slipped away. With mild surprise he realized daylight had dawned. What was taking so long? Had there been complications?

"Mr. McComb?" a soft voice inquired.

Jon jumped. "Yes?"

A young, attractive, kinder nurse smiled and said, "Congratulations, you have a fine, healthy, baby boy."

"A boy? Is Betsy okay?"

"Sure. He'll be in the window at the head of the hall in just a few minutes. Your wife is tired from her prolonged labor, but she's okay."

Jon gathered his things, feeling no emotion except relief that the long vigil was over.

Jon waited at the window; the nursery window drapes were still drawn. The absurdity of his newborn son being kept behind glass in a sterile environment to protect him from the dangerous contamination of his father amused Jon!

The curtains parted and a nurse held up a tiny, red, wrinkled, hairless, shrunken monkey! Despite the long night and previous lack of emotion, Jon felt a gush of love and protectiveness over this little guy who'd invaded his life. He'd cherish his little 'monkey' without any effort.

A bed whisked behind Jon. Betsy was being taken to her room. Jon memorized every wrinkled detail of his son's face then followed the bed-pushers. A delivery room nurse caught him by the arm, admonishing him to stay only a few minutes.

Jon stood over his wife, looking fondly on as she napped. Her face was flushed, her hair matted, but the creases so evident during labor were gone. Her eyes were closed in peaceful slumber. Jon kissed her forehead.

Her eyes flickered open. "Hi," she said softly.

"He's beautiful, Hon. Did you tell them his name is Jay?"

"Uh-huh."

"Jay McComb, our son. Well, I'd better be going. I'll be back tonight. You rest, okay?"

"'Kay." She closed her eyes.

Jon paused once more at the nursery window. Jay was front and center, wrapped in the traditional baby-boy-blue. Pride, love and joy swelled in Jon's chest.

Jon arrived at their Tannersville apartment mid-morning. The air was frosty; a bright sun glinted through a break in the clouds. "I'm a father," Jon reminded himself as he climbed the drafty stairway to their apartment. Remembering that he needed to contact some people, Jon grabbed the phone. Minnie was first on his list; loyalties to the Move were above family and job.

"Hello," a sleepy voice answered.

"Minnie? It's Jonathan."

"Jonathan, are you all right?"

Wanting to sound spiritual, he announced, "A man child has been born."

"What do you mean?"

"I... I mean we've had a baby boy, Betsy and I. We have a son," Jon said, embarrassed that she hadn't caught his play on words from Revelation 12.

"Oh, I see. Well, I trust everyone's healthy?"

"Yes. Betsy is weary; they induced labor and it lasted all night. But both are fine, Praise the Lord."

Jon was disappointed that Minnie hadn't shown more enthusiasm. They chatted a few more minutes, then Jon called his folks and then Betsy's. Mom Rutlidge planned on coming to stay with them a few days.

Lastly, Jon called his job and explained why he wasn't there.

That night when Jon visited his expanded family, Betsy said, "I'll be able to come home Sunday. Oh, you should see the little guy breast feed, he does it so well... and what little poo-poos he makes... and grunts and sighs when he snuggles close." Betsy's eyes shone with joy.

That Sunday Jon brought his family home, proud to be invested with the care, nurture and protection of this woman and the son she'd borne him. Jon wanted to be the absolute best husband and dad in the world. He intended to do everything right, keeping them safe from evil, harm and want.

That Sunday was also notable for the Body; Sam Fife's airplane had buzzed Sonya and Doug Trevor's farm earlier, announcing his arrival so they'd send someone to fetch him from the local airport. He arrived at Minnie's house later that afternoon.

Jon stayed home from the meeting that night to be with Betsy and Jay, even though he was curious about meeting Sam Fife. He was also somewhat intimidated to meet a real apostle.

Monday morning Jon, assured everything was under control, reluctantly left Betsy and their son to go to work. Mom Rutlidge was on her way, and she always showed up with a carload of groceries, clothing and a whirlwind of activity that made a house shine. Her presence would be a tremendous boon.

Betsy had confided to her mother over the phone that she'd claimed healing and independence from lithium. Mom Rutlidge took the information with caution, but went along for the sake of Jay's breast-feeding. Even so, she'd be on the lookout for any symptoms that had marked Betsy's original psychotic breakdown.

Jon arrived home from work that night and found the house neat and tidy. Betsy's Mom tended simmering pots on the stove while Betsy gently rocked their son. Betsy had just finished nursing and was aglow with the joy of motherhood. She was dressed in her pink and brown peasant dress that Jon liked so much. "Stay just like that, Hon, I'll get the camera."

"Let's get Grandma in the picture," Betsy teased.

"Oh, no you don't," Minnie Rutlidge said. "I'm busy making dinner."

"Aw, come on Mom, you can't stay camera-shy forever," Jon said. "Especially with a brand-new grandson. Come on 'Grandma.'"

She consented and sat beside Betsy. As soon as Jon released the shutter Minnie scolded, "Enough of that. There's work to be done," and bustled out to the kitchen.

Betsy lowered her voice and said, "Minnie Eastman called this afternoon."

"Oh?"

"She said Brother Sam's meetings are really good. They're meeting every night— he wants to lay the foundations of the church, since there are so many newcomers who don't understand what the Move is all about." She hesitated, then added, "I'd really like to go."

"Oh Betts, you're in no shape to go to anywhere, especially since the weather is so cold."

"Why not? All I'd do is sit and listen. Mom could watch Jay... and besides, I feel so cooped up in this apartment."

Jon knew how Betsy hated confinement. "I'll think about it."

Betsy pressed her case, "If the Lord could heal me from needing lithium, couldn't He heal me from childbirth as well?" This reasoning challenged Jon. "I believe the Lord wants me to hear Brother Sam, and He'll heal me quicker if I act on my faith and go to the meetings."

Jon had his doubts, but he'd already waded knee-deep by trusting for healing of Betsy's mental condition; wouldn't it be faithless to not trust Him for physical healing too? After all, Brother Sam would only be there for another couple of days. A chance like this might not come again for years.

"I'll break it to my Mom," Betsy said, sensing her husband's weakening resolve.

Mom Rutlidge didn't like the idea, but was a firm believer in not meddling. She consented to watch the baby while Jon and Betsy went out.

As it turned out, Betsy was too tired to go that night, but promised she'd do nothing but rest all the next day in anticipation of going to the meeting that night. Jon stayed home too.

Later, Mom Rutlidge, finally finished with the day's chores, sat down across the table from Jon. Jon had been poring over the Minor Prophets in pursuit of reading through the whole Bible. His Bible-reading agenda had suffered lately and he was anxious to get back on track. Not knowing the Bible well would hinder his apostolic calling.

"It's good to see a man so interested in God's Word."

Jon looked up. 'Oh, well, I'm... just studying. I've never hungered for the Word like this before."

"Betsy's asleep now," Minnie said quietly, "...tell me more about this group."

Her question was a desire for reassurance. She had every right to be concerned, after all, Jon had been in the family less than a year. What did she really know about him? She'd been forced to accept Betsy's assessment, even so, Jon sensed trust in his mother-in-law's manner. He wanted to assure her that he was going to act responsibly and be a sensible provider.

"These people love the Lord," Jon said, "and understand the Bible better than any group or church I've ever known. They care deeply for one another—I really feel at home with them, and so does Betsy. We believe this is a move of God's Spirit; that soon believers everywhere will forsake spiritually weak churches and join this move that walks in the whole truth." Jon hadn't meant to say so much.

"Well," Minnie said after consideration, "...I trust you to seek the Lord, and I trust Him to lead you. Please be very careful; don't make any snap decisions. 'Think things through."

"I will," Jon promised.

Minnie Rutlidge went into the bathroom and changed into her nightclothes in preparation to sleep on the living room couch.

CHAPTER SIX

For we wrestle not against flesh and blood, but against principalities,
against powers, against the rulers of the darkness of this world,
against spiritual wickedness in high places... Ephesians 6:12

WEDNESDAY, FEBRUARY 9, 1972

Betsy and Jon traveled in relative silence to the meeting, but their thoughts were on the same frequency. What powers did someone of Sam Fife's spiritual stature have? Would he see their faults, their sins? Would he recognize Jon's calling? Would he prophesy over Jon—maybe set him in as an elder? Jon finally broke the silence, "So, this is supposed to be like meeting Paul."

Jon studied Betsy's face in the glare of oncoming traffic. Yes, she was musing on the same things. Before they had even met each other, both Jon and Betsy had anticipated God's call on their lives. The tales of the nighttime voice to Samuel, Moses' burning bush, and Paul's Damascus Road conversion spoke to Jon of a very personal God—and of the possibility that He might call Jon to ministry. Betsy also had anticipated a call to some exotic mission field. Now it seemed that they were closing in on their dreams—as an apostolic couple. Of course, there was much yet to learn, but they were ready to pick up stakes and go anytime, anywhere. They weren't rooted to Jon's job, or a house, or any of the status symbols of American life. Brother Sam might just be the catalyst they needed.

"Oh my," Betsy said as they pulled into Minnie's street. "Look at all the cars." Parking close to Minnie's house would prove difficult. Several of the cars crowding the narrow street bore empire state registrations. "The New York Body must have joined us tonight," Jon said.

"And the Jersey body," added Betsy. "And we're late. I hate being late."

"I'll let you off at the door. Go in and find us seats. Are you sure you're up to this?"

"I'm fine," Betsy said. "I feel so much better just getting out of our apartment."

Jon opened her car door and held her hand as she stepped onto the icy sidewalk. "I'll be right along."

Jon parked thirty yards up the road and slipped and slid his way over the ice-crusted sidewalk back to Minnie's where he found Betsy still waiting on the porch. "Hon, you should have gone in. It's too cold out here."

"Oh, I'm all right. I looked in the window and saw all those strangers... I just couldn't go in without you."

Jon smiled, proudly took her by the arm and ushered her inside.

Body members were happily surprised at seeing them. Sonya smiled warmly as she picked up her autoharp. Jack and Alice Dymond smiled, expressing surprise that Betsy was out and about so soon after giving birth. Larry Filmore volunteered his easy chair to Betsy, which she gratefully accepted. Jon slid onto a wooden folding chair beside her and scanned the room, hoping to catch a glimpse of the apostle.

Sonya strummed a few chords and the hubbub quieted down. She started singing:

> "Lord make us one,
>
> Lord make us one,
>
> Lord make us one every day,"

progressing through the various verses of: "I'll walk upright" and "I'll be a son." There was a stir from the back of the room; Jon turned to see a man who looked vaguely like TV's Carroll O'Connor, only younger and better looking. His hair was brownish-blond with tinges of gray; but his eyes, of all his features, stood out the most. They were light blue, almost aglow. Brother Sam!

Minnie followed in Fife's train along with several people Jon didn't recognize.

Fife picked up a guitar then took a position at the front of the assemblage. Sonya relinquished song leading to him. Brother Sam strummed a chord and animatedly launched into singing:

> "Hallelujah! I want to sing all about Him...

Hands waved in the air like a crop of wheat swaying in the breeze as the assembly repeated the peppy chorus. The song eventually ended and the polyphony of personal worship spontaneously broke forth as the instruments strummed. The crescendo of harmonic voices was more intense than Jon had ever experienced; each person seemed extra-inspired due to Sam's presence. Fife led several more choruses, some fast-paced, others slow and emotional; between every song was the polyphony of praise. An hour of singing and worship passed; then Brother Sam paused, waiting quietly.

The room became quiet.

Then Sam prophesied: "Hallelujah! Behold, says the Lord God, I am bringing my true church to the unity of the faith. I am pouring out revelation upon my holy apostles like never before. I am perfecting the saints. I am bringing forth my sons, manifesting them as my sons so they will grow up into my likeness and burst forth in my glory and deliver the earth from the bondage of corruption."

Jon was astounded; he was going to be one of those apostles. He eventually roused from his reverie to find that Brother Sam had progressed from prophesying into preaching.

"... simply as God's revelation from the Bible of His glorious plan for the sons of God in these last days. The foundation for this great truth is found in Romans 8:19-21:

'for the earnest expectation of the creation waiteth for the manifestation of the sons of God... because the creature itself... shall be delivered from the bondage of corruption into the glorious liberty of the children of God.'

"Hallelujah. Here we are told that all creation is to be set free from the wickedness of corruptible flesh that knows sickness, sorrow, suffering and death."

Fife pointed out that many Christians mistakenly believed that Jesus was going to deliver creation from bondage. "But," Sam continued, "... God's purpose is to bring forth sons of God who will deliver the earth. This Move of God is the first fruits—the first sons of God manifested to start the momentum that will ultimately bring deliverance to the entire earth."

Jon was overwhelmed. God had directed every step of his life bringing him to this climactic moment. All these events had been fore-ordained: his evangelical up-bringing, the coffeehouse ministry, being baptized in the Holy Spirit, Betsy meeting Alice Dymond which led to their involvement in the "Move," and finally the prophecy of calling to high spiritual office.

Jon glanced at Betsy to see if she was thinking the same thing. Betsy's face had taken on a blank, trance-like appearance; she moved her lips and stared intently at Sam.

Jon's stomach tensed. He touched her wrist and asked, "Betts, are you all right?"

Betsy stared blankly at Jon, blinked, then said, "Of course. I'm just listening carefully." Expression returned to her face.

Sam continued detailing the five-fold ministry, starting with apostles. Jon's ears perked up. He dismissed Betsy's strange reaction.

Sam said, "...never did pass away, but was covered over by Satan's trickery. The idea that Jesus only ordained twelve apostles is not borne out in Scripture. It is an assumption of man because God found few and far between who were committed to becoming apostles.

"Acts 14:14 makes it clear that there were more than the original twelve and Paul," said Fife. "All over the world today, God is calling out apostles, supernaturally anointing them to bring His last day message to those who are hungry for truth. They are revealing what God is planning to do in these last days through His body—The Church. Hallelujah!"

Sam mentioned specific ministries: Gerald Derstein, Oral Roberts, Johnny Osteen; relating how the Lord had spoken to them in their youth, calling them to the apostolic ministry. Then he modestly related his own calling to apostleship, "I can speak of a time when the Spirit of the Lord came upon me for four hours, and I heard the voice of the Lord commanding me to establish a revival center in Miami and to bring forth God's Last Days message."

Sam taught that along with apostles, the other offices of prophet, evangelist, pastor and teacher were to bring the Church to a state of perfection: to the full measure of the stature of the fullness of Christ. Sam shouted, "In the here and now, Christians are called to be manifested sons of God—in this life, before the Lord's return!"

"Most Christians assume," Brother Sam paced to and fro, "... that sooner or later we'd end up sort of like Jesus in heaven. They have assumed it would be far off in heaven somewhere, and that after Jesus returned He would gather together all the lazy, unconcerned, unspiritual Christians that fill our churches today, performing an instantaneous miracle upon them, making them all perfect like Him. It sounds very nice and beautiful, but it is not what the scriptures reveal. Ephesians 4:15 says: 'but speaking the truth in love, may grow up into Him which is the Head, even Christ'. Hallelujah! Here you see we are to grow up into Him—in revelation, faith, in knowledge, and power, so that when He appears we shall be like Him. This is to be a matter of growth."

Jon had never heard any pastor, conference speaker or Bible School professor push these verses to that conclusion.

Fife continued, "Jesus is not going to do anything He doesn't do through the rest of His body anymore than your head doesn't do anything without your body. When the Bible speaks of Satan being bound in the bottomless pit so that the millennium may begin, it's speaking of the sons of God growing up into His likeness in all things, having come to perfection, moving against Lucifer and his demonic kingdom, uncovering every spirit and invisible demon, bringing them into the light, and by faith, casting them from earth. Hallelujah. By faith they will bind them outside earth's atmosphere so that Jesus, our blessed Head, can return and begin the millennium."

Jon's head spun. The Church was to bring Jesus back?

"The night before I preached this great truth," Fife continued, "... several years ago now, God revealed all this to me in a vision as I lay on my bed. A great herd of black cattle was being driven across the face of the earth by rays of light sweeping up and down behind them. I saw the scope of the earth in this vision; there were hundreds of thousands of these black cattle. Over to the right I saw a small herd of cattle driven out of a city and joined to the main herd. Ahead another herd was brought out of the jungle and joined to the main herd. Sometimes a few of the dark cattle darted off to one side but a ray of light would sweep behind them and drive them back into the main herd. These rays of light kept driving the herd across the face of the earth. Then up ahead, Hallelujah, I saw wave after wave of these black cattle going over a cliff until the last one toppled over the edge. Then the rays of light lit up all the earth and I heard the Lord say:

'Then shall the righteous shine in the Kingdom of their Father'.

"The vision represented the manifested sons of God driving the demoniac kingdom out of the earth, binding Satan in outer space—the bottomless pit—so that the millennial reign of Christ might begin. Hallelujah! Hallelujah!"

Fife jumped from teaching to prophesying, " He that overcometh and keepeth My words unto the end, to him will I give power over the nations: And he shall rule them with a rod of iron—even as I received of my Father. I say to those who will be My manifested sons, to those who overcome the flesh nature, to those who go all the way, I will give power over the nations."

All over the room hands shot into the air as people prayed in tongues. It was all so... heady... so wondrous to have such an important message coming through Jesus' apostle!

Nothing like this had ever happened in a Baptist church! Jon glanced at his watch. Sam had been speaking for over an hour, yet it seemed like minutes. This was what it must have been like in the first century, before man's conventions, traditions, and watered-down doctrines polluted the Church.

Sam grabbed his guitar and led in another song:

"Not my will, but Thine be done, prayed Jesus...

Worship gradually ended, and Sam, after some additional encouragements, dismissed the meeting. Minnie served refreshments as people gravitated to engage Sam in conversation.

Jon brought Betsy a glass of punch and some cookies. "That was some word, huh?" Jon said, surveying the throng surrounding Sam.

"I guess so, I didn't quite hear all that he said with his mouth," Betsy said, nibbling on a cookie.

"What do you mean?"

"Jonathan, Sam is on such a deep spiritual level, he can communicate on more than one level at a time."

The faraway look in Betsy's eye and wistful tone made Jon's stomach clench. "Wha-what are you talking about, Betts?"

She shifted her gaze to where Sam talked to the people around him about a farm in South America. "Well... like now, he's speaking to those people, but at the same time he's communicating mentally with me about something entirely different."

"Betsy, that doesn't make sense."

"Well, I guess only those who are really growing in the Spirit can hear him on this level," she said. "Just ask Sonya or Minnie, I'm sure they know all about it."

"I'll do that."

Sonya sat near Sam, paying rapt attention, so Jon went in search of Minnie. He found her in the kitchen talking to an elder from the New York body.

"Excuse me," Jon interrupted, "It's important that I speak with Minnie."

"Jonathan?" Minnie beamed. Then to the New York elder, she explained, "This is the young man I told you about."

"Ah," the elder said, giving Jon the once over. "Brother Harry." He grasped Jon's hand in a vise-like grip. "I—uh, think I'll see what's happening in the other room."

"Minnie," Jon said, "... is it possible to read minds?"

Minnie's expression turned serious. "What do you mean?"

"Well, Betsy says she's getting special messages from Brother Sam—things that he's thinking to her, like mental telepathy."

Minnie's voice was grave as she replied, "No, it isn't. Where is she now?"

"Where we sat during the meeting."

Without another word Minnie left the kitchen. Jon followed.

Betsy sat nibbling on a cookie, listening to Sam.

Minnie broke in on Betsy's concentration. "How are you feeling, Betsy?"

"Oh, I'm fine," Betsy said with a smile. "It must be very nice in South America where the end-time farm is. I'm just sitting here listening to Brother Sam tell all about it."

"Would you like to see pictures?" Sam called from across the room. "I have a photo album of people and projects, if you'd like to see."

"This is the young couple I told you about—you know, the ones who just had a baby," Minnie introduced, "Jonathan McComb, and his wife, Betsy."

"Come, sit by me where you can see better." Sam patted an empty cushion on the sofa.

Betsy said, "I'd like that very much." So Jon and Betsy sat in the enviable positions on either side of Sam on the couch, looking at his pictures, listening to him explain who was who and what was what.

"You know," Sam said, "...all that farm needs is a bright, young, energetic couple willing to be used by the Lord."

Betsy and Jon glanced at each other. Neither dared give voice to their thoughts until they could discuss this development in private. Forgotten was the uneasy feeling Jon had had about Betsy.

Minnie retired to the kitchen, leaving the matter to Sam's discernment.

Jon asked, "What might such a young couple do on the Caqueta?"

Sam gave vague answers, nevertheless, both Betsy and Jon were eager to start packing.

Jon looked at his watch and remembered his mother-in-law. "We'd better go." Slipping out the back door was easier than pushing through the mass of people milling around Sam Fife in the living room.

Minnie saw them out onto the backdoor porch, wishing, "Godspeed."

"Good night..." Betsy called back, and then after Minnie closed the door, added, "...child!"

Up until that moment Betsy had been acting normal. Now, however, she uncharacteristically manifested a smug, arrogant attitude. "Betsy, you shouldn't mock," Jon said.

"She's just a child, Jon. She doesn't understand deep spiritual things after all."

Alarmed, Jon silently prayed for wisdom.

"It all became clear as Brother Sam talked," Betsy said. "We already are the Body of Christ. We just need to fully realize it; when we do, we'll be able to do absolutely anything. You understand that, don't you?"

"I—I'm not quite sure I do," Jon said.

"Never mind, you will," Betsy stated unemotionally. "After all, you're called to be an apostle."

The couple said little as they rode home.

"Jonathan! Wake up!" Betsy whispered in her husband's ear. She lay motionless beside him in the dark. Jon glanced at the alarm clock. 2:00 A.M. The only sound was Jay's breathing from his bassinet at the foot of their bed. "Jon, wake up," she pleaded again.

"What's the matter?"

"Do you see that hand."

"Hand? What hand?"

"The gigantic, black hand hovering over Jay's bassinet."

Jon peered through the darkness at their son's cradle. "I don't see anything. It's too dark to see anything, especially a black hand. You've had a nightmare."

"No, Jon," she insisted, "I still see it. Oh no, it's descending!" Then she added, "It's Satan coming to kill our baby." She threw back the covers and jumped out of bed.

Bewildered, Jon watched the light shade of her nightgown moving through the darkness toward the cradle. Was it possible that Betsy saw something in the spiritual realm?

Jon shook his head. "Betsy, honey, come back to bed. The Lord won't let any harm come to our baby."

"I must intercede for Jay. I must let this hand descend upon me, and envelop me instead of him, because I know how to make the Devil flee."

"Betts…." Jon's internal alarms went off full blast, though outwardly, Jon tried to maintain calm, "… come back to—."

"It's enveloping me now. In the name of Jesus, I rebuke you, Satan. In the name of Jesus I command you to leave, Satan. It's leaving now… and I see a white hand, the hand of God, coming to rest on me. It's all over now, Jay is safe."

Jon got out of bed and flipped on the light just in time to stop her as she reached for the baby. "Betsy," Jon said, "… don't, you'll wake him."

Betsy said in a whining, little girl's voice, "But he needs to be nursed."

A wave of vertigo momentarily hit Jon.

Then suddenly, Betsy was herself. She looked at Jon as if puzzled. "Why are we out of bed?"

"Come lay down, Betsy, you need your rest."

She complied and snuggled in the crook of Jon's arm. She was trembling, but not from the chill in the room. "What's happening to me?" she asked in a small, frightened voice.

"Satan doesn't want us learning the deep things of the Spirit; he's trying to frighten us. If you have any more visions—hands, or... or whatever, just ignore them. Now, close your eyes and pray yourself to sleep, okay?"

"Okay." Then as an afterthought she said, "Jon?"

"Hmmm?"

"Do you see dark shadows around our bed?"

"No Honey, it's just your imagination. There's nothing there. The Devil is trying to frighten you. There's nothing there. Trust me."

Sleep was elusive for both. Betsy lay rigid. Sometime in the wee hours Jon drifted off to sleep.

Insistent buzzing jolted Jon awake. He hit the alarm clock, only then realizing Betsy wasn't in bed. He checked the cradle and was relieved to see Jay asleep. Could Betsy be trusted? But... perhaps the madness had passed with the coming of daylight and things would be better now. Betsy was out in a living room chair reading her Bible. Her mother was still asleep on the couch.

"Hi," Jon whispered. "How do you feel?"

Betsy's eyes were wide and her brows upraised as she said, "I feel funny, different inside—I can't explain it but... something is ... different."

If Minnie and Sonya were right—that Christians could have demons—Betsy was a classic case. If they weren't right, this was post-partum depression aggravated by a lack of lithium. But to admit the latter would be to renounce all that Jon and Betsy had learned in the Move—as well as his apostolic call.

"Will you be all right?" Jon asked, wondering if he should take the day off from work.

"Mom's here." Betsy tried to sound confident. "I'm okay, really. Look, I'll fix you breakfast. What would you like?"

She was putting on a brave front and Jon loved her for it. "Toast, I guess." He played along so she wouldn't worry about him worrying. "Listen Hon, if you need help, call Sonya or Minnie for prayer."

"Oh, I'll be all right," Betsy insisted, then changed the subject. "Here, Mom made your lunch last night. I have no idea what it is. Hope you like it."

Jon took a sip of coffee. Yes, she'd be okay; last night was a passing thing. He needn't burden Betsy's Mom by mentioning last night's weirdness. "Love ya," Jon called on his way out the door. "I'll be home about five."

Jon arrived home shortly after 5:00 p.m. as promised, and climbed the creaky stairwell. The tantalizing aroma of Italian cooking overwhelmed his nostrils as soon as he opened the door. Betsy's Mom stood by the stove, stirring a pot. Jon smiled in greeting. She all but ignored him, staring into the living room; her expression conveying that things weren't well.

Jon's appetite disappeared. He slipped out of his jacket and drew near his wife. Betsy sat cross-legged on the floor, nursing Jay. Instead of enjoying the moment, Betsy glared at the infant.

Jon approached. "I'm home, Betsy. Is everything okay?"

Her dour mood suddenly broke; she smiled as though she'd never had an angry thought, much less been glaring at their baby. "Oh we've had a lovely day, haven't we Mom?"

"It's time to switch sides now," Minnie said.

Betsy shifted Jay to her other breast and then all but ignored the baby as she smiled sweetly up at Jon.

Jon wandered back out into the kitchen and whispered, "What's going on?"

Minnie looked up with concern. "I'm not sure. She's been in an ugly mood for about half an hour now. She was in a strange mood earlier on in the day, but that passed after a few minutes." Then Minnie's expression changed as she said, "At the Laundromat Betsy said something about going to South America?"

Jon explained that Sam Fife had broached the topic; and they thought that maybe they were called to serve the Lord in Columbia—but nothing was decided.

"Jonathan, come and tell me about your day," Betsy called. She was herself again, gently cooing to Jay as he nursed. The transformation was amazing. Jon left the kitchen and sat on the floor beside Betsy.

"I told Mom about the Caqueta River. She's really excited for us."

"But we haven't decided anything, and especially won't go any time soon."

"Oh, I can dream, can't I?" She hoisted the baby to her shoulder and gently tapped his back. Jay responded by giving two little 'errrps' and a contented sigh. She then hugged him and squealed, "Oooh! I just love him to pieces." Then her eyes met Jon's and she suggested quietly, "Let's go to the meeting tonight, and take him."

"I—uh, I was planning to go alone tonight. I think you should stay home and rest."

"But I'm bored in this tiny apartment; I really want to hear Brother Sam again. Please, let's go. I'll be okay, I promise."

"It's too cold to take the baby outside—he's just a week old," Betsy's Mom said from the kitchen.

Jon followed her cue, adding, "Your mom's right, Betts. Stay home. I'll tell you all about it."

She dejectedly nodded.

"Dinner will be ready in just a minute, then I've got to go," said Mrs. Rutlidge.

"Go? Go where?" Jon asked.

"Dad called and said he needs me home to take calls and such. You'll be fine." She wordlessly dished the spaghetti, then donned her coat.

Jon got up. "I'll, uh, carry your luggage out."

He leaned against the car door as she started the engine. "What do I do about tomorrow? I can't go to work if she's acting strange."

"Can't you take a couple of days off? Or… can you get someone to stay with her?"

"Taking off is out of the question. I've missed too many days as it is. But maybe I can get someone to watch her."

"Meanwhile, I'll call Dr. Hotchkiss and get him to send you some lithium, or at least a prescription."

Jon didn't know what to say. Betsy's strangeness might just be a test of faith; he must commit to believing that Betsy was healed. Jon nodded but said nothing. Mrs. Rutlidge wished him God's blessings, then drove out.

When he came back in, Betsy was on the phone with Jon's folks. "It's your mom and dad, they'd like to see us tonight."

Jon weighed the option of hearing Brother Sam but leaving Betsy alone with Jay against visiting his folks. "Well, they're taping the meetings, so it's not as if I'll miss anything," Jon said. "Okay, tell them we'll be there around 7:30."

Jon and Betsy visited his parents that night, showing Jay off and watching TV. Jon's dad, a newspaper photographer, stayed home later than usual to visit with his first grandchild. Betsy especially enjoyed all the attention Jay received.

FRIDAY, FEBRUARY 11

After a fitful night, Jon called work and told them he was needed at home. He didn't know if his excuse would be accepted, but he truly was needed at home. He didn't want to say he was sick because he wasn't; but neither could he explain that his wife was either having a mental breakdown or under demonic attack.

Jon spent the day reading the Bible or playing Scrabble with Betsy and admiring their littlest family member. Betsy's behavior was normal. They shared a quiet, uneventful day enjoying each other and their newborn.

Near the middle of the afternoon Betsy posed, "Do you suppose we could go to meeting tonight?"

"Oh Betts, I don't know..." Jon hedged. "It's so cold outside."

"Well what's the difference between going to your parent's or to a meeting? It's still going out. Besides..." she implored, "I'm afraid to be left alone. I keep thinking the Devil is going to get me when I'm alone."

"When you use Jesus' name the Devil has to flee. Just tell him to go, and he must." Jon said.

"But... I'm still afraid. And this is Brother Sam's last night. We might miss something important."

The same thought had occurred to Jon. This was the last chance that Sam might have a prophetic word for them.

"Well, I guess it'll be alright if you bundle Jay up real good. Are you sure you're up to it?"

Betsy's eyes sparkled. "Oh yes! Don't worry about me. I've been fine all day. What happened the other day was the result of doing too much too soon. Last night with your parents did me a world of good. Watching TV and laughing and talking helped get life back in perspective."

"Yeah, I know what you mean. Just a little break like that helps keep your head clear," Jon agreed.

— ·�֍· —

Snow crunched underfoot as Jon and Betsy approached Minnie Eastman's back door. They'd come early to be assured of seats in the rear so Betsy could slip out and attend Jay's needs without being a distraction.

"Well praise the Lord," Minnie greeted with a look of relief. "Where have you two been? We've been so concerned."

"Oh Minnie, we've had quite a time of it," Jon said.

"I just knew it," Minnie said. "I knew in my spirit that something was wrong. Tell me."

Jon related Betsy's visions of the black hand and communicating with Brother Sam via mental telepathy as well as Betsy's mom's description of her behavior during the previous day. "But Betsy hasn't had any more weird thoughts or visions since, so we think it's over and done."

Minnie listened, her eyes narrowing and her mouth a thin, straight line. "Wait right here. I'd better tell Brother Sam about this; I'm pretty sure he'll want to pray for you." Minnie then headed upstairs to where Sam and others were preparing before the meeting.

In the outer rooms other worshippers arrived, greeting one another. The front door kept opening, admitting believers from the frosty outside into the congenial warmth of Minnie's house.

Jay, unbundled and muttering, was due for another feeding. There was a half bathroom just off the kitchen and Betsy decided to nurse him in there. She was nearly finished by the time Minnie returned.

"Where's Betsy?" Minnie asked with a no-nonsense air.

"In there, feeding Jay," Jon pointed to the bathroom door.

"As soon as she's done, send her upstairs to the bedroom at the end of the hall. Brother Sam and others are waiting to pray for her." She turned to go.

"Wait a minute," Jon called. "I don't know what's going on, but I want to be with her when you do this... this praying. I told you that I think the problem has passed and there's no more cause for alarm."

"Yes, I think he should be there, too," said a young man who was standing just behind Minnie. It was Carmen, one of Sam's traveling companions.

The bathroom door opened and Betsy emerged with a sleepy, satisfied baby. Betsy looked questioningly at Jon.

"Betts, they want to pray for you, upstairs," Jon said.

"Okay. Should I bring Jay?"

"No," Minnie said firmly. "Mary Filmore will watch him." So saying, she bustled out to the noisy atmosphere of the living room to fetch Mary. Betsy, Jon and Carmen, waited at the base of the stairs.

Mary was delighted to babysit the McCombs small infant. "Don't you worry," she said, "he's in good hands."

The foursome ascended the steps. Why was everyone suddenly so serious? What were they going to do? Were they going to try to cast demons out of Betsy? Stories of flagellation, bloodletting, and other strange rituals arose as specters in Jon's mind.

Who were these people really? Could he trust them? What if they tried something bizarre? Would he intervene? Would they overpower him?

With each upward step Jon felt as if he was traveling back through time to the Middle Ages.

CHAPTER SEVEN

I command thee in the name of Jesus Christ,
come out of her.' And he came out... Acts 16:18

"Lord Jesus," Jon silently prayed following the entourage up the steps, "protect us. We're so vulnerable. If these people are deceivers, please get us safely out of this. But if they are of You, help me to trust them." At the bedroom door Betsy turned and looked at Jon, her eyes round with fright.

The door swung inward; in the dim lighting Jon saw half a dozen people on their knees around a bed. Minnie took her place beside Sonya. Everyone else was unknown to Jon except Carmen and Brother Sam who stood beneath the room's only light source—a bare bulb dangling from the ceiling; it was like a garish scene from a Hitchcock thriller.

"Her husband wanted to be here," Carmen explained Jon's presence to Sam. "I thought it was a good idea."

Sam nodded then turned his attention to Betsy, gently instructing, "Betsy, sit on the foot of the bed. I understand you've been having some difficulties?"

Betsy sat. "No, everything's okay." Betsy twisted her fingers over and under as she stared directly into Sam's eyes, unable to look elsewhere.

Jon's lips parted at Betsy's bold-faced lie; he was about to remind Betsy of the vision of the descending black hand, but Carmen touched his forearm, staying him.

"Heavenly Father," Sam prayed, his steely blue eyes holding Betsy's terrified gaze, "We put our trust in the blood of Jesus Christ, and ask that You make any evil spirits manifest." He then looked into Betsy's eyes, demanding, "In the name of Jesus Christ, tell me your name."

Betsy's eyelids fluttered; she tried to twist away and stuttered in a thin voice, "I—I—I'm Betsy."

Sam placed a hand on Betsy's forehead. "You are a liar, demon. Now, I command you in Jesus' name, tell me, who are you?"

Betsy tried to rise. Two men gently seized her shoulders from behind, keeping her seated. "Get your hand off my head, you're burning me," she whined.

Jon longed to step in to hug and comfort her, but… why should Brother Sam's hand burn? Whatever was manifesting through Betsy's voice wasn't Jon's wife; the facial expressions, tone of voice, agitated temperament—definitely not his Betsy!

Chills ran down Jon's spine; a demon was using the lips of the woman he loved! The reality of the spiritual world crashed in on him like a runaway freight train. Angels and demons were loose in the room! Jonathan's Baptist upbringing had not prepared him for anything like this.

And Jon wasn't the only one frightened by the demonic manifestation; Sonya, the other local body elder, backed away to the wall, staring unblinkingly at Betsy, praying in tongues.

The others in the room, however, were unperturbed. Someone moved beside Sonya, comforting her.

"It—it's just that I've never encountered—you know, a demon's actual speaking before," Sonya whispered.

Jon shared her terror. Were it not for the fact that it was his Betsy sitting there saying those things in a strange voice, he'd have bolted from the room, the house, the neighborhood and never looked back.

"I command in Jesus' name, tell me who are you," Sam persisted.

"Ooh, you're burning me. Take your hand away," a little girl's voice whined. Betsy again tried twisting away.

"Satan writhes under the Anointing. I command you to tell me who you are, in Jesus' name."

"Mmmmmph!" Betsy clamped her lips and threw herself backward.

Minnie said lowly in Sam's ear, "I see a vision of a little girl with a sad look on her face."

"Hallelujah! Spirit of rejection, the Holy Spirit has identified you. I bind you in the name of Jesus."

Betsy's eyes locked onto Sam's.

"How long have you been in Betsy?" Fife demanded.

All struggling ceased; Betsy hunched over, head hanging low like a reprimanded child. "A long, long time. This is my house; I have a right to be here. Let me alone."

"The blood of Jesus has cancelled all your claims on this young woman. I command you in the name of Jesus, come out of her."

Tears flowed down Betsy's cheeks as the thin, quavering voice begged, "I don't want to come out. I like it here. I've been here a long time. Let me alone."

"Come out, in Jesus' name."

"I don't want to come out. Where will I go?"

"You will walk through dry places, as scripture says. You are no longer allowed in this child of God. Come out of her in Jesus' name."

"No-oo!" Betsy choked. "I don't want to go out. This is—my—home. I have—a right—." The rest of the sentence went unfinished. Betsy gagged, yet nothing visible passed her lips except saliva, which someone caught in a handkerchief.

"Hallelujah, Father!" Sam said. "Now please, reveal the next one."

Betsy's body stiffened, her shoulders squared, her eyes were fierce and her face hard as a rock. "I hate you Sam Fife! I wish you'd burn in hell forever!"

"I'm sure you do," Sam said with a chuckle. "Spirit of hate, I bind you in Jesus' name and command you to come out of her."

"Gaaahhhh!" Betsy growled, struggling against the hands on her shoulders. Then she lurched forward and gnashed her teeth, as if to bite.

"You don't frighten me, spirit of hate. Release her Bob, Andy." The two men let go of Betsy. "Spirit of hate, I command you in Jesus' name to sit still; in Jesus' name."

"You can't make me." But Betsy sat still.

Sam leaned forward and again placed his hand on Betsy's forehead. "In Jesus' name, come out of her."

"Owww! It burns, it burns, it burns."

"Come out of her, in Jesus' name."

"Take your hand away, it burns. You're hurting her."

"She's not harmed by the Holy Spirit's touch, but you are tormented by the Anointing. Come out of her, in Jesus' name."

"Eaahrrg! Eaahrrg!" Betsy retched in dry heaves, throwing her head between her knees.

Sonya, still against the wall, her eyes wide, pointed at Betsy. "I see it! It's a blue snake, and very large. It's slithering out of her mouth!"

Jon only saw Betsy doubled over.

"Hallelujah. Hallelujah, Jesus!" Sam said. "The Anointing prevails in Jesus' name. Come out of her, keep coming out, keep coming."

For several more seconds Betsy spasmodically heaved, then Sonya said, "There's its tail. It's all out." Betsy sat upright, breathing deeply. She looked at Jon and smiled weakly.

"Is it over?" Jon asked.

"Shhh!" cautioned Carmen. "Demons of mental illness haven't been approached yet. These are just the weaker ones sent up to try to wear us out. These spirits haven't had much control over her like the stronger ones. Don't be deceived by whatever she says; they'll try to get you to interfere. Even that smile she just gave you wasn't her, but one of them trying to get your pity."

Jon's heart sank. "How many more?"

"Shhh."

Sam again, gently insisted, "I command you to tell me who you are, in Jesus' name."

"Hallelujah, I'm Jesus!" Betsy said. "Hallelujah, Praise the Lord!"

"Religious spirit, I bind you in Jesus' name, and command you to come out of her, now, in Jesus' name."

"HallelujahhallelujahhallelujahJesushallelujah!" Betsy spat out like a machine gun. "I am God!"

"You are a demon, and you are coming out of this young lady in Jesus' name."

"PraisetheLordPraisetheLordPraisetheLordPraisetheLord!"

One of the men standing behind her said in a low voice, "I believe there are several of them—all religious spirits. False doctrine, false revelation, emotionalism, hypocrisy, condemnation of others..."

"All right, hallelujah! We'll do them all at once. You religious spirits, I bind you all in the name of Jesus, and in Jesus name, I command you all to come out of her, all at once. Come out of her, in Jesus' name."

"Hallelujahhallelujahhallelu—yeech!" Betsy coughed again and again.

Sonya said, "I see small white crows flying out of her mouth each time she coughs."

Jon only saw the coughing fit, but no longer doubted that the unseen realm was responding to the authority of this modern day apostle.

Betsy looked up, drained, pale, her hair clinging in clumps to her forehead.

Minnie whispered to Sonya, "I told you the Lord might want to use you here tonight."

"Yes, you were right. I just didn't want to actually combat them," Sonya whispered back.

Jon was glad that he hadn't seen the spirits. It was terrifying enough to watch Betsy's visible convulsions; they were proof enough. Any objection to Christians having indwelling demons was gone. Betsy dearly loved the Lord, and was a true, born-again Christian. In addition, this deliverance followed scriptural guidelines as practiced by Jesus and Paul. Deliverance was no longer theory or an ancient story written on a page.

Jon wondered, where had the evicted demons gone? Were they still in the room trying to enter somebody else... him?

"Who are you, I command you to tell me, in Jesus' name." Sam gave the demons no respite.

"You cannot dislodge me," a deep, almost masculine voice boasted. "I am too strong even for your anointing, Sam Fife."

A tremor of doubt ran through Jon. Was Sam strong enough to complete what he'd begun? Maybe this demon was stronger than any Sam had previously come across.

Sam wasn't in the least disturbed. "Aha! The Strongman! When a stronger than he comes and binds him, then is his house plundered. Hallelujah! Strongman, I bind you in Jesus' name, and command you to come out of Betsy, in Jesus' name." He replaced his hand on her head.

"This is my house. I have won it by right. You cannot force me out." Betsy reached up and grabbed Sam's wrist.

"In Jesus' name, be still."

Betsy's hand lowered, but defiance glared from her eyes.

Sam replaced his palm on her forehead.

"Don't put that hand on me!" Betsy wriggled but made no other evasive moves. "I'm warning you..."

"Come out of her in Jesus' name, you foul spirit."

"Nnnyaah! Errrgh! Unnnnh! I won't come out."

"Yes, you will. The Holy Spirit is driving you out this very instant. Come out of her in Jesus' name."

"Ahhhhh! It burns. Take it away, take it away."

"No, you go away. The Anointing of the Lord is setting this young woman free. Who are you? How long have you been in her?"

Betsy's eyes locked with Sam's as she snarled, "Insanity. I have a right to her family from generations. That's why you can't make me go."

"Look how bestial insanity is," Sam commented to those in the room. "It growls its answers. Every time I meet a spirit of mental illness, they are vile and low, animalistic, unclean."

Betsy bared her teeth.

"Come out, in Jesus' name, spirit of insanity."

"I told you—errrgh—I have a right—ugh—to be here."

"The blood of Jesus has cancelled all your claims. She is washed in the blood of the Lamb, and is free from you and your mental illness. We now break all generational claims you've had on her family, in Jesus' name, and set her free. Betsy, I know you can hear me, you must renounce all family practices of occultism and place them under the blood of Jesus."

Betsy's own voice and facial expression surfaced briefly. "I do, I place all occultism in my family under the blood of Jesus,"

"Going back for three and four generations," Sam prompted.

"Going back three and four generations," Betsy said.

"Now then, spirit of insanity, I command you in Jesus' name, come out of her."

Betsy moaned lowly; the moan increased in volume until she howled like a wolf. Then tears ran from her eyes as she shouted, "I don't want to come out. She doesn't mind me being here, really."

"You have no place in this child of God. Come out of her, I command you in Jesus' name."

"No! No, she's been my home so long, I have nowhere to go. Don't force me out."

"You must go, in Jesus' name."

"I have... a right... to... ahhhhhh!" Betsy's voice trailed off.

"I see a large dog with huge eyes emerging from her mouth," Sonya said.

"It's gone, hallelujah!" Sam's hand still rested on Betsy's forehead as he waited for another demon to manifest. After some minutes of silence he prayed "Father, if there are any more demons here, manifest them now, we ask in Jesus' name."

Betsy sat meekly hunched over, exhausted, her eyes darting around the room.

"Betsy?" Sam asked, lifting her chin so their eyes met.

"Yes?" she answered timidly.

"How do you feel?"

"Tired."

"Can you stand and lift your hands and say 'thank you, Jesus?'"

"Thank you, Jesus," Betsy said, raising her hands. Jon caught a furtive, frightened look in her eyes as she rose to her feet.

Jon embraced Betsy. "Oh Hon, are you all right?"

"Yes, just very tired."

"Take good care of her, son," Sam said, laying his hand on Jon's shoulder. "She'll need your love and protection more than ever. She's still in a vulnerable state."

"Is—is she really healed of her need for medication now? She's really free from demons of mental illness?"

"Yes, she's free. You'll find her quite a different woman from the one you've been living with, hallelujah."

Sam headed downstairs to the meeting, followed by everyone else. Jon and Betsy came last, Jon's arm draped around her. Betsy's hair was mussed and sticking to her forehead, her face was drained of color, her eyes red from crying. Jon felt bad, taking her into the meeting in such a state, yet neither of them wanted to be far from Sam Fife's side.

CHAPTER EIGHT

... hath delivered us from the power of darkness... Colossians 1:13

Jonathan felt the eyes of the assembled body as the troupe descended the stairs. How could they not have heard all the growling, retching and screaming?

Seats were cleared for Jon and Betsy beside Marion Filmore who lovingly held baby Jay in her arms.

Sam picked up his guitar, took his place at the fore of the meeting and banged out some chords and sang:

"He's setting me free, with the Holy Ghost power..."

People enthusiastically joined the celebration. Betsy remained seated. Jon stayed seated beside her, singing along, but his worship was hollow. He was in shock. Coming face to face with the spiritual realm was like something straight out of the Twilight Zone, and no amount of singing was going to return normality.

Sam launched into another song, mopping sweat from his brow, glancing every now and then at Jon and Betsy. Betsy's head kept drooping. Jon would have taken Betsy home except he was worried that the expelled demons were possibly lurking in their Tannersville apartment.

After several more songs Sam put his guitar down, placed the podium in the front and said, "Tonight I want to talk on the subject of deliverance, from Ephesians chapter six, verses 10-12. I want to remind you that this is not just a scripture lesson, but a real life and death issue—it is life in the Spirit, for those who overcome, and death in the flesh for those who stay subjugated to Satan's control.

"As I travel around this country I'm continually approached by people who have family members under the control of demonic spirits: hearing voices, delusional, having nervous breakdowns, compelled to sin and so forth. God's people are woefully ignorant of how to deal with Satan, or else they are too afraid to do battle. There is a tremendous fear of Satan among Christians today, and that is why the Church is in the state it's in.

"The first Christians were fearless when confronted by demonic spirits. The Lord Jesus commissioned his disciples, '…And these signs shall follow them that believe…' The very first sign He set before them was this: '…they shall cast out devils.' If this is the word of the Master, surely there is something wrong when Christians are afraid to even mention Satan's name, much less be unable to cast him out of people.

"Let me tell you how God led me into spiritual warfare. Now, we had already been established in salvation truth, but the Holy Spirit began to reveal the lost truths of the gifts of the Holy Spirit. I received healing from stomach ulcers, and one of my deacons had his deaf ear healed, hallelujah! Then God spoke to me in a dream. All the people in my church were little children, about nine years old. We were playing in some woods when we came upon this huge snake, about twenty feet long. He looked dead, and we all said so; but then one of the men picked him up by the head and suddenly the great serpent came to life, wriggling and squirming. The man—who was a child in the dream—dropped the snake which then slithered off into the woods. We all sat down and covenanted to hunt that snake down and destroy it. Hallelujah."

Sam explained the dream's symbols—that the people in his congregation were children in the Spirit, that the forest was the world, and the snake was Satan.

"I want to make it clear that I'm not just talking about the eldership casting evil spirits out, for when Christians are educated from the Word of God, and take what it says seriously, they'll be able to defeat demons themselves and not need deliverance, hallelujah! Now Jesus did not say these signs might follow those who believe, but these signs will follow.… If these signs are not following us, then something is wrong in our believing, amen?"

"Amen!" chorused the crowded room.

"Amen. Now the apostle tells us to 'be strong in the Lord and the power of His might'. That is so we aren't wrestling these evil beings in our own strength, but His. Oh, if only believers would realize how much satanic activity guides the events in this world, we'd quit being angry with people and begin to resist the demoniac powers that manipulate people like puppets. Demons will infest someone in your family and that person vexes everyone else in the house so they can't stay in the Spirit. We get mad at the person and harbor unforgiveness toward them instead of getting mad at the spirits, and then wonder why we are powerless.

"This truth was drilled home to me when my own sister had what the world calls a mental breakdown. She became a babbling idiot, so much so that we had to lock her up for a long time while casting spirits out of her. There were times when the demons toyed with us, making us think we were making progress. We'd let her out of the room to come to the table for something to eat. She'd walk to the table and sit down while my mother put food out. Then she'd sweep all the food off the table to the floor, breaking dishes and ruining all the food. Then she'd stand and laugh at us; of course it was the demons in her. Those demons got us so furious with her that we were unable to operate in the Spirit.

"When we realized we couldn't bring her to the table, we'd take a banana to her. She'd calmly peel the banana, then the demons caused her to mush it in her hair! Demonic laughter would erupt from her as if to say: 'What are you going to do about it?'"

Jon listened intently; so... Sam had to walk out what he'd learned, following the Spirit's step by step guidance. It hadn't just come as revelation.

"Hallelujah! When the Lord revealed that we were divided and angry, we repented and found the Lord's power to overcome and drive them out of her. Today she's an apostle, traveling and strengthening the churches down south. That's how I learned this chief trick of Satan's that keeps churches divided and believers stirred up against each other so that they lack the power to defeat the Devil's kingdom. This is why there is no healing, no power, no glorious outpouring of the Holy Spirit across the land. Satan keeps us divided by making us judge and be angry and bitter against one another."

Sam broke into tongues followed by interpretation: "'Therefore the Lord thy God would say unto thee, walk no longer in the flesh, but walk in My Spirit. See no longer in the flesh, but see in My Spirit. Think no longer in the flesh, but think in My Spirit. Then shalt thou have victory over the enemy of thy soul.' Hallelujah! Hallelujah!"

Fife then resumed preaching, "The Devil doesn't care how many college degrees you have, not even how many theological degrees you have; he doesn't care about your position in the church, or your future calling." He glanced momentarily at Jon. "The only thing that's going to make him tremble is when you speak the word of faith and believe it in the Spirit! Then you'll have power in Jesus' name, and the heavenlies will tremble at your word.

"All over the world the people of God are hearing the call to join the fight against the demonic overlords that have held sway too long. The manifest sons of God are rising up to hunt Satan and his hordes and remove them from power."

Jon still felt nervous. He didn't have the faith Sam was talking about. But how was he going to arrive at that faith except to face the battles? If he was called to be an apostle, could he depend on mere theory? Didn't he need first hand experience? But... tomorrow would be a better day to begin.

Sam picked up his guitar and started singing:

"Victory in Jesus, My Savior forever…"

Several choruses followed, then Sam committed the gathering to God's keeping. The meeting broke up with people milling around, pressing close to Sam one last time; he was leaving in the morning. Jon sought out Minnie and found her in the kitchen; her hands dripping with dish water. He said, "Minnie, I—I get this feeling that things still aren't right with Betsy."

"What do you mean?"

"I think the demons will try to get back in when we get home."

Minnie paused, then said, "No. It's out of the question. My house is full with Sam and his traveling companions. There's just no room for the three of you."

"I think they should stay," said Carmen, coming up behind Jon. "This was no ordinary deliverance. Powerful spirits were cast out of her tonight, and they won't take it lying down. Let me talk to Brother Sam, and see if something can't be arranged."

Jon looked imploringly at Minnie.

Minnie dried her hands and said, "I know what you must feel, Jon. Be courageous and strong."

Carmen went and whispered in Sam's ear. Sam turned to look at Betsy who was sitting in her chair, playfully tugging at a strand of hair. He spoke to Carmen who gave Jon a slight nod.

"Well, that's that, I guess," said Minnie. "I'll shift all the men into one room and their wives into another. That'll make the middle upstairs room available to you. Your baby can sleep in his little car seat. I'll get fresh linens."

Relief flooded Jon's mind. This truly was the body of Christ.

Jon told Betsy that they were staying the night at Minnie's.

"I'm glad," Betsy said. "I dreaded that dark stairway at home and those miserable little rooms." She laid her head on Jon's shoulder. "Those thoughts weren't really from Sam, were they?"

"No, Honey, they weren't. People don't communicate by mental telepathy, and especially not servants of God."

"Then all those things he said to me, uh, that I thought he said to me, weren't really true?"

"What things?"

"Never mind. They weren't true, I guess. Jon?"

"What?"

"Will they come back?"

"Sam?"

"No, the demons. Will they get back in me?"

"I don't think so, but that's why we're staying here tonight."

"Oh, yeah, I forgot."

Jon chalked it up to Betsy's exhausted state.

"We'll go to bed soon," Jon said, "… as soon as Minnie makes up our bed. Then you can get some rest, okay?"

"All right. Where's my baby? He needs to be fed and changed."

"Right here, and such a little darling he is, too," cooed Mary, handing Jay to Betsy. "We've got to go, but it was delightful looking after him. We'll be praying for you both."

Jon looked up gratefully. Larry squeezed Jon's shoulder. "We're committed to praying for you until everything is back to normal."

Tears welled up in Jon's eyes; he bit his lip and nodded. Sam and his traveling companions had already retired upstairs. They were flying out early and needed to be rested. Only Carmen remained downstairs, taking over the clean-up details.

"Jon, I need some things that Minnie doesn't have. Will you go and get them?" Betsy asked. She detailed the particulars that she and Jay needed. No pharmacies were open at that hour, so Jon had no choice but to go home for them. Fear hit him afresh; he felt like he was going to a haunted house.

"Carmen, can I ask a favor?"

Carmen was about to ascend to the bedroom. "What is it?"

"I, uh, need to get some things from our apartment for Betsy and the baby, but I'm sort of frightened to go there alone…. Could you, possibly… ride along?"

Carmen bowed his head. Finally he looked up. "Okay. I'll tell Sam and get my coat."

Within minutes they were on the way to Tannersville, their breath frosting the inside windshield. Jon asked, "What took you so long to decide to come along?"

"I was discerning your motives. We had a brother go with someone once in a similar situation, and there was a gang of thugs waiting. They beat the brother mercilessly. I was just being careful not to walk into any setups."

"Oh."

"I felt it was a good thing to come with you."

"I'm glad. I was afraid I might encounter demons waiting at our apartment."

As they traveled Jon asked questions about deliverance, about the Move and what it was like to travel with Sam.

"You'll have a new wife," said Carmen. "Those demons have affected her personality since before you knew her. You'll see a dramatic change. A stronger person will be the outcome, more loving, less self-centered—."

"Betsy's a very loving, unselfish person as it is. Truth is, I'm the self-centered one."

"Nonetheless, you'll see better qualities coming forth from Betsy now. You had nothing to fear from those demons. It's not easy for them to transfer from one person to another. They have to learn the personality they overtake—what weaknesses they can exploit, what deceptions will be swallowed, what temptations or vexations they can attack with. All you have to do is stay in the Spirit and they can't get any readings on you; they won't know how to trap you."

"Just the same, I'm glad you came along. I never heard demons actually talking through a person like tonight. That really scared me."

"Yes, a lot of people feel the same way the first time they encounter deliverance. But think about it, those demons were in Betsy all along, weren't they? They're most dangerous when they're not recognized. Now that you know, they won't have the same influence on you. Your marriage will be wonderful without their interference."

"Yeah, come to think of it, we did argue a lot over silly things."

"And in time they would have caused more breakdowns. Now Satan's work in her life has been halted. Hallelujah!"

"Yeah, Praise the Lord! Well, here we are." Jon pulled into the icy driveway and shut off the ignition.

CHAPTER NINE

... thy rod and thy staff, they comfort me... Psalm 23:4

Jon turned on every light in the apartment, then gathered the things Betsy and Jay needed. Spying his classical guitar in the corner, Jon remembered that Sam had said the farm on the Caqueta River needed musical instruments. Considering how much Sam had done for them, how could he not give it? Soon, they were back in the car heading toward Minnie's house again.

Minnie was up awaiting their return. She said, " Betsy is upstairs in the middle room. I think she's asleep. I loaned her one of my nightgowns. It's a little large, but will do in a pinch. Sam and everyone will be leaving about five in the morning, so if you hear any commotion, just ignore it and go back to sleep. Well, goodnight." With that, she went up to her crowded room.

"Goodnight, Minnie. Thanks. And thank you too, Carmen, for coming with me. Since I won't see him, will you give this to Brother Sam, tell him it's for the Caqueta?" Jon placed the guitar case on the floor.

"Sure, glad to do it."

Upstairs, Jon opened the door and saw Betsy already under the quilt. Though he crept quietly in she sat bolt upright demanding, "Who's that?"

"It's me, Betts. Who'd you expect?"

"Oh, Jon. I've been so frightened."

"Of what?"

"They're talking to me."

"Who?" Jon slipped beneath the quilt.

"The demons. They say they're going to get back in when I fall asleep."

"Well… we just won't let them." Jon tried to exude confidence.

"How?"

"We have authority in Jesus' name. Brother Sam taught that demons must obey when believers speak in Jesus' name. So, demons, we command, in Jesus' name, do not come into Betsy while she sleeps. Or me, or… or anyone. Just leave this house and never come back. There, that ought to do it."

"Do you think so?"

"Yes," Jon hoped.

Betsy trembled as she snuggled in the crook of his arm.

"Keep praying," she begged. "I still hear them."

"I am, Betts, I am. I'll keep praying till I fall asleep."

"Hideous faces are leering at me out of the darkness. Make them stop."

Jon propped up on an elbow and said, "You demons, quit tormenting my wife, I command it in Jesus' name."

"I don't see them any more."

"There, you see? They must obey when we speak in Jesus' name. Now if they bother you again, you just command them, and you'll see that you have authority over them, too."

"I… I… okay. Just don't fall asleep 'til I do."

"Envision Jesus, like a shepherd, whacking them on the head with his staff every time you rebuke them."

"It's like that? Jesus comes and whacks them one?"

"Something like that, I'm sure. Now, just relax and try to sleep."

Jon rolled away, praying.

Betsy was still tense. "Jon, let me sleep in the crook of your arm. I'm not as frightened with your arm around me."

"Okay," Jon rolled back, letting her get close. "Do you… still see things?"

"Yes," Betsy said in a small, weak voice. "They're all around the bed threatening me."

"Envision Jesus smacking them a good one."

She laughed a frightened little giggle, and said, "Come whack them, Lord Jesus. Drive them away."

"Amen," Jon fervently agreed.

Jon slept fitfully, strange voices and vile faces filling his dreams. He woke in the early morning, around two or three, each time finding Betsy awake. Sometime later Jon roused and heard people going down downstairs.

Jon woke to sunlight. It was seven o'clock. Betsy wasn't in bed. He got up, dressed and went downstairs. Betsy was feeding Jay in the front room. She didn't even notice Jon. Instead she stared intently down at Jay, her eyes narrow, brows furrowed.

"Betts?"

She jerked her head up. "Wha—what?"

"How do you feel?"

Fear filled Betsy's eyes as she regarded Jon. "I'm feeling fine, and how are you feeling, Jonathan?"

Jon's heart sank. His Betsy wouldn't have responded so formally.

Minnie, in the kitchen doing dishes, stuck her head around the corner. "Good morning, Jon. Did you sleep well?"

"Not too well, under the circumstances."

"I can imagine." She rolled her eyes and nodded toward the living room. "You go watch while Betsy feeds the baby. I'll make your breakfast. What would you like?"

"Scrambled eggs and toast?"

"And coffee?"

"Please, with milk and sugar."

"I'll call you."

Jon sat and slipped his arm around Betsy.

She pulled away, declaring, "I'm nursing the baby, can't you see?"

"I'm sorry Hon, I didn't mean to—."

Betsy's face softened. "That's okay Jon. I don't mind." She relaxed, snuggling close.

"Did you get any sleep last night?" Jon asked as she hoisted Jay to her shoulder to burp him.

"Oh, I slept fine."

"You slept fine?" Jon asked.

"Umm—mm." She laid Jay across her legs and gently bounced him, evoking a frightened response. "There, there baby, Momma's not going to let you drop."

"Jon, your breakfast is ready," Minnie called from the dining room.

Minnie sipped tea as Jon sat at the table. "She came down right after Sam and his party left, manifesting demons all over the place. Sam and them weren't even out the road yet," she whispered. " She seems better now. I had to take authority over them just to make her feed the baby. Those demons knew the minute Sam was out of the house."

"Can you cast them out?"

Minnie looked up through tired, sad eyes. "I wish I had half the anointing Sam does. I'm afraid we're going to have more of a struggle than Sam had."

"Even if we get the whole body together?"

"Even then. Anointing like Sam's is rare, even in this Move of God. And those demons know it."

Jon watched Betsy who was glowering at the infant on her lap. "Is she dangerous?"

"I doubt it. One of the strongest natural bonds is between a mother and child. I doubt they'll make her harm him. Besides, she seems pretty much herself right now. I did have a time coaxing her to nurse. And even then her milk wouldn't come until I commanded it in Jesus' name."

"She's not herself."

"It's possible she'll snap right out of it. She had been bound by those demons so long she might not have quite gotten the idea that she really is free."

"Oh, I hope so. This might be a good time to listen to the Jane tape."

"I was thinking that very thing. I also found Sam's tapes on demonology and deliverance. We might as well get right into it," Minnie said, rising to get the tape player.

For the next three hours they listened to Sam's teaching from scripture and personal experience about demons and deliverance. Jon and Minnie listened to one tape after another until they had completed the series.

Then Minnie brought out The Jane Tape, the actual deliverance of a young Texas woman who had had a series of nervous breakdowns, and as a result tried to commit suicide. "Sam Fife was called in," Minnie said, "… as a last ditch effort to help the poor girl who was by that time in a miserable condition, unable to care for herself, let alone her children and husband. She was on the verge of being permanently institutionalized. Sam ministered and set the woman free. Her life returned to normal for several months until the demons got back in and made her life hell again. Sam came again and made a tape of this second session as a teaching tool about deliverance. Jane joined the Move and became an elder somewhere in Texas, and is now being used to cast evil spirits out of people."

"So, this tape we're about to hear is the second deliverance?"

"Yes. As a matter of fact, copies have been so widely distributed that the psychology department at Tulane University experimented on some of their most severe cases by commanding in Jesus' name to see what would happen, or at least that's the rumor."

Betsy lay on the couch staring at the ceiling. Jon cradled his sleeping son as he listened.

The tape was of poor quality, yet the conversation between Sam Fife and the young woman with a deep Texas drawl was intelligible. The struggle with Jane's demons was even more intense than Betsy's had been. Sam forced them to reveal: how they'd gained entry, their activities, how they made her forgetful or careless, and how they made her irritating to others. They also admitted to setting up harmful accidents. There were so many things mentioned that reminded Jon of Betsy.

After hearing the tape, Jon needed to get alone and digest what he'd heard. "Minnie, I need to check our apartment. Will you be all right?"

"Sure. Just… don't be gone too long."

"I appreciate you letting us stay here."

"I understand. And you're quite welcome. I guess this is how God makes apostles, eh?"

"Yeah, I guess so."

"No mistake about it Jon. What you're going through is the fulfillment of the vision Sonya had of you kneeling on an altar and fire consuming you 'til nothing was left."

"But doesn't that mean we'll be destroyed?"

"Not you," she smiled, "… your flesh. This is God's chastening every son He receives. He burns up your flesh nature, leaving only what's of Him. Endure this trial to the end, and you'll be refined gold, fit for His use."

Jon stepped into the bleak February sunshine, snuggling his collar against the wind, his heart heavy. This wasn't how life was supposed to be. Betsy and he were young and in love; these should've been the happiest days of their lives. Instead, they were unfairly thrust into a struggle against unseen, evil entities.

The car started grudgingly; a flume of exhaust billowed from the tailpipe, he put it into gear and the tires crackled and popped as they broke free of ice.

Had Jon ever known the real Betsy? Or had he only known Betsy under the influence of her spiritual squatters? Tears rose in his eyes. Now that he was alone, he could release his pent-up emotions. The road ahead blurred.

Betsy seemed oblivious, and maybe that was for the best. But she was slipping away. The telltale signs that had accompanied her weirdness of a few nights ago were reoccurring. Would she continue to slip away, or as Minnie suggested, snap out of it?

In his spirit, Jon sensed it was far from over.

"Why God? Why?" he screamed as he pounded the steering wheel. "Why is this happening? Are we worse sinners than other believers that we need such a strong discipline? You have the power to make those demons just pick up and get out, why don't You do it? Why do You allow her to be tormented? You just... let it get worse. You can stop it! Why don't You?" Jon no longer cared what God thought of his weak faith. He wanted the trial to end; he wanted Betsy to be in her right mind. He wanted them to live as a family in their own place. Alternating between pleading and blaming, Jon made promises, entertained taking vows, was ready to yield whatever it took, as long as, when he arrived back at Minnie's, Betsy would be herself.

Jon went upstairs to gather clothing, perishable food and more diapers. Jon placed everything on the table then sat in a borrowed chair, morosely considering his options, praying for alternatives. Sam Fife needed to come deliver Betsy again; or else she should be taken to a hospital. Jon briefly considered bringing her home in the hopes that familiar surroundings might jolt her back to reality. It boiled down to either trusting the Move, or relying on psychiatry.

If Jon hadn't actually seen the demons exorcised... if he hadn't heard them plead and threaten and growl, if he hadn't seen Betsy get 'torn' (the biblical word for retching).... he wouldn't think twice about leaving the Move. But there was no denying what his eyes and ears had witnessed. The Move was the truest form of Christianity he'd ever seen, unlike the lip service of so many churches. To turn to psychiatry would be to deny all he now believed. He would never forget the night demons were cast out of Betsy. He'd always know for the rest of their lives that they'd gotten back in and were lurking just below the surface, wreaking havoc.

There was no choice but to stay in the Move. Did Jon want to follow this course of action? No, not anymore! Too much was demanded. Not even the calling of apostleship was worth this price. What good was any of that if his wife was under such torment?

Jon groaned, wanting life to return to the way it was. But how could he go back? But... was it possible he wasn't accurately interpreting the events?

Jon sat in the chair, painstakingly reviewing every detail of the exorcism. Nothing even hinted of taint or evil in Sam Fife. In fact, it was all very scriptural. But, what if Sam, being spiritually powerful, had hypnotized Betsy to say and do the things she did, making it appear as if demons were talking through her? What if Sam was a deceiver? Was that possible?

But neither Jon nor Betsy had known how demons would respond during deliverance. Even scripture didn't give much in the way of detail. Only by direct experience could a person know such things. No, Jon had witnessed a genuine, biblical deliverance session. To fault Sam's methodology or character would be like when the Pharisees accused Jesus of casting out spirits by Beelzebub's power. No matter what Jon personally wanted to believe, he knew the truth.

Jon rose from brooding and loaded the car, still stung by the troubles plaguing his family.

CHAPTER TEN

... prove all things, hold fast to that which is good... I Thessalonians 5:21

"Hi Jon," Betsy greeted as he stepped inside the door. "I'm so glad you're home. Little Jay is staring at me, I'm sure he knows I'm his mother."

Tears filled Jon's eyes. "Betsy? You're you?"

"I—I feel a little dazed, but, yes, I'm all right."

"She's been this way about half an hour," Minnie said, coming around the corner with a ladle in her hand. "I think the worst is over. I was about to call Brother Sam in Canton, Ohio; all of a sudden she snapped out of it."

Still wearing coat and gloves, Jon sat beside his wife as she dandled Jay on her knees. "Betts, I'm so relieved." So, it had been a test, and evidently he—they passed.

"Soup's on," Minnie called, placing a pot of steaming chicken noodle soup on the dining room table. There were three places set and a loaf of bread. "Betsy, since you're feeling better, you can help with the dishes after supper."

"Yes, of course, I'll be glad to." Betsy put Jay in his car seat and joined Jon and Minnie at the table.

"Well, I guess we'll soon go home," Jon said. "Minnie, how can we ever repay you? I don't know what I would've done."

"Tush, child, that's what the body of Christ is for—to help one another. Actually, it's been a blessing to me as well, for just before all this happened, I'd been complaining to the Lord about being lonely. And He provided you three. So this has been good all around."

Betsy's fist slammed the table.

Minnie and Jon jumped.

"Tush child, tush child, tush child, that's what the body of Chreee—ist is for."

"Oh Lord, they're back!" Minnie said.

Betsy sat still and very quiet, her lips quivering, looking to Jon.

"Betts?" Jon said.

"What's happening to me?"

"Demons, Betsy," said Minnie, "…trying to get back in. Keep your mind on Jesus or else all you went through will be for nothing."

But might Betsy's rapid swings from lucidity to psychosis be mental illness? Jon shook his head; he mustn't lose faith now.

"Betsy, listen to me," Minnie said. "You must not entertain bad thoughts about people. You must be forgiving, and not be critical, or else you'll give the Devil entry. Your mind has to heal, and if you let them back in before it heals, they'll get firmly entrenched behind a wall of bitterness and judgmentalism. Do you understand?"

Betsy nodded, then weakly said to Jon, "I'm tired."

"Don't you want to finish supper?" Minnie asked.

"You really should, Hon," Jon said. "You've been through an ordeal and need to keep your strength up."

"Especially since you're nursing. Now come on, I won't take no for an answer. You have to eat to keep up a good milk supply."

Betsy resumed eating.

Minnie carried on as if nothing out of the ordinary had taken place, which helped Betsy more than Jon's fearful stares.

After supper Jon helped with dishes while Betsy sat on the couch and read the Bible, or at least stared at the open book on her lap.

"I still think she'll snap out of it," Minnie said. "Post-partum depression happens with young mothers. Not so much in the Move, but it does happen. With Betsy, it's more severe because of her deliverance from demons of mental illness. It's like she's had them in her mind so long that she's used to their thoughts flooding her mind, thinking it's herself. But now that she's had a taste of freedom, I believe she'll wake up one day and decide she's not going to let the devils do that to her anymore."

Jon peeked into the living room; Betsy was staring at them.

"She knows we're talking about her."

"I'm not surprised. People manifesting demons sometimes hear people whispering about them three or four rooms away."

"How long do you think it'll take 'til she fights back?"

"Hard to say, but I shouldn't think more than two, maybe three weeks."

"Three weeks? What'll I tell our folks?"

"You can't serve God and be concerned what people—even your own family—think. Jesus said that we had to hate father and mother, brother and sister... you get the drift."

"It's not an easy path, is it?" Jon said.

"No, but it's the best. It beats being in a dead church system that doesn't even know how to worship properly, much less drive out demons."

They finished drying dishes in silence. The next day was Sunday; the body would gather. Some might now regard the McComb's with suspicion...or pity. Yet, if Sam's sister overcame demonic possession to become an apostle, and if Jane from the Jane Tape became an elder...

Jon joined Betsy on the couch, took the Bible and opened to the Minor Prophets. There was uneasiness about Betsy that made concentration difficult.

"Jon?" Betsy asked, "When can we go home? Why are we staying with Minnie when we have our own apartment?"

"Well..." Jon wondered how much he should say, "... do you remember Sam casting demons out of you?"

"Uh-huh. That was yesterday, wasn't it? So why are we still here? I think we should go to our own place and not bother Minnie anymore"

"You're no bother child," Minnie said, entering the room and sitting in her upholstered rocker. She picked up her knitting. "Take my word for it, you and your husband and baby are better off here for a little while until we're sure things are what they should be."

Betsy fell silent.

The evening passed as they read and talked, or just sat and watched Betsy tend Jay's needs.

"Well, I'm going to bed. I need to be up early to prepare for the meeting tomorrow." Betsy and Jon also decided to turn in.

"I fixed up the room at the head of the stairs for you two instead of the middle bedroom, which is mine. But if you'd rather, I can move your stuff down to the room at the far end where you'll have more privacy."

"Where the deliverance took place?" Jon said. "No thanks. The room at the head of the stairs is fine," Jon picked up Jay's baby seat and followed Betsy upstairs. Minnie went last, after locking the front door and turning out the lights.

They tended Jay, and finally slipped under the covers. Betsy snuggled close, nudging Jon's arm around her and burrowing her head into his shoulder. "I'm so frightened. I hear them again, telling me they're going to get back in when I sleep."

"Betsy, remember how you fought them off last night? Just picture Jesus like a shepherd brandishing his staff like they were a pack of wolves."

"I'm trying, but... I'm so scared. What if they get in again?"

"They won't. But, if they do, Minnie and I will cast them out. Besides, tomorrow is church, and we'll have a house full of holy warriors. I don't think we have anything to worry about."

Betsy lay quiet for several minutes. Eventually she rolled over and began breathing heavily. Jon thought she was sleeping, but a short time later she rolled back and said, "Jon, I believe the Lord has healed me."

"That's wonderful Betts."

"No, I don't mean like that. I believe the Lord healed me from the ripping and tearing of childbirth."

"It's only been a week Betts, the doctor said it would take six weeks till you healed."

"I know, but the Lord just now healed me."

"How do you know?"

"I just heard Him say so, and I felt warm all over."

Jon was apprehensive.

Betsy leaned up on an elbow and whispered in Jon's ear.

"Betts, we can't. You know the doctor said—."

"But I'm healed! I know I am!" Betsy said, loud and angry.

"Betsy, I...."

"Don't you believe God healed me?"

"He could, but..."

"I'm telling you I'm healed. You don't have faith. The woman always has to show the way; the man is faithless. I see it now; Sarah had the faith to conceive Isaac, not Abraham. Abraham doubted God's ability to do what He promised, and wouldn't have received Isaac if Sarah hadn't had the faith. I'm telling you, I'm healed, and we can be together as man and wife again without waiting the six weeks the foolish doctors think it takes. I have the faith of Sarah, I have the faith to receive my healing, but you doubt. You are no man of God!"

"Betsy, think about what you're saying. The Bible clearly says it was Abraham's faith, Abraham believed God and it was counted to him as righteousness."

"It was Sarah who had the faith!" she screamed. "You have no faith, Jonathan McComb. You're an unbeliever, and you will burn in hell forever."

"What's going on in there?" Minnie rapped on the door. Without waiting an invitation she entered, dressed in pajamas and robe.

"I am healed, I have the faith of Sarah."

"She wants us to resume lovemaking, believing she's healed," Jon said. "And she's got the story of Abraham and Sarah all twisted..."

"I knew it, I just knew it," Minnie said. "Well, I recognize you, spirit of lust. God knows I've had enough go arounds with you myself."

Jon gladly yielded to Minnie's expertise, standing away from the bed while she sat beside Betsy and commanded unseen foes.

"But I'm healed," Betsy said. "Any evil spirits were driven out by Brother Sam."

"Oh poor girl, they've been tricking you with false revelations, getting back inside to harm you. If you have relations with your husband before you're healed, you'll do damage to yourself down there that will never be fixed. Now you just cooperate and let us cast these spirits out."

Betsy sat up and glared at Minnie and then at Jon as she spat out, "I don't want you to cast any spirits out of me. I like them here just fine."

"Betsy!" Jon gasped.

"That's not her speaking, Jon. It's the demons. Maybe you'd better let me handle them since they're of a sensual nature—you might be tempted."

"I...uh, yeah, okay. You know best." Jon backed away.

"Now Betsy, I know you hear me, you fight from in there as I fight from out here and drive those nasty spirits out. It'll go much faster if you resist them, too. Understand?"

"Leave me alone! I hate you Minnie Eastman, I hate you I hate you I hate you."

"Betsy don't talk like that—."

"You've got to get a hold of yourself, Jon. These are demons speaking, not your wife. Don't pity her; that only strengthens their resistance."

"But, she's tormented."

"Not half as bad as they let on. Believe me, I know, I was delivered of lots of them, including this one of lust. Now you take the baby and go down to the room at the far end and sleep there. I'll take care of business here."

"Are you sure?"

"This one I have power over, for I took authority over lust in my own life. Never you mind about us, we'll be all right. Go on now."

Jon took Jay, who, thankfully, was still asleep, and went down to the deliverance room. "Lord, please protect us," he prayed. Jon sat on the edge of the bed listening to Minnie's commands and Betsy's shouts and howls. After several minutes Jon closed the door, muffling the ruckus from the far end of the hall.

An hour later things quieted down. A door opened, then closed, followed by a lock clicking. Footsteps padded quietly to Jon's door and Minnie said, "Well, that one came out, but things are worse than ever. I don't have the stamina to keep going all night, so I locked her door. She can't get out. The key is in the hall side of the lock, but she'll be all right for the night. Try to get some sleep. There's formula in the fridge if the baby needs any, and pampers on the table. See you in the morning, Jonathan."

"Is she going to be okay?"

"They have her mind going so fast right now… she doesn't even know who she is. She won't likely remember much, if any, of this. Goodnight now."

"Goodnight." Jon lay back on his pillow and listened to the mutterings from Betsy's room. Just before he drifted off to sleep Jon heard voices close by.

"So when the next one comes around it's my turn, do you understand?"

"Of course, of course. But we each take a turn you know. And don't be so— hey! He can hear us! How is that possible?"

Jon sat up fully awake, looking around the dark room.

The voices continued, "I don't know, but it doesn't matter. Ignore him. He'll forget he even heard any of this. It doesn't apply to him anyway."

"Well, okay. As I was saying..."

Jon shook his head. The voices faded away, but he had definitely heard them as clearly as if they had been on a radio. And he had the uncanny feeling that he was the "he" the voices had referred to. Had he eavesdropped on a conversation from the spiritual realm? Or, was he also losing his mind?

"Lord Jesus, protect me, and my son. And Minnie. Please Lord, set Betsy totally, forever free."

Jon tossed and turned for nearly an hour. Doubts about the Move pressed in on him again. Was Betsy displaying classic psychosis? If she took lithium would she become herself? With such misgivings, Jon eventually fell asleep.

CHAPTER ELEVEN

… for I reckon that the sufferings of this present time… Romans 8:18

SUNDAY, FEBRUARY 13

> 'We're flowing, flowing, flowing into God,
> It takes a breaking, it takes a melting,
> Flowing into God.'

The words wafted up through the heating vent to where Jon sat on his bed brooding about the fact that few of those gathered below glibly singing about flowing into God had ever had as painful a trial as he faced.

He slipped out of bed and dressed, trying to keep the ancient floorboards from creaking. The assembly downstairs needn't know he was up. He tiptoed down the hall to the head of the stairs. The meeting was subdued, as if the weight of Jon's battle was felt by all.

Behind him, coming from the locked door, sounds of quite a different nature erupted. Betsy chattered incoherently. Jon peeked through the keyhole. Betsy, her hair disheveled, sat on the edge of the bed wrapped in sheets like an Arab. Madness glared from her eyes as she stared into the mirror, raving about the royal party clothes she'd wear to the Marriage Supper of the Lamb. Jon's stomach knotted; he turned away, unable to bear the sight. Would she ever be herself again?

Jon sneaked back to his bedroom, crawled onto the creaky bed and stared at the ceiling; reliving events, conversations, prayers… searching for clues that would indicate these people were not of God and could, therefore, leave with his family. But he couldn't fault their adherence to the Bible—their interpretation of it, that is. Their lives reflected a greater degree of faith than he'd encountered in any denominational church, manifesting joy and freedom in the Spirit. And dealing with demons? Baptists acted as if they'd never heard of demons, let alone knew how to cast them out.

No, no people Jon had ever met lived out the precepts of the Bible like these in the Move. They must be of God… and yet… doubts plagued him. All the external evidence shouted, "Truth," yet Jon's spirit was uneasy. Was that uneasiness from the Lord or the Devil?

There was no third party to seek counsel from. Everyone in the Move would be biased, as would those outside the Move. Jon faced this decision alone. All he could do was replay the same scenes in the theater of his mind, hoping for some overlooked piece of evidence to come to light. But, no matter how many times he reviewed the evidence, flaws in what he'd experienced proved elusive.

—·✄·—

The living room door closed with a thud, waking Jon. The meeting had dismissed. Jon checked his watch; two-and-a-half-hours had passed. Indecision weighed like an elephant on his chest. Hearing no activity, Jon ventured downstairs, pausing to peek through Betsy's keyhole again. She laid face-up on her bed, as if asleep.

Downstairs he found Minnie bottle-feeding Jay.

"Larry and Mary brought some formula by, thinking we might need it," Minnie said with a smile. "See how the Lord provides?"

"Betsy won't feed him?" In the crisis of the moment, Jon had forgotten all about Jay's needs.

"I tried to get Betsy to feed him earlier, but she's so confused, I don't think she recognized him. It's such a shame. But don't you worry. He'll get proper nourishment. Why, I could even nurse him myself if I had to. Once you've nursed a baby you can always begin lactation again by suckling." Minnie tenderly gazed at the baby in her arms sleepily tugging on a bottle. Then she looked up. "How is she now?"

"Asleep, I think."

"That's good. She needs rest. We'll try her later with the baby."

Jon waited for the other shoe to fall—for Minnie to challenge his absence from the meeting. She never mentioned it.

Jon sat on a dining room chair. "Minnie, what are we going to do? It just can't go on like this."

"Let's wait a little longer and see if things don't improve."

"You still think it'll pass?" Jon asked. "I mean, in light of all that's happened?"

"Even so, it just might. Post-partum can get severe, with mental delusions, paranoia; even the complete loss of reality, for a while."

"What are you saying, that you think it's not demons?"

"That's not what I said. I said it might pass. Her physical condition is weak, but when Betsy has had enough of those demons messing up her mind, she'll resist them. I've seen it happen. Sooner or later the victims come around and start praising the Lord again, making the demons flee. I think there's a good chance that will happen. A mother's love for her newborn is one of the strongest natural bonds God ever created. Not even demons can overwhelm a mother's love for long."

"Really?"

"Yep, it may take only a couple of hours, or it may take days, possibly weeks, but she'll come 'round in the end. I doubt it'll take as long as a month."

"A month! Minnie—I… we can't stay here a month. My folks are already suspicious. And if my father-in-law decides to get involved, things could get ugly."

Minnie gently rocked Jay and said, "Well, we'll just have to trust the Lord then, won't we?" Her eyes brightened as she posed, "Maybe there is something else you could do."

"What?"

"Would you be willing to take her to a deliverance farm?'

"Deliverance farm? What's that?"

"A farm established by the Move where they deal with people even worse than Betsy. There are mature elders there who are experienced in casting out evil spirits. Once delivered, people like Betsy are taught to walk in the Spirit, preventing demons from getting back in."

"Where are these farms?"

"There's one in Mississippi. I stayed overnight there on my way back from the Lubbock convention. I've never met such sweet, considerate young people in all my life. They go around singing praise songs, quoting the Bible—and polite! I tell you, the things they do on that farm for kids in trouble with the law has convinced me that I'm in the true Move of God. The girls just help do the dishes without being asked, happy to serve. Everybody down there is full of God's Spirit; it really is something to see."

"Sounds wonderful," Jon said. "Where's the nearest deliverance farm?"

"I'll call Sam later, he would know," Minnie replied. "Right now, how about some lunch?"

"Lunch? Sounds good." Jon had a glimmer of hope. This was what Betsy needed—deliverance and training to prevent demons from getting back in.

In the mid-afternoon Minnie escorted Betsy downstairs. She was docile, but not herself. Minnie brought Jay to Betsy, hovering over them like a mother hen. Betsy cuddled Jay like a child with a puppy; yet there was no evidence that she recognized him. And she didn't nurse him. Eventually Minnie gave up hoping and prepared some formula.

Jon sat beside Betsy, not knowing what to say, and so, said nothing. Instead he communicated by looking lovingly into her eyes.

Suddenly there was a flash of recognition. "Jonathan?" Betsy said.

"Yes, it's me, Betsy. It's me."

"I'm so glad. They told me you were dead."

"Dead? No, I'm not dead. Betsy, don't listen to the spirits. Set your mind on Jesus," Jon said.

Minnie came into the room. "What's going on?"

"Betsy's back," Jon said, hoping that this wasn't a tease. "Maybe we won't need to go to a farm after all."

Betsy looked from Jon to Minnie and back again, blinking, smiling, then asked, "Where's Jay? I think he should be fed."

Minnie's eyes widened. She said, "I'll just go get him," and scurried off toward the kitchen.

She was a bit dazed, but in every other way, was herself. "Oh Betsy, if only you knew the scare you've given me."

"Yeah, boy! I've had quite a scare too!" Betsy shot back too hilariously. She dropped her gaze to her lap.

"Easy Betsy, easy," urged Minnie, re-entering the room with Jay. "You've been through an ordeal, and need to take it easy. Don't worry about things, just relax and feed your baby."

Betsy fondly took Jay, undid her nursing bra and fed him. As Jay guzzled, Betsy examined him, saying lowly, "What have they done to you, my baby? What have they done to you?" Then apparently satisfied that he was healthy, she returned her attention to her husband. "Where have you been?"

"I've been here all along. You're the one that's not quite been here. But everything's going to be all right now." Jon glanced up at Minnie who just shrugged. "Oh Lord, let it be over," Jon silently begged.

Within minutes the all too familiar glaze shrouded Betsy's eyes again. Jon's heart sank; he wanted to shout angrily toward the sky, "Why don't You put an end to this?" But... that wasn't faith. He must endure, believing, as the Move taught, that all things worked together for good.

Betsy slipped back to insanity. But, there was a glimmer of hope that deep inside, despite her delirium, Betsy was still herself. She had recognized her baby and her husband. Had she somehow managed to temporarily elude her demonic wardens, or... was it a cruel ploy they used to demoralize him by letting her regain reason, then snatch it back again?

"When will You make an end?" Jon silently cried. The words had a familiar ring. Where had he heard that phrase before? Then he remembered; it was the persistent question asked of Michaelangelo by the pope in the Agony and the Ecstasy. The master artist always replied: "When I am finished." That same reply echoed to Jon, and he understood; a death to self and a stretching of faith was underway. Even so, the pain wasn't buffered.

Jon watched helplessly as Betsy's mind became ensnarled in terrors, fantasies and illusions.

Minnie's eyes welled up too. "Jonathan," she said, still cradling Jay, "...you might want to take a look at the first five verses of Romans five sometime soon."

CHAPTER TWELVE

…prove all things… I Thessalonians 5:21

MONDAY, FEBRUARY 14

Sleep provided but a temporary respite of dreaming about the way life used to be. Waking brought reality oppressively back. Jonathan dressed and went downstairs, Bible in hand. No one else was up. What passage would yield the comfort and strength he needed before heading to work?

"Lord, I know this isn't usually valid, but, will You let the Bible fall open to what You want me to read?" The Bible in his lap fell open to Matthew 12:43-45: When the unclean spirit is gone out of a man, he walketh through dry places seeking rest, and finding none. Then he saith I will return into mine house from whence I came out; and when he is come, he findeth it swept and garnished. Then goeth he and taketh with himself seven other spirits more wicked than himself, and they enter in and dwell there; and the last state of that man is worse than the first.

"No, God! This can't be what You wanted me to read. Don't let Betsy get worse. Please."

Minnie's bed creaked; she was rising and preparing for her morning devotions. Remembering Minnie's suggestion, Jon turned to Romans chapter five and read: … but we glory in tribulations also, knowing that tribulation worketh patience; and patience experience; and experience hope, And hope maketh not ashamed…

If Jon took Betsy and left the Move, knowing what he now knew, he'd be declaring the Move was false. But if Sam Fife really was an apostle—and Jon had no evidence to the contrary—then Sam's interpretation of scripture was superior to any church leader or pastor Jon had previously encountered. And after Jon saw what he saw... how could he not believe?

Jon prayed until Minnie came downstairs. She and Jon discussed the options; it was decided that Jon should go to work, leaving Betsy and Jay in Minnie's care. If things got out of hand, Minnie would call Sonya.

So, Jon left for work with a heavy heart.

The hours drudged by. Jon was worried because of the ominous scripture to which he'd flipped open. Around noon Jon's mood lifted. His prayers became optimistic; he again believed he was doing the right thing by sticking with the Move. All afternoon Jon prayed and sang praises under his breath and tried to remember Sam's messages.

The buzzer sounded; Jon filed out the door, got in his car and headed towards Tannersville.

Jon gathered a few items from their apartment; a quick glance at his watch revealed he had but ten minutes to get to the post office.

Among the bills handed to Jon by the clerk was a letter from his mother-in-law. He sat in the car for several moments staring at the Sunbury postmark. Dare he read it? Somehow he knew that this letter would unsettle him all over again. But, he owed her the respect of reading what she'd written… Mom Rutlidge had her own heart and soul bound up in the matter. Jon slit the envelope and unfolded the handwritten pages.

FEBRUARY 12, 1972

Dear Jonathan,

I am praying that you receive and read this letter. I know you want to obey the Lord and do what is right by your family. I love you and respect you for that. I do not believe that Betsy is healed from needing lithium though. The Lord uses doctors and psychiatrists to help people now days. Please understand that I'm not trying to tell you what to believe, but I am very concerned about Betsy's and Jay's well being. What is happening to her now is exactly what happened to her before, and only lithium straightened out her mind the last time. For the sake of your family and your own sake as well, please pray about getting her medicine.

I also talked to a Pastor Keifer from Shamokin about all this. He believes in spiritual healing and the other spiritual gifts of the Holy Spirit. When He asked me what church or group you were associated with I told him that Sam Fife was

your main apostle. At that his face fell and he told me that Sam Fife was possessed
of an evil spirit himself; that he was teaching deceptions and even faking healings
and exorcisms of demons. He said he is luring Christians away to live on farms in
other countries and nobody ever hears from them again.

Please Jon, listen to me. I trust God to show you to do what is right. Take Betsy
out of that Minnie woman's house, and get some lithium for her before it's too late.

love, Mom Rutlidge

Jon sighed and sat back. As much as he wanted to, he couldn't dismiss her letter. Minnie Rutlidge wouldn't lie. This other spirit-filled pastor believed Sam Fife was
demon possessed.

What did Jon really know about Sam Fife? He'd met him only twice. Was it possible that Sam was demon-possessed? If so, all his radical interpretations of scripture
were "doctrines of demons." It wasn't altogether impossible, Jon supposed, for Sam to
subliminally suggest to Betsy how demons should respond. But, Jon had been in the
deliverance room the entire time; such an idea was remote. The possibility that Sam
was a deceiver, however, threw Jon into turmoil. He had to settle the issue once and for
all. He couldn't bear going back to Minnie's in confusion. He needed to get alone and
pray, and not return till he'd heard from God.

He knew of a scenic overlook of the Delaware Water Gap that had little traffic and
no nearby residents; just the privacy Jon needed. He headed toward Brushy Mountain
determined to either irrevocably commit to the Move or else take his wife out of Minnie's and go straight to the hospital.

A half-hour of daylight remained when Jon shut off the engine and stared across the
snow-covered fields at the gap locals called the "Eighth Natural Wonder of the World."

"Okay Lord," Jon breathed aloud, fogging the windshield, "... help me sort this mess
out. What I've seen in the Move lines up with scripture. I can't deny my experiences,
though I'm not sure I understand them. It would be easier to take the medical path that
helped Betsy before; but the Move says I should take the more difficult road of faith.

"Now my mother-in-law sends a letter telling me that Sam Fife is under an evil spirit.
Lord, I need to know the truth..."

Night descended over the landscape; the eastern sky turned cobalt; stars appeared.
Lights in the town below blinked on; silvery clouds, as if caught in a tug-o-war, hung
in the gap between the two granite mountains. Jon felt like one of those clouds being
tugged this way then that way.

Jon remembered waiting for God to speak to him once before, when he'd argued doctrines with a Jehovah's Witness in a coffeehouse debate. After grueling hours of point and counterpoint, the two sat across a table from each other, mentally exhausted from the effort to convert the other. "Well," the Witness observed, "...one of us has the truth, and one of us has a lie." He leaned forward and declared, "At this point, I don't think either one of us is sure who has what."

Afterward, Jon sat on the dock staring across Lake Wawasee, praying with all his heart to know truth from error. He didn't want to embrace a belief system because of how he'd been raised. What if he had been born Muslim, or Buddhist, or Hindu?

Stars twinkled in the inky sky. Jon had received no immediate answer back then; no angelic herald, no blaring trumpets, no sudden epiphany. He had prayed his heart out, only to receive an answer of silence. Yet, in the following months as he continued to read the Bible, his faith had grown stronger.

The answer he'd received back then was apparently the same answer he was going to receive now. God would only reveal one step at a time. That being the case, how could Jon draw any other conclusion than that God had maneuvered him into the Move? Until such a time as God revealed otherwise, he would follow the Move.

Jon arrived at Minnie's in a clearer frame of mind.

Minnie however, was frazzled. All day Betsy swung between sanity and psychosis, and as the hours grew later she was more out than in her right mind.

Minnie looked up suspiciously. "Where have you been so long?"

"My mother-in-law sent me a letter saying she'd heard things about Sam Fife. So I went up on Brushy Mountain to be alone and pray."

"Are you at peace yet?"

"Not totally; all I know is that the Lord has led me so far," Jon said.

"I got hold of Sam."

"Is he coming back?"

"He's much too busy to come here from Georgia. He suggested we take her to the Mississippi farm."

Jon plopped down on the couch. "Mississippi? I thought Sam was in Ohio?"

"Oh, he's so busy. He was in Canton, then Georgia, which is where I finally tracked him down. I told him what's been going on, and asked what he suggested."

"And he suggested the deliverance farm in Mississippi," Jon said. "Isn't there one closer?"

"I'm afraid not," Minnie said. "It's the only one anywhere, right now. I know some of the people there," she added, "… some are almost as anointed as Sam."

"That's so far away... I need to think about it." He wasn't about to have his wife a thousand miles away on a deliverance farm while he was in Pennsylvania. He'd need to quit his job, close out their apartment, give away most of their belongings as well as return the borrowed furniture—if he could locate the owners. Whatever he decided, someone would hold him culpable of wrongdoing. This decision affected many lives beyond his own little family. Nevertheless, if this was God's leading...

CHAPTER THIRTEEN

...for how long shall thy journey be, and when wilt thou return? Nehemiah. 2:6

WEDNESDAY, FEBRUARY 16

"Victory in Jesus, My Savior forever, He sought me, and bought me,

With His redeeming blood, He loved me 'ere I knew Him,

So all my love is to Him, He plunged me to victory,

Beneath the cleansing flow." (Eugene Monroe Bartlett, 1939)

The body repeated the chorus, as if just singing could generate victory. Minnie's house was full; body members had come from all quarters to assist in the spiritual conflict. A sense of unity permeated the gathering. Many had awkwardly greeted Jon, unsure what to say, uncertain of how he was holding up, but all offered encouragement. Jon appreciated their concern.

He was, however, still hesitant about going to Mississippi.

Minnie and Sonya brought Betsy down to the meeting thinking the exposure to worship might set her free. Betsy however—or the religious spirits controlling her—gustily sang along in obvious mockery.

After the worship, Minnie went to the podium and said, "I believe the Lord has shown me why we haven't gotten victory over Satan. Turn to Joshua chapter seven."

Everyone followed as she read the account of the Israelites losing a battle to the insignificant town of Ai. She read the execution of Achan, whose greed and disobedience had brought defeat. She paused and looked out over the group. "There's an Achan in the camp," she said. "That's why we haven't had victory over these demons. Someone in our midst has displeased the Lord by allowing some accursed thing in his possession. Before Betsy can be delivered, this betrayer must openly confess his sin. Then we'll see a difference."

Jon examined his heart. He glanced up, certain everyone was waiting for him to confess since it was his wife that was under the dominion of evil spirits, but everyone was likewise absorbed in self-examination. The meeting remained hushed, waiting for the guilty one to admit their sin.

Betsy startled everyone by suddenly singing out loudly:

"There's an Achan in the camp,

Yes, an Achan in the camp…"

Sonya and Mary Filmore, seated on either side of Betsy, led her from the room. Betsy offered no resistance, but heartily continued singing, "There's an Achan in the camp," as she was led upstairs. The song was only slightly muffled when they closed the door to her room. Minnie sighed and dismissed the meeting, warning each to look into his or her own heart.

Jon didn't think it possible to feel worse. Even after attempting to sing praises, his depression was unabated.

After the meeting a few people milled about, talking in hushed tones. The harsh jangling of the telephone intruded, giving them an excuse to leave.

Minnie answered, "Yes, yes, he's right here." Putting her hand over the mouthpiece, she called, "Jonathan, it's for you. It's a man."

Jon cautiously took the receiver, breathed a silent prayer, and answered, "Hello?"

"Yeah," Jon recognized his father-in-law's voice, "… is that you Jon?"

"Yes, it's me."

"What's goin' on there, boss? My wife tells me things don't go so well with Betsy?"

Betsy's dad was a tough-minded, successful businessman accustomed to getting his way. He didn't live by other men's norms and was known far and wide as someone not to cross. "Well Dad," Jon began, "… things are bit rocky right now. But God has the answers to Betsy's needs."

"I'll tell you what that girl needs: lithium! I spent over $10,000 to find out she's got to have lithium to keep sane. I told you that the day you asked to marry her. I said 'she'll be all right as long as you make sure she takes her medicine'. Now you get out of that nut house you're in, take Betsy to a hospital, and see to it she gets her lithium."

"I can't do that, Dad…"

"Well then," Mr. Rutlidge said, "… take her over to your parent's home. "She don't need the hospital so much as she needs lithium and peace and quiet."

Jon swallowed a hard lump that had lodged in his throat and said, "Well, I don't believe that's the way the Lord wants to do this. He's going to heal her so she doesn't ever need lithium again."

"Now lookee here sonny-boy," Betsy's dad said, "… that girl needs her medicine, no matter what those religious crack-pots tell you. You get her out of there and get her some lithium. Even Dr. Hotchkiss told you she'd need to take it all her life."

"Dad, listen to me. There's more involved than mental illness. I've seen things that are beyond medical science. Only the Lord can help Betsy."

Betsy's Dad paused as though listening to someone, and then demanded, "Are you saying she has demons?"

Jon looked helplessly at Minnie who was standing by. Telling Charles Rutlidge that Betsy's problem was demonic was akin to taunting an un-caged tiger. Well...so be it! God had allowed this mess; if this was God's will, God would handle Betsy's dad. Betsy's dad was capable of coming down on them like the Hitler on Holland. Might this be God's way of getting Jon and Betsy out of the Move? Jon prayed silently then replied, "Yes Dad, she's been delivered of demons, but some got back in. I was there and saw them coming out—well, I saw her vomiting, which was the demons coming out."

Jon cringed, waiting for a torrent of abuse.

Instead, it was as if Charles Rutlidge hadn't heard Jon's idiotic reply. "I'll see to it that some lithium gets in the mail. Do you still get your mail in Tannersville?"

"Yes," Jon said, relieved.

"Day after tomorrow there'll be medicine at the post office. Make sure she gets it; you'll be amazed how quick she gets better."

"Well," Jon said, "...thanks for your concern."

"Now you know that I don't believe in interfering in your personal life. I gave that girl away. But you've got to exercise some common sense. Make sure she gets her lithium, and I don't care where you go to church."

"I've got to go now, Dad, thanks for calling." Dad Rutlidge didn't brook disagreement; Jon was expected to do exactly as told. To Jonathan however, obeying his father-in-law would be tantamount to denying the Faith. But failure to comply with Charles Rutlidge's orders could bring an unpleasant confrontation. Jon hung up the phone with a shudder.

THURSDAY, FEBRUARY 17

Jon woke to demented chatter from the far end of the hall. Minnie, having fed Jay around 4:a.m., was still asleep. Jon descended the stairs and called his employer. "Hello, Cliff? Uh, yeah it's Jonathan McComb, I—."

"Look Jon, I understand you're wife isn't feeling well, but I can't let you stay out any more unless you tell me that you're the one who's sick, understand? I'd like to help you, but that's company policy."

"I can't lie about it, Cliff, it's my wife, she's had complications related to giving birth... she's real depressed and needs me with her."

"I'm sorry Jon, but... look... come see me when you do come in."

"Okay." Jon hung up; his standing with his employer was the least of his worries.

Sparkles of sunlight coming through the window curtains off the glazed snow promised a beautiful day. "Maybe spring will be early this year," Jon mused, reaching for his Bible. He found concentration difficult. He kept rehashing the conversation with his father-in-law. Dad Rutlidge wasn't the type to sit patiently by and let things work themselves out. He had powerful friends, including some among the state police. If he had Betsy nabbed and put in a hospital—would Jon be able to resume life with a woman he knew to be inhabited by demons?

Jon shook his head and tried yet again to focus on the verses before him: For we wrestle not against flesh and blood, but against principalities, against powers, against the rulers of the darkness of this world, against spiritual wickedness in high places. Wherefore take unto you the whole armor of God that ye may be able to withstand in the evil day, and having done all, to stand.

Stand therefore, having your loins girded about with truth, and having on the breastplate of righteousness; And your feet shod with the preparation of the gospel of peace;

Above all, taking the shield of faith, with which ye shall quench all the fiery darts of the wicked. And take the helmet of salvation, and the sword of the Spirit, which is the Word of God...

These familiar verses took on a very personal application. Jon and Betsy were swept up in a spiritual battle for which their previous religious experience had left them totally unprepared. Jon had always assumed that they had this spiritual armor because they were Born Again Christians, and all the more so when they were "filled with the Spirit." But the present situation pointed out how ill-equipped they really were.

Directly overhead he heard Minnie rising from bed.

Jon silently prayed, "Lord, You know I'm weak. Please Lord, I need the helmet, breastplate, girdle, shoes, shield and sword of Your Spirit, and the wisdom to know how to use them. Help me, Jesus." Jon wiped at his eyes.

Minnie came downstairs carrying Jay and dumped him in Jon's arms. "Here Dada, you take him while I go fix a bottle. Oh, by the way, Larry and Mary Filmore are coming by later."

That was welcome news. Larry was rock-solid; a man's man, yet gentle and full of the Spirit. It would be good to have him to talk to. Jon snuggled his son.

Later in the morning they brought Betsy down to eat. Dark circles under her eyes revealed she hadn't slept. She had no problem eating, however.

"Poor girl," Minnie mused, watching Betsy devour her oatmeal. "I heard her chattering away the livelong night."

The phone rang. Jon answered it. It was Larry, calling to see if it was too early to come by. They'd breakfasted at a diner and were ready to come over.

"Good," said Minnie. "When they get here I'll go upstairs and have my devotions." She rose and started to clear away the dirty dishes.

"Where's my baby?" Betsy asked, searching the room, her eyes full of recognition. "Isn't it time for his feeding?"

Minnie answered, "But he's already fed. Don't you worry about him, he's in the next room sound asleep."

Jon took Betsy's hand and implored, "Betts, honey, try to stay with us. Set your mind on the Lord. 'He will keep him in perfect peace whose mind is stayed on Thee,'" he quoted.

"I'm—I'm trying," she said. "It's so hard. I feel so weird." Even as she spoke, the glazed look came over her eyes again. "Achan, Achan, who's got the Achan in the camp?" she babbled.

"No! Betsy don't give in to it," Jon shouted, jumping to his feet. "You demons, I command you in Jesus' name, come out of her."

Betsy fixed her eyes on Jon with an intense hatred. Jon's blood ran chill.

"You don't scare me, you old devil." Minnie stepped in front of Jon, demanding, "Come out in Jesus' name. Come out now, in Jesus' name." She stared right back at the demonic expression on Betsy's face. "The blood of Jesus is against you, demon, you must come out, in Jesus' name."

Jon took courage and joined Minnie, insisting the spirit come out. Betsy writhed as if being held down, though neither Jon nor Minnie laid a hand on her. But the more they commanded the more Betsy thrashed about, gnashing her teeth and glaring. Jon began fearing for Betsy's safety.

Minnie had the same thought, ordering, "Stop that thrashing, in Jesus' name." Betsy stopped immediately.

Through clenched teeth, Betsy growled, "Why don't you just leave me alone? I just want to be left alone."

"I won't leave you alone, demon, because you don't belong here. Now, get out, in Jesus' name." Minnie pressed.

Betsy threw her head back so violently that Jon feared she'd hit it on the table.

"Minnie," Jon said, "… maybe we should do this in a padded chair in the living room."

"Good idea. Now demon, let her come peaceful, in Jesus' name," Minnie ordered.

Betsy was led into the living room and deposited in an overstuffed chair. Despite all the commotion, Jay was still asleep.

Once there they recommenced the exorcism in earnest, keeping at it for several minutes. Betsy glared and occasionally shouted, "Stop it, leave me alone!" Jon was about to give up, feeling the attempt was useless, when Betsy began gagging, "Aaaaggg-hhh!" She rose out of the chair despite both Minnie and Jon holding her down. Betsy screamed, then went limp, and fell back into the chair, dazed, but conscious.

"Betsy, do you know me?" Jon asked, hoping with all his heart that the ordeal was over. "Betts… Betsy, can you hear me?"

She breathed deep and looked straight ahead.

Jon looked at Minnie, who stood akimbo in concentration, working her jaw muscles.

"Did it come out or didn't it?" Jon asked.

"Oh, it came out all right. Didn't you hear it scream?"

"But, why is she like this?"

"I don't know. I don't sense any more evil spirits, but… I'm not sure." Then, nose to nose with Betsy, Minnie said, "All right, the rest of you, manifest and come out, in Jesus' name."

Betsy stared calmly straight ahead, not twitching a muscle.

Minnie stepped back, puzzled.

A car pulled up outside. It was the Filmores. Jon broke away from the scene and opened the door welcoming them. They unwrapped themselves by layers. Larry was 6 feet 3 inches tall, with a balding pate, and eyes that emanated kindness. Mary was short and plump, obviously of Irish extraction, sporting red hair and a round, impish face, which, like Larry's, reflected loving concern. They were in their mid-fifties, and were accompanied by their thirteen year-old daughter, Joanne.

Jon took their wraps as Minnie described the battle they'd just had. Larry put his arm around Jon's shoulders, saying, "I know how difficult this must be, Jon. The Lord doesn't test every man this severely. He must be preparing you for a special ministry. Be strong in Him. Endure what must be endured, and remember that we're hurting with you."

Tears welled up. Jon could only nod. Mary likewise encouraged Betsy as if she was able to comprehend.

"Well," Minnie broke in with a clap of her hands, "... it's time for my devotions. Just make yourselves at home," she said, ascending the stairs.

Jon asked the Filmore's if they'd like a cup of coffee with him. They declined, having had their fill at the diner. Jon went out to the kitchen, put the kettle on and settled into a chair to wait while the water heated.

Jon heard Minnie begin her devotions, praying softly in tongues, her voice filtering down through heating ducts to Jon sitting just below. Gradually her high soprano singing faded, and Jon heard indistinct, mumbled prayers, as if her head was buried in a pillow. There followed several moments of silence. Jon, embarrassed at eavesdropping, was about to leave, when Minnie suddenly spoke out loud, "My son, you have asked for weapons of battle. I have given you salvation as a helmet, truth to gird your loins; righteousness as your breastplate; preparation of the gospel to shod your feet; faith to be your shield, quenching all the fiery darts of your enemy; and the Word of My Spirit, which is a mighty, two-edged sword. I will strengthen you to do battle in My Spirit. Stand firm then, be not shaken in your faith. Follow the path I have shown you. Thus saith the Lord."

Jon gulped. Had the Lord just spoken directly to him through Minnie? What else could it be? Everything Jon had silently prayed earlier that morning had been in that prophecy. Minnie's words again became muffled.

A sense of peace settled over Jon.

Later that afternoon Larry and Jon were involved in a chess game as a temporary diversion and to pass the time.

The phone rang.

Minnie answered, then called Jon to the phone. "Sounds like your father-in-law again," she warned.

Shooting a quick prayer to heaven, Jon took the phone. "Hello?"

"Yeah, boss, it's me again. Have you done anything about getting that girl her lithium?"

Jon hesitated.

"I didn't think so. Well listen, I'm coming down there tomorrow with a doctor and the police to get her outta that house. I believe Betsy is being held against her will, so I'll have a warrant some time tomorrow. You can come out with her, or you can stay with them crackpots. That's your choice. After Betsy gets to be herself again, she can choose for herself what kind of church she wants to go to. But come tomorrow, Sonny-boy, we're gonna get her out. And don't think you can take and hide her somewhere either, 'cause I've got the place under surveillance. That's all. See you tomorrow." The phone clicked dead.

Jon was stunned. "He—he's coming tomorrow, with a warrant and police and a doctor."

Minnie and Larry exchanged worried looks. "You must make a decision now, Jon, or else it will be made for you," Larry said.

"I just don't know for sure," Jon said. "If only I had complete peace…"

"You told me that you thought the prophecy I spoke in my devotions was for you," Minnie reminded. "Didn't the Lord say to follow the path He has shown you?"

"But which path is His? Let her be taken to a hospital, or take her to Mississippi? You tell me, Minnie, which way is the Lord's?" Jon held her gaze: angry, frightened, frustrated.

"You already know what I believe Jon; you're the one who has to make the decision."

"I know." Jon looked out the window to the few remaining patches of snow on the ground. "I just don't want to make a mistake. The welfare of my wife and son depend on my decision. I'm not prepared to risk their lives and well being. And I can't be sure unless I have complete peace, one way or the other."

"Ah," Minnie said with a wink at Larry, "…that's a father ministry's heart coming forth. Do you see how the Lord does that?"

Jon knew what she meant, but it didn't help.

"Jon, give me your hands." Minnie took his proffered hands and said, "Now pull away from me." Jon did, wondering what the point was. "Do you feel the strain as we pull?"

He nodded.

"Now, relax your arms, let me control them. Now, do you feel any strain?"

"Of course not. I stopped resisting."

"Exactly." She smiled and departed into the kitchen.

Understanding dawned. "Okay, call Brother Sam; tell him we're going to Mississippi."

Minnie switched off the TV news. "Well, the weatherman says its going to be a nice day for traveling. No bad weather expected for days. That'll give us time to go down to the farm and back again, I expect." It had been decided that Minnie and Mary Filmore would accompany Jon and Betsy to Mississippi.

A knock came on the front door; Larry rose to answer.

"We'll leave about 9 o'clock then?" Jon asked.

"Sounds about right. I don't think your father-in-law will get here until noon. By then we'll be long gone," Minnie said. "And any spies keeping watch can trail us all the way to Mississippi if they want."

Larry led Gladys, a body member, into the room. She approached Jon saying, "Jonathan, the Lord woke me up at 3 A.M. this morning and told me to give you this."

Jon took the piece of paper. It was her endorsed paycheck for $207.00. Gladys smiled and said, "I don't know what it's for, but He knows you need it." Then to Minnie she said, "I'd like to stay, but my family is waiting dinner for me. Jon, God bless you." With that she scurried out the door.

Mary Filmore raised her hands and marveled, "He's even provided money for the journey down and back!"

"I hadn't even thought about money," Jon said. "And after I bring you two back, I'll close out our apartment, quit my job—officially that is—and head back down. I think this is enough for three trips."

"And food along the way," Minnie said. "See how the Lord moves on your behalf once you make up your mind?"

Jon smiled. "I guess we're set then." Now that the decision was made, it seemed foolish to have considered anything else.

CHAPTER FOURTEEN

...like a man traveling into a far country... Matthew 25:14

FRIDAY, FEBRUARY 18

Jon woke to dazzling light flooding the room. It was 7:a.m., but the brilliance filtering through Minnie's lace curtains suggested it was much later. He quickly dressed, then paused to look out the window. A deep blanket of snow covered the ground. "I thought the weatherman said no bad weather..."

Jon hurried downstairs wondering about their plans. He didn't want to risk staying later than 9 a.m.; Betsy's Dad wasn't one to let something as insignificant as a foot of new snow hinder him.

Minnie and Mary were already fixing breakfast. Betsy was eating toast, eggs and drinking a glass of milk in one gulp—something that she wouldn't normally do; she detested milk.

"Hi Betts," Jon said. Getting no response, he settled into a chair and asked, "What are we going to do now, Minnie? There must be eighteen inches of snow out there. We'll never get out of here before my father-in-law comes."

"How you talk," Minnie said. "Don't you remember that this snow was unpredicted?"

"Well, yeah," Jon said.

"Then it caught your father-in-law off guard as well, didn't it?"

Jon nodded as he bit into toast smeared with raspberry jam.

Minnie continued, "The Lord sent this snow to slow him down while we get away. They're plowing now; we shouldn't have any trouble. The radio said that the roads west of here were blocked off."

"I hope you're right," Jon said. "But... what if they put out an all points bulletin on us? He did say he'd have state police with him."

"Will you quit worrying and just praise the Lord that He's provided an escape?"

"I'll try," Jon said as he dug into the eggs. "I'll go and clean off the car. Oh, did you ever get in touch with Brother Sam and tell him that we're going?"

"I left a message at his next stop. By the way, Sonya has cash on hand to cover Gladys' check, so we'll head over there as soon as the car is packed."

"But... but that's right past my folk's house. There's a good chance they'll see us."

"If the Lord brought eighteen inches of snow out of a clear sky, don't you suppose He'll blind the eyes of anyone He doesn't want observing us?"

"Just thought I'd mention it," Jon said, retreating out the front door with a broom. He jumped into the knee-high snow and waded to the car. After clearing the car he found a snow shovel and dug a path to the street.

Within the hour they were on their way. Betsy and Minnie sat in the back; Mary occupied the front passenger seat holding Jay.

Sonya came out as soon as they pulled into her driveway; Jon and Sonya exchanged envelopes and the fivesome headed back to the interstate, passing the lane to Jon's parent's house. Might Charles Rutlidge, be at that very moment, sitting there discussing plans for invading Minnie Eastman's home? Jon held his breath. "Lord, this is the place to stop us... and now is the time." They drove past; the lane hadn't even been plowed.

Jon and Betsy were on their way to the Mississippi deliverance farm.

It was early evening; they'd been back on the road after a gas and restroom stop for nearly an hour. Mile markers passed in endless procession. The others had had refreshment earlier at a restaurant, but Jon was unable to eat. Jon had stayed in the car with Betsy while Minnie and Mary took little Jay into the restaurant. Minnie brought food out for Jon and Betsy, but Jon couldn't touch it.

Storm clouds scudded across the horizon as they crossed into Tennessee. Minnie and Mary were silent, meditative, watching the passing scenery. Jay fretted, cranky from being bundled in his snowsuit all day. As Betsy fed the baby Mary commented that Jay was wheezing more lately.

Betsy sat directly behind Jon, rigid, alert. Jon glanced at her in the rear view mirror and she started, then glared back with open hostility.

Minnie asked, "What's the matter Betsy?"

Betsy whispered, "He's the Devil."

"Who is?" Minnie asked. Then realizing she meant Jon, said, "No child, he's your husband."

"He's pretending to be Jon, but I know that he's really the Devil."

"No, Betsy, listen to me, Jon loves you very much," Minnie said.

"I've seen him do magic. That's how I know he's really the Devil. He doesn't think that I see him, but I have, at night, when he thought I was sleeping. I would wake up and watch him pretend to be asleep. Things appeared and disappeared all around him. That's how I know who he really is."

Jon's knuckles grew white on the steering wheel; he stared at the blurred road through his tears. "Lord, use me to help destroy Satan's kingdom."

Mile after mile passed. Night deepened, and with it, Jon's depression.

Betsy and Minnie talked occasionally—mostly nonsense on Betsy's part. One time however, when Betsy was briefly herself, she asked, "Where are we going, and why is it taking so long?"

Minnie said, "We're going to a farm in Mississippi."

Betsy fell silent, and soon receded back to confusion.

Another hour passed; Jon pulled off I-40 for gas. Mary and Minnie led Betsy into the restrooms as the station attendant stared.

"What's the weather forecast?" Jon asked, drawing the man's attention away from the two older women dragging his wife across the lot.

"Storm," he spat out suspiciously. Jon didn't blame him. They were, no doubt, a sorry-looking bunch of Yankees. Most travelers had already settled into motels by this hour of the night. The attendant bobbed his head and turned his attention to the pump; tobacco juice spattered to the ground. "Hard rain, an' mebbe thunder an' lightnin'. Rough night fer travelin'."

Jon paid for the gas. Minnie and Mary escorted Betsy from the restroom back to the car. Betsy put up a fuss, having qualms about entering a car with "the Devil" inside. Would the gas jockey call the police? Jon didn't feature explaining to a southern state trooper that they were enroute to a deliverance farm to have demons cast out of his wife. Betsy was finally persuaded to get in the car when Minnie and Mary switched places.

A few miles down the road Minnie said, "We'd better look for a motel."

"No," Jon said. Catching Minnie's questioning glance he added, "I'd rather keep driving. I'm not the least bit tired; it keeps my mind occupied. Besides, I want to get there as soon as possible."

Minnie drew a deep breath. "Okay," she agreed, "...but if you feel tired, pull over and take a nap, all right?"

"Okay." Jon was wired; he could drive forever. They'd been on the road over fourteen hours, and though his legs were restless, he was mentally keen. Driving kept despair at bay.

Minnie, Jay and Mary dropped off to sleep one by one; Betsy glumly stared at the back of Jon's head.

Raindrops splattered on the windshield. Now and then a brilliant flash lit up the countryside with blinding light. Then rain pelted down until it was so loud that Jon couldn't hear the accompanying thunder claps. Quick checks of everyone revealed all were sleeping, including Betsy, though she maintained a rigid, upright position.

SATURDAY, FEBRUARY 19

Midnight…

Jon drove on into the storm, peering out at the rain-distorted highway in the glare of his headlights. The rain; the dark; the long, long miles; fasting; sleeplessness; grief; being misunderstood… all took a toll on Jon's depleted emotions. "God, what are You doing to me?" he silently pled. "I can't continue like this. I want to call it quits… to turn the car around… just go back home. I'm not cut out to be an apostle. I'm too weak. Make an end of it, please God. Where are You? Do You even care?"

In that deepest moment of despair, when all was futile and lost, as grief and hopelessness crashed in, a verse from a song learned in childhood came to mind:

Turn your eyes upon Jesus...

Was the Holy Spirit answering?

And the things of earth will grow strangely dim…

Jon sang it softly, drinking in the healing message, whispering it over and over, letting it saturate his distraught spirit. Only by keeping his eyes on Jesus would he get through this.

Jon's mood lifted with each repetition; he didn't remember the entire song, but what he did remember was enough to sustain him; he'd keep heading to the farm where they set people free from demons.

J.M. MACLEOD

Jay whimpered.

Jon's eyes opened a slit; he was surrounded by the grayness of a foggy pre-dawn. It took a moment to recollect where he was. Jon glanced at his watch: 6 A.M.; he'd pulled into a rest area and managed to sleep about three hours. It was raining steadily, but at least it wasn't torrential. The brief interlude of the previous night's peace was gone; a weight of doubt again sat heavily on his chest. A dull neck ache promised to add just a little more misery to his day.

Jon stretched and started the engine. No one stirred except Jay, who snuggled next to Jon making little wheezing noises as he breathed.

Jon turned onto route 45 just south of Jackson, TN. "This farm had better be something special," he muttered, "... or I'm going straight back to Pennsylvania."

A thick fog hampered driving; Jon had to keep well below the posted speed limit, adding to his impatience. Run-down shacks and shanties loomed out of the fog on either side; mud was everywhere: ugly, red, oozy mud; no grass, not even frozen ground. There was no pavement other than the two-lane road; just muddy fields and muddy lanes connecting to the asphalt artery. Jon gritted his teeth and drove on.

The others in the car stirred, stretching, yawning, muttering, "Good morning." Even Betsy's eyes looked a little clearer for the sleep she'd had.

"Better find a rest area," said Minnie, yawning and arching her back.

"We're off the four-lane now, no more rest areas," Jon said. "But I'll find a diner so you can get some breakfast."

Mary asked, "Are we in Mississippi yet?"

"A sign said 'Corinth, Mississippi, 40 miles', about three or four miles back. That's right at the top of Mississippi. Minnie, are you sure you know where to go once we get to Mississippi?"

"The farm... I seem to remember... is by a little town called Eupora. I'll check the map," Minnie said. "Ah yes, here it is... keep on 45 south till it turns into the Natchez Trace, which will take us close to Eupora. I think I'll remember the road when I see it."

Jon was doubtful. The last thing he wanted to do was drive up and down mud-wallow, southern back roads searching for a demon-deliverance farm. The neon glare of a diner's lights appeared through the fog. Jon slowed to turn in.

Car doors popped open even before the car came to a complete halt. "C'mon Betsy, you come, too," said Minnie as she clambered out of the car. "Oooh, I'm cramped from sitting so long. Don't you worry Jon, she'll be good. Besides, there's nobody in there this time of day that'd care. Why don't you eat something too? It'll keep your strength up."

"No thanks. Order me a coffee, though. I'm going down the road apiece to that Esso station and fill up. I'll be right back."

When Jon joined them in the diner he found a large Styrofoam cup of coffee that he correctly assumed was his. They sat and chatted, but Jon, protective of Betsy, wanted to get moving again. Betsy tried to join in the conversation, though she had no clue as to the topic. Only when she looked at Jon did her nostrils flare and her eyes blaze. No one in the diner paid the slightest attention.

"Jon," Minnie said after they were back on the road, "I didn't say anything last night, but I had a vision while we were driving in all that heavy rain."

Jon looked over expectantly.

"I saw Betsy, in her right mind… in a large room with lots of little children climbing on her lap. All the time she smiled the most beautiful smile." Minnie's eyes twinkled. "Do you see what that means?"

Jon shrugged.

Betsy looked from Minnie to her husband and back again, shrugging her shoulders in mimicry.

"That means that she'll be delivered, and the Lord will give her a ministry."

"Well that's a relief!" said Betsy, grinning widely.

All laughed, caught off-guard by Betsy's outburst. Mary recovered first, saying, "Well, glory. Even in all her confusion, she still wants to serve God."

The farther south they went the buildings became more dilapidated. The cold, misty landscape was void of anything attractive, and was instead littered with derelict shanties and rusted automobiles. Though the rain eventually let up, the skies remained dark and foreboding, matching Jon's mood.

Minnie wanted to find a diner before noon, since they still had well over a hundred miles to go. Although Jon's stomach revolted at the thought of food, the needs of the others prevailed

Jay happily dined on mommy's milk whenever Betsy recognized him. His wheezing, however, was worsening.

The prolonged trek and dismal weather had taken a toll on Jon's attitude. He resented Minnie fulfilling her elder's role by coaxing them all to sing praise songs. She was probably right, but Jon wanted the privacy of his own thoughts, worries and prayers— and not to have to join a sing-along.

Jon tried to envision the farm's elders immediately casting the devils out of Betsy upon their arrival. Now, however, after twenty-six straight hours of exposure to Betsy's dementia, Jon doubted the demons would ever leave. "Oh God," he prayed, "... please don't let us have come all this way for nothing."

Minnie prevailed upon Jon to stop at the Twilight Star Diner in Booneville. Again Jon stayed in the car with Betsy and Jay while Mary and Minnie went in and ordered hot food. Jon repeatedly checked his watch, frustrated at how long they took. Jon said nothing when they finally did come out, but they sensed his irritation and, in turn, were miffed at Jon's lack of appreciation for their sacrifice in undertaking the journey.

Mile after muddy mile passed. The sky lifted, but not enough to promise clearing. They passed through Tupelo, birthplace of Elvis, as Minnie commented. Jon thought it strange that an elder in the Move even cared, much less knew, where Elvis was born. "What a waste of talent," she sighed.

"What do you mean?" Jon said.

"Elvis was raised in an Assemblies church, but he got off track and now serves the Devil. What a waste." she sighed again.

The narrow road became the Natchez Trace Parkway—a four-lane highway with a windbreak of trees separating opposing traffic lanes. Deep forest surrounded them, a refreshing contrast to the landscape of run-down shanties and junk autos they'd been passing.

At Matheson Minnie spotted a sign for Eupora, and Jon reluctantly left the enchanting, timeless beauty of the Natchez Trace and re-entered twentieth-century Mississippi with its billboards and squalor.

A tiny signpost nailed to a tree read: "Eupora: 8 miles." The journey's end loomed.

"There should be a road about two or three miles before Eupora," Minnie said.

"Don't you know the name of the road?" Jon asked

"Well, we'll see a 'Church of Sapa' sign on a tree."

"Sapa? What's that, a Greek word?" Mary asked.

"No," said Minnie, "I think it's the name of the township or parish or whatever they call them down here. That's the New Testament way, you know, to call a church after its locality. Hence, the Church at Sapa."

"Oh, you mean like the Church of Corinth, or the Church of Rome?" Mary said.

Minnie nodded.

Jon studied every tree alongside the road, loath to have to run back and forth on this dreary highway, hunting for some obscure lane. Then he saw a sign: "Entering Eupora".

"I thought you said the farm was before we got to town," Jon said through tight lips.

Minnie ignored him, saying instead, "I thought so, too. We probably missed it. Ask at that gas station if anyone here knows the road we should take."

Jon hated Mississippi already. He pulled over and Minnie rolled her window down asking an elderly man, "Excuse me, do you know the road to the Church of Sapa?"

"Church of—Sapa did you say? Cain't say's I recollects any church hereabouts called Sapa."

Minnie said, "They have a special school there for disturbed children. It's somewhere along this road."

"Oh," he smiled, "Y'all wants that religious school. Well, y'all turn an' go back thataways fer 'bout two, mebbe three mile. Anyways, it's the secont right onto a dirt road. Then jest keep lookin' fer a row o' mailboxes on yer left. Y'all wants the right turn directly acrost from them mailboxes."

Jon bobbed his head. "Thanks. Believe I've got it."

"Shore 'nuff. Y'all take keer now."

They located a tiny, weather-beaten sign pinned to a tree twenty feet off the road declaring: "Church at Sapa."

"No wonder we missed it," Jon grumbled. Three-quarters of a mile along the gullied track they saw a row of mailboxes and the road opposite.

"This is the driveway," Minnie said, leaning forward. "Just wait till you meet these people. I know you're going to love them."

Coming around a bend they encountered several mobile homes forming a large semicircle. Jon pulled into a gravel parking lot and turned off the engine.

A couple of teenaged boys walking by stopped and watched as the four adults and infant emerged from the car.

"Hi, I'm David. Can I help y'all?" said one of the boys. His eyes twinkled as he extended his hand.

The sun broke through at that moment. Jon took the teen's proffered hand; everything would be all right.

PART TWO

CHAPTER FIFTEEN

...ye shall see their way, and their doings, and ye shall be comforted... Ezekiel 14:22

The travel-weary company stood stretching and blinking beside the car, as if waking from a deep sleep. Indeed, the whole journey seemed but a dark, dreary dream.

Minnie introduced the party to the young man, explaining, "The elders are expecting us. Sam Fife said we should come here."

"Well, praise the Lord," David said. "Y'all just follow me and I'll take you to the Main Trailer. I believe the elders are in a meeting right now." David's eyes twinkled; he obviously loved being there.

David led past a dozen trailers that connected to a narrow, pebbled walkway. "These three trailers are where the boys sleep," David explained, "... and we call this yellow warehouse-type-building The Golden Tabernacle. This is where we meet for services and meals. Those on the other side of the Golden Tabernacle are the girls' trailers; and those other, larger ones are family trailers."

They came to a bend in the path where the largest trailer stood. It had a built-on extension that overhung the yard. "The Main Trailer," David announced as he mounted the steps of the addition and rapped on the door.

A balding, thin-faced, narrow-eyed man opened the door and stared out inquiringly.

"Brother Chester," David said, "... these folks said Brother Sam sent them."

Chester nodded at David then turned to the group; his attention lingered on Betsy. He invited, "Come in, come in. David, you may resume your duties."

Minnie went first into the addition that appeared to serve as both office and lounge. A desk and chair were set in the bay window looking out over the semi-circled trailers. A microphone on a stand, telephone and typewriter were the only items on the desk. A dozen people were seated on folding chairs and couches around the room. Several men rose, offering the newcomers seats.

"These folks say Brother Sam sent them," Chester said.

Jon and Betsy settled into seats, aware of the group's scrutiny.

"Jack Halstead," said Minnie abruptly, "… don't you remember me?"

"Why, yes, I believe I do," said a man with a slightly receding hairline. His countenance, accent and mannerisms reminded Jon of Mayberry's Sherriff Andy. Bright-blue, friendly eyes sparkled beneath Jack's bushy eyebrows; a playful smile revealed gleaming white teeth. "Y'all are an elder from up north, aren't you?" Jack said. "Why, I remember now, y'all stayed with us on your way back from the Lubbock convention—was it two years ago? Well, it's ni-ice to see y'all again. What is it we can do for you?"

Minnie was at a loss, her face reddened as she said, "Well, I thought Brother Sam would have let you know we were coming."

"Brother Sam hasn't called lately, has he?" Jack asked, glancing around the room.

"I'll ask Marie," said a stout woman sitting beside Jack. Her auburn hair was coifed in the same style as most of the women in the room—light and puffy on top with a flip on either side. The lady disappeared behind a curtain.

Jack turned to Minnie. "Maybe you could tell us what this is all about, er…."

"Minnie Eastman," Minnie said.

"Yes, Minnie. Why is it y'all have come from—Pennsylvania?"

"I'm so embarrassed. I thought Sam would have called by now. Well, I guess I'd better start by telling about the recent meetings we had with Brother Sam. About the middle of the week, this young lady began manifesting demons."

"That always happens wherever Sam goes," said a dark-haired woman seated by the desk. "There's just so much of the Spirit in Sam that no matter where he goes, demons get all agitated and can't hide, just like when Jesus went places."

Minnie continued, "So, we had us a deliverance session. Brother Sam cast out about a dozen spirits. But after he left, the demons got back in. Jonathan—this is her husband—and I got a couple of them to come out, but for some reason we couldn't keep them out. So we tracked Sam down and he said we should bring her here. By the way, there was quite a prophecy said over this young man."

Jon blushed.

The stout lady returned, lifting the curtain saying, "Jack dea-ah, Marie says no such call has come from Brother Sam."

Jack smiled at Jon. "Well, how convenient that we're having an elder's meeting just now."

Betsy pretended to follow the conversation, looking at each person as they spoke. But whenever Jack's eyes rested on her she stiffened. Despite her confusion Betsy knew that she was the topic of conversation.

"Jonathan, what's your last name?" Jack asked.

"McComb."

"And your baby's name?"

"Jay," Jon said. "I'm concerned about him, too; he's been wheezing."

"May I hold him?" asked an attractive blonde from across the room, she was the only woman with a simple hairstyle.

Jon yielded Jay to her arms.

"Ooh, there now, little fella," she cooed. "My son's name is Jay, too. Is your wife able to feed and care for him?"

Minnie said, "We tried to get her to nurse, but it's hit or miss. She doesn't recognize him much of the time. As for changing and dressing him and so forth, I've been doing most of that."

"I see," said the blonde. Then addressing Jon, "My name is Jill Rine. If it's all right with you, I'd like to care for your baby until your wife is herself again. I'm still nursing my own son, but he's nearly two and doesn't need as much milk. It would be no trouble…"

"Thank you, that would be a great help," Jonathan said. "I haven't thought that far ahead. Up till now my focus has been getting here."

"Well, that takes care of this little guy's needs, all except this nasty cold, that is," said Jill. "But prayer will take care of that. If it's all right with you, Brother Jack, I'll go see if this little guy is hungry."

"Goo-od idea, Sister Jill," Jack said, smiling broadly. "In fact," he added, looking around the room, "… why don't we dismiss? Brother William would you and your wife, Wanda, remain, and oh yes, you too, Brother Chester?"

Everyone else rose to go.

"Brother Jonathan," said Jill, "I'm in the teeny travel trailer right next door. Anytime you want, just come and visit your son."

"Bunny, dear," said Jack to the stout, auburn-haired woman, "… why don't y'all take Minnie and…."

"Mary," Marion Filmore introduced herself.

"And Mary... and get them settled in Brother Wallace's trailer?"

"Right away, Brother Jack. If you ladies will come with me, I'll see to your accommodations."

Brother William flashed a pearly-white smile at Jon, his clear blue eyes contrasted with his deep tan. He was ruggedly-built from his sandy-brown hair down to his highly polished cowboy boots. Like most of the elders, Brother William appeared to be in his mid-forties. The exceptions were: Sister Jill, who was at most, only a couple of years older than Betsy and Jon; and a tall, lanky fellow named Don, who appeared to be in his early thirties. Brother Chester seemed the oldest, somewhere in his fifties.

The four elders sat silently in front of Jon and Betsy for several minutes. Betsy squirmed when Jack looked her way.

Jack suddenly got in Betsy's face and commanded, "Tell me who you are?"

Betsy jumped, riveting full attention on her inquisitor. After a moment of angry but silent defiance, she averted her eyes to the floor.

"Tell me who you are," Jack said again.

"Be-Be-Betsy," she whispered, still averting her eyes.

"Betsy who?"

"Betsy Rutlidge, uh, I mean McComb," she replied, trembling.

Jon was amazed at Betsy's lucidity.

William rose from his seat and knelt before Betsy, placing his hand on her forehead, forcing her to look him in the eye. "The blood of Jesus is against you, devil!"

"The blood of Jesus is against you, devil," Betsy spat back.

Caught off guard, William jerked back.

"Hah!" Betsy sneered.

"What's your name?" Jack said.

Chester rose to his feet, arms folded, eyes half closed.

The jangling of the phone disrupted their probing.

Wanda leaned across the desk and lifted the receiver. "Praise the Lord; this is the Church at Sapa." Her eyes grew round as she cupped her hand over the mouthpiece, saying, "It's Brother Sam!"

Jack took the phone. "Praise the Lord, Brother. Oh yes! Umm-mm. In fact, they're here right now... Yes, pulled in a few minutes ago.... Is that right?" he smiled briefly at Jon. "Umm-mm. We were, in fact, just having us a meeting, discussing that very topic when they arrived... Well, y'all do as you see fit. Yes... yes. The end of April? Not till then? Well, y'all have yourself a blessed journey, and we'll see y'all the end of April."

Jack replaced the receiver. "We can pray with the McComb's later," he said to his fellow elders.

The outside door opened. "Where are we going to put this young lady and her husband, Brother Jack?" asked Bunny, returning from escorting Minnie and Mary to their lodgings.

"For now we can unfold the studio couch and let them sleep in this room. After her deliverance we'll make other arrangements if they decide to stay with us…" he turned to Jon and added with a big smile, "… which would be no trouble ay-tall!" What are your plans, Brother Jonathan?"

"Well… I need to take Minnie and Mary back to Pennsylvania, and then settle our affairs. Then… come back here."

"I see. And what do your folks think of y'all coming to a deliverance farm?"

Jon laughed nervously. "Oh, they don't have any idea where we are."

Jack's face grew serious. "What will they think when they find out?"

"They'll be upset, I imagine. You see, they don't believe in the gifts of the Spirit, much less that a Christian can be demon possessed."

Chester asked, "Are they saved?"

"Yes, my folks are Baptist, and Betsy's are Bible Fellowship."

The next couple of hours was spent in question and answer as the elders got to know a little more about this young couple that had appeared on their doorstep.

Later in the afternoon the door opened admitting several girls who had been summoned by Sister Bunny. One of these girls, Marie, switched on the public address system and announced, "Brothers and Sisters, it's time to cease your labors and prepare for the evening meal." Loudspeakers strategically placed around the farm echoed her message.

"Y'all will come with us to the Golden Tabernacle to share our dinner, won't you?" Bunny said to Jon and Betsy.

Jack and Bunny escorted the McComb's down the pebbled trail as teenaged girls left their trailers and joined the entourage. From the opposite side men and boys likewise filed toward the door of the large steel building.

Jack said, "You can see how large our little family has grown. There are almost ninety of us now."

The Golden Tabernacle served as dining hall, meeting hall, recreation room, schoolroom and whatever other purpose required a large, indoor area. Eight-foot-long folding tables and chairs were set up for the meal. Jon noticed that men and boys migrated to one side while girls and single women went to the other. This was not strictly true however, for each table appeared to have at least one married couple. Everyone went to a table and stood behind a chair, waiting for the signal to be seated.

Betsy and Jon were directed to the table nearest the door—Jack's table. Minnie and Mary were already there. Betsy and Jon sat between Jack and Bunny.

When the parade of arrivals slowed to a trickle, someone started singing Gaither's The Family of God.

After all three verses, Jack pronounced, "Ay-men!" Scuffling, scraping sounds filled the room as everyone took their seats.

Serving girls carrying platters of food streamed from behind a makeshift wall that separated the kitchen from the dining area. It all reminded Jon of summer camp.

"Why, thank you, Sister Diane," said Jack to the pert teenager placing a steaming plate of potatoes on the table. "It's so ni-ice of you to be a servant to us."

The girl blushed, murmuring something about her duty, then scurried away to fetch another dish for another table.

Betsy darted angry glances at everyone but was otherwise well behaved.

"So, what do you think of this farm, Jon?" Minnie asked. "Is it everything I said it would be?"

Jon looked around at people eating, chatting, and laughing, then out the window at the red mud and simple trailers huddled along the thin pebble pathway. He could live here; at least until Betsy got delivered; he might even enjoy the experience. "Certainly is," he said.

CHAPTER SIXTEEN

...let me not be ashamed, for I put my trust in Thee... Psalm 25:20

After dinner Jack questioned Jon more closely about Betsy's personality and family history. Wanting Betsy to keep touch with her baby, Bunny and Wanda escorted her to Jill's trailer.

Jonathan watched them go, saddened that Betsy was no longer directly under his care; but, the same would have been true had he committed her to a psychiatric ward.

Jack intruded on Jon's thoughts. "Has your wife ever been involved in the occult?"

"Not willingly. She told me about a youth fellowship party at her house once; one of the girls convinced the others to do a seance. She didn't participate and tried to get her Mom to stop it. The whole thing really scared Betsy."

"And you say she had a breakdown before you even met her?"

"That's right. Her dad took her to a Mennonite psychiatric hospital. For six weeks they tried this and that, but when they gave her lithium she snapped right out of it."

"Uh-huh... well, Brother Sam indicated that she needs deliverance, and then day by day training to help her maintain her deliverance."

Jon nodded.

"And what about you? What kind of work have you done?"

"I've done lots of different things," Jon said. "I worked on a menagerie, in a meat packing plant, a factory, and as a lab tech analyzing plating vats."

Brother Jack looked out the window toward the Rine's tiny trailer where Bunny and Wanda were bringing Betsy back to the Main Trailer from an unsuccessful attempt to get Betsy to suckle Jay.

"I don't think we'll need metal-plating expertise here, but your zoo-farm experience might prove useful. We don't have any animals yet, but we'll be getting some shortly."

"It's pretty serious," Bunny said coming in the door. "She doesn't seem to want anything to do with her baby."

"That's right, Brother Jack," said Wanda, "…she thought that her child was Jill's two year old."

Betsy mumbled, "What have they done to my boy?" under her breath, fluttering her eyelids.

Jack went to the hallway, pulled the curtain back and called, "Marie."

She appeared immediately.

"Marie," said Jack, "…announce an elder's meeting tonight at 7:30."

Marie went to the microphone and made the announcement.

"I'll take care of the meeting then, Brother Jack, if that's alright with you," said Bunny.

Jon swallowed a lump in his throat. Was the "elder's meeting" going to be a deliverance session… for Betsy? But then, wasn't that why he'd brought her to Mississippi?

"Y'all come down to the meeting in the Golden Tabernacle with us," said Bunny to Minnie, Mary and Jon.

Jon hesitated, wanting to be at the deliverance, but Jack smiled, encouraging Jon to go along to the meeting.

"Okay," Jon finally agreed.

"Fi-ine," said Jack.

Jon longed to stay for Betsy's sake—to be a familiar face among the strangers. His eyes brimmed.

Jack smiled and said, "Now don't you worry 'bout a thing. We're jest gonna have a little prayer time with your wife while y'all are down there getting blessed."

As Jon, Minnie and Mary fell in with the procession on the way to the Golden Tabernacle, Minnie asked, "Bunny, how often do you have meetings?"

"We meet every night and twice on Sunday. At first I took exception, telling my husband that it was just too much, that we needed some free time. But he remained adamant that we needed meetings more than we needed free time. Of course, when the weather turns nicer, we have our Friday night meetings outside around the campfire,"

Bunny said, pointing to a ring of felled tree trunks encircling a stone firepit. "Everyone looks forward to that; and then it doesn't seem like all we do is have meetings."

"My goodness," exclaimed Minnie, " …with working all day and meetings every night you sure do keep everybody busy. Isn't it difficult to make sure the teens have private devotions?"

"We don't encourage private devotions. In fact, that's why we have meetings all the time. The elders supply all the spiritual food they'll need, giving deeper insights than they'd get on their own; besides, many would likely get deceived."

The tables inside the Golden Tabernacle had been moved to the back of the building; chairs were now in rows facing a platform replete with microphone, piano and lectern.

The crowd was predominantly teens, with a smattering of other age groups. A half dozen older men looked uncomfortably out of place as they clustered in the very back row.

"Well, Praise the Lord, brother," said David, the teen who'd first welcomed Jon to the farm. "I sure am glad to see y'all here tonight. Would y'all mind if I sat with you?"

"I'd like that," Jon said, hoping to pump him for information about the farm. Before he could ask any questions, however, Bunny took the microphone, saying, "All right, now, settle down; get a seat."

Everyone immediately hushed as a young woman at the piano played a lively tune.

A blind, frail, red-haired girl in the front row stood up and played along on an accordion. "Well GLORY!" the blind girl exclaimed with alarming volume for one so slight. She then launched into a gusty rendition of Jesus is My Strength and Song.

The crowd rose to their feet and the rafters reverberated with the thunderous clapping and singing. When that song stopped, Loretta—the blind accordionist— launched into another song based on Isaiah Six.

Hands waved aloft as individuals surrendered in worship. Jon timidly raised his hands shoulder high. When the song finally ended nearly everyone sang or spoke in tongues.

Several more songs followed. David occasionally flashed a bright smile at Jon, then shut his eyes and resumed singing. Presently the singing stopped and the polyphony of praise faded.

Jon wondered why everybody still stayed on their feet.

"Behold," boomed David from alongside Jon, "…I am the Lord. Is there anything too difficult for me? Have I not chosen you to be my Bride, to restore the earth to purity? Do not consider your own weakness, says the Lord, for I have put my Spirit in you that you may glorify me with your works. Let the weak say, 'I am strong'; let the barren say she has many children. It is time to rise up and overcome the Wicked One. Prepare your hearts for the day of battle, for behold I send judgments on the earth, a dividing of my sheep from the goats; a separating of the wheat from the chaff. Have I not selected you to be my divine instruments to purge that rebel, Lucifer, off the earth? Prepare yourselves for the battle; your enemy like a roaring lion walks about seeking whom he may devour. The fainthearted will not stand before him; those divided by denominations will not overcome him. Those corrupted by the Babylonian world system will not even recognize him when he comes. But you, my children, I have chosen you to confound the mighty. Thus says the Lord."

"Furthermore, my children," a young man with curly, blond hair and horn-rimmed glasses across the room continued the theme, "I will give you the weapons you need to fight. I will equip you with holy armor. I will steady your weak knees and strengthen your feeble hands that hang down. Arise and face your enemy. Thus saith the Lord."

"Ay-men!" said Sister Bunny into the microphone. "Y'all be seated now. "Yes, Brother David, what is it?" she asked, noting David's upraised hand.

David stood. "I had a vision during the praises, Sister Bunny, There were several dark clouds over different people in the meeting. And as we began singing, pillars of light entered the building and chased the dark clouds out the door. Then I saw a golden throne hanging in the air over the platform. There was an embroidered, linen robe draped over the arm of the chair. On the throne was a crown studded with jewels. In the last part of the vision, the pillars of light came and bowed before the throne."

"Hallelujah!" Bunny said, "The Lord is saying that as we rise up in praise, the enemy will be driven from our camp, and we can assume our rightful position on the throne beside the Lord, wearing our redeemed garment, crowned with His glory."

"Amen," and "Praise the Lord," resounded all around the room while Loretta boomed, "Well glory!"

"Tonight, brothers and sisters," Bunny said, "… we're going to have a test on the tape we heard last night, 'Israel, Prince of God." Several groans greeted this announcement. "Sister Connie Ann, will you and a couple of other sisters please pass out these tests? That's a good servant. Now everyone put your name at the top of the page so you can be sure y'all will get your own paper back."

Jon hadn't heard the tape, but thought that, being raised a Baptist, as well as his own studies, he ought to do fairly well. He signed his name. Only then did he glance over the questions. People around Jon were already writing answers, so he too, bent to the task.

After forty-five minutes, aside from not knowing the answers, his mind kept wandering to the Main Trailer.

Bunny's voice caught Jon wool-gathering. "All right, that should be enough time. Exchange papers."

Someone put a paper in Jon's hands and waited for him to reciprocate. Then Bunny went over the test question by question. "Alright now, who has the answer to number one, 'What is the meaning of Israel?'"

Jon winced when someone volunteered, "Prince of God." Jonathan had written "God's chosen nation." But the second question he got right: Jacob meant "schemer, supplanter". Several wrong answers later, it became evident that Jon didn't know the code to even comprehend the questions. To the initiated, terms like "first born" or "second born" meant much more than just birth order. Each name like Jacob, Esau, Leah or Rachel had significance. He hoped the person grading his test would be merciful.

"And the last question, 'Give another connotation of the name Israel'?" asked Bunny, holding up her test copy.

"One through whom God fights," came the quick response from up front.

Jon sighed, another wrong answer.

Seeing the "fifty-six" grade when his paper came back, Jon quickly folded and put it away. David had scored a ninety-two. Aware of Jon's embarrassment, David encouraged, "If y'all had heard the tape, y'all wouldda done as good as everybody else. Brother Sam makes the Bible so understandable; you can feel his anointing even from tape."

After the meeting David and Jon lined up for the evening snack. Minnie and Mary decided to forego the snack, retiring to their quarters so as to be fresh in the morning for the journey back to Pennsylvania.

As they moved through the queue Jon told David why he'd come to the farm. "When Betsy is better we'll return to Pennsylvania. Then our folks will see God still does miracles."

"Praise the Lord! That really blesses me to see such strong faith. I've been here almost three weeks now, and get more blessed every day," David said with a grin. "I came here to learn how to be a prophet. The Lord sent me here for training. Brother Jack and Sister Bunny both confirmed my calling."

Bunny, coming up behind, broke in, chiding, "Brother David, we do not announce what we think God's calling is on our life."

David's face flushed and he dropped his gaze to the floor. But he recovered quickly, regaining his broad smile when Bunny suggested, "Why don't you show Brother Jonathan around and introduce him to some of the family?" Then to Jon, "I'm going to see how the prayer for your wife is going. Wait here another twenty or thirty minutes and meet some of the other brothers and sisters."

As the clean-up crew began sweeping the floor David led Jon around, introducing him to various people. Eventually, those still milling about were advised to return to their trailers. Jon stepped out into the crisp night air, took a deep breath and thanked David. Minnie was right; this truly was a special place.

An ugly cacophony of loud, angry voices incongruous with the serenity Jon had just experienced bombarded him as he neared the Main Trailer. This was a prayer meeting? Had this din been going on the last three hours? How could anyone bear up under that?

One voice rose above the general hubbub, "In the name of Jee-sus, in the name of Jee-sus!"

Jon bit his lip. His poor, darling Betsy—already so confused; how could she survive all that angry shouting? Of course, the anger wasn't directed at her, but how was she to know the difference? Brother Sam's deliverance had been so calm and controlled…

Jon shook his head. Doubt mustn't be allowed; he must trust these people; he must remember what he'd witnessed. Betsy wasn't mentally ill; she didn't have a chemical imbalance. He must believe that coming here was for Betsy's good, else he'd never be able to live with himself. The die was cast: either God led him to Mississippi and all would turn out well, or he was deceived and in the process of destroying his family.

Jon turned the doorknob. Sister Bunny was waiting just inside as if expecting him. She put her hands on both doorjambs blocking the entry. "It's a good report, Brother Jonathan. We'll be here a short while yet, so why don't y'all go next door to Sister Jill's and visit your darling son? We'll send someone over to fetch you when we're finished."

Jon peeked beneath Bunny's outstretched arms. Betsy was seated on a chair—or was she tied to it?—in the middle of the room, glaring at everyone like a trapped animal. She didn't see Jon; for that, he was thankful. A man knelt in front of Betsy, tracing a cross on her forehead, chanting, "The blood of Jesus is against you, devil. The blood of Jesus is against you, devil." Someone else shouted in her ears, "Come out of her NOW! In the name of Jee-sus!" Others stood around, praying in tongues.

Bunny's firm hand on his arm guided Jon back outside. The cool, night air stung his tear-filled eyes. The door closed.

Through trembling lips Jon cried out, "Oh God! This had better be of You!"

Jill and her husband, Claude, received Jonathan warmly. Jon cuddled and played with his son for half an hour, feeding, burping, rocking and lulling him to sleep. But his thoughts were focused on the larger trailer just a hundred feet away.

Jill's husband, Claude, though deaf, was an expert lip-reader. He was swarthy with wavy, black hair and olive skin. His eyes, like his wife's, were clear and friendly. Jon told them how Betsy and he had gotten involved in the Move and how they believed God for Betsy's healing.

Jill told Jon that she had been an elder in another body, but felt the Lord sent her to the deliverance farm. Claude, the only qualified plumber on the farm, was kept busy maintaining the camp's water lines, flush toilets and drains.

Half an hour later a girl with long, red hair came from the Main Trailer and asked, "Is Jonathan McComb here?"

"Yes, Sister Kim, he's right here," Jill said.

"You can come back now," said the teen. "The prayer session for your wife is ended... for now."

"How is she?" Jon asked, donning his coat.

"Well... you'll see."

That answer comforted like a bed of nettles.

"Brother Jonathan," Bunny greeted as Jon stepped inside, "... you and your lovely wife will sleep on this fold-out couch, is that alright?"

Jon nodded, searching the room for Betsy. There was no trace of her.

"I'll just get a couple of the girls to make it up then." She went to the curtained- hallway and called, "Marie, Agnes..."

Would Betsy be herself? Dare Jon hope?

Marie and another girl Jon presumed to be Agnes entered bearing blankets, sheets and pillows. While they prepared the foldout couch, Bunny led Betsy into the room. "Here she is, Brother Jonathan. Doesn't she look lovely? It's a good report from the prayer session tonight. My husband says to tell you that everything is going just fine, so don't you worry none."

Betsy shuffled along, her eyes downcast, face expressionless, fists clenched.

Jon rose to greet her, "Hi Betts, how do you feel?"

Betsy didn't look up.

Jon's heart sank. This was the good report? Betsy was as psychotic as ever. Jon looked at Bunny, frustration and grief fueling the challenge rising in his thoughts . He blurted, "She's no better! After all that shouting she endured, she's still the same?"

"Now, now, Brother Jonathan, don't you fret none. Tonight was just to see what we're up against. At this very moment my husband and Brother William are seeking God for a sign. Didn't I tell you it was a good report? Just believe it. Y'all will just have to be patient."

Elders were to be trusted, Minnie had taught.

Jon's spiritual immaturity was challenged in that he hadn't seen anything accomplished during those hours of screaming. "But in this Move of God," Minnie had said, "we walk by faith, not by sight." Jon bit his lip and meekly nodded.

Bunny smiled then turned to Marie and Agnes, nudging, "Come on now girls, it's time we were all asleep in our own beds."

Agnes said to Betsy in a tough, Brooklyn accent, "You hang in there, Sis, ya hear? Jesus is gonna set you free." Then to Jon, "Don't you worry, Brother. I was in worse shape than her when they brung me here, 'cause of all the drugs I fried my brains with. But I got delivered, and then learned how to keep my victory, glory to Jesus. You'll see; she'll be fine."

"Thanks."

Agnes smiled, then disappeared behind the curtained doorway of the hall.

Jon switched off the light, undressed to his underwear and slipped beneath the covers. Betsy remained huddled on the foot of the bed.

"Betsy, Hon, come lay down," Jon said.

"We mustn't sleep. We must watch and pray," Betsy said in a monotone.

"Hon, we're amongst God's people, you can relax."

"She's an angel of light sent to deceive." Betsy suddenly whirled around demanding, "What have they done to my baby?"

"He's right next door, with Sister Jill."

"I want my baby. They can't give him away to somebody else!"

"Sister Jill is just taking care of him till you feel better."

"I want my baby! They can't have my baby!" Betsy cried hysterically. She climbed over the bed on her hands and knees, whining, "I won't let them take my baby away."

"Calm down, Betts. Jay is with Sister Jill until you're feeling better." Jon went to put his arm around her shoulder.

Betsy yelped and jumped out of bed and stood trembling in the middle of the floor. "Don't you touch me," she shouted.

The curtain opened. Bunny and Jack Halstead rushed into the room. "What's the trouble?" Jack asked turning on the desk lamp.

"She's afraid we won't get our son back. I tried to comfort her, but she jumped out of bed and started yelling."

"Um—mm. Sister Betsy, y'all best come to the back room with my wife and me tonight."

" Brother Jack, those demons want to hide in her baby," Bunny said. "They don't want us to know where they hid when we chase 'em out. Well, we're on to their little tricks." Then to Jon, "See, they're all riled up and looking for a place to hide. I told you it was a good report."

Jack and Bunny led Betsy back to their quarters, leaving Jonathan in the dark, confused, softly praying, "Oh Lord, oh Lord," till sleep overtook him.

CHAPTER SEVENTEEN

They departed into their own country another way... Matthew 2:12

SUNDAY, FEBRUARY 20

Jonathan, Minnie and Mary had been northbound since early morning. Darkness descended as they neared the Tennessee—Virginia border.

Jon had hugged Jay to his chest before he left the farm, but when he tried to say goodbye to Betsy, she turned away, giving no sign that she even knew him.

Bunny's parting words rang in Jon's ears: "Remember who you are and what you're called to." Although she said that every time anyone left the camp, it reminded Jon that God was shaping into an apostle him through all these trials.

"We'd better find a motel," Minnie said in such a manner that wasn't open to discussion. Bristol was twenty miles behind. A snowy expanse lay on either side of the road. The rainstorm that had greeted them on the way south had been a monster snowstorm in the northerly regions.

Jon spied a Motel 6 sign. "How about there?" he asked.

"Well, I know they don't mean anything by it," Minnie said, "… but six is the number of carnal man."

"That's a no, I take it? I sure have a lot to learn about types and shadows. At least I'll be in the right place to learn it."

"You're right about that," Minnie said with a twinkle in her eye. "You'll learn things at that farm that Sonya and I could never teach you. You'll probably come back to Stroudsburg teaching us."

Mary pointed out another motel sign and Jon took the next exit.

MONDAY, FEBRUARY 21

The travelers hit the road early the next morning.

The pressure of decision making was off Jon's shoulders. The die had been cast; only consequences remained—be they blessed or condemned.

By late morning they neared Staunton, Virginia. Minnie sighed as they passed a sign for the Skyline Drive. "I remember going up there on my honeymoon with my ex-husband," she said wistfully.

"I didn't know you were married," Mary said from the back seat.

"Oh yes, he was a good man, but he had no heart for the Lord. When I got saved and started going to church he took to drinking. He eventually moved out."

"He's still alive?" Jon was also intrigued.

"Well… but he's dead to me."

"You mean he's reprobate?" Jon asked.

"I'm free from him," Minnie said. "If I met a man, and the Lord so led, I could marry again. I'm alive in Christ; my husband is dead in trespasses and sins; therefore I'm free to marry again."

Jon asked, "You mean that you're not bound because he's not a Christian?"

"That, and the fact that he left me," she explained. "Brother Sam had a teaching about that in one of the conventions; Lubbock I believe."

"Man, I need to relearn the whole Bible," Jon said.

"Jonathan, let's go up there. It's such a beautiful, scenic drive," Minnie said.

"Where?"

"The Skyline Drive. It runs parallel to the interstate, so we won't lose much time. After forty or so miles we could come back down."

"I don't think we should squander our time. It'll take us out of our way, and the road won't be a four-lane highway like this."

"Oh, it's been so long since I was up there…. Who knows when I'll be back this way again? It's so high you can see for miles. Yes, I think we should go," she decided.

"Jon is right, Minnie," said Mary from the back seat. "All this traveling is tiresome. Even an extra half-hour is too much."

"And besides, look at all the snow," said Jon. "Up there, it's got to be deeper. Roads will be drifted shut. We'd get stuck."

"Oh, bosh," said Minnie. "Virginia has snow plows. I'm sure they keep that road open. In this Move of God you'll learn that when an elder suggests something, you obey as a matter of submission."

Jon bit the inside of his lip.

Minnie, just gazed at the passing scenery.

Jon sullenly took the Skyline Drive exit.

"There aren't any other cars," Mary commented.

Snowdrifts did indeed cover the road the higher they went. Jon gunned through a large one, sliding sideways. But he dutifully pressed on until they finally encountered a barricade with a sign stating, "CLOSED FOR THE WINTER—OPEN APRIL 1".

Jon swallowed the rising rebuke. If Minnie, as an elder, had truly heard from the Lord, why was the road closed? Was it possible that elders didn't always hear from the Spirit? Dare Jon even consider that possibility, having turned his family and future over to the Move?

Jon nearly got stuck turning the car around on the narrow, snow-covered road. As they went back down the road had become even worse; a whipping wind had made the snowdrifts deeper and longer. The detour had added four unnecessary hours to their journey.

They crossed into Pennsylvania long after dark rather than late afternoon. Mary called her husband, Larry, from a diner, telling him when they'd arrive at Minnie's. The three resumed their journey with a minimum of conversation.

Jon turned down Minnie's street. Larry, leaning against his car, waved in greeting. Soon Larry and Mary were on their way to New Jersey.

Jon, too tired to drive to Tannersville, accepted Minnie's invitation to spend the night.

It felt surreal at being back where the spiritual battle had begun. Jon was half way up the stairs when the phone rang. He paused in mid-step, his hand tightly gripping the railing.

"Now who knows we're back at this hour?" muttered Minnie, shuffling to the phone. "Hello?" After a moment she looked at Jon and said, "Yes, he's right here." Cupping her hand over the phone she whispered, "I think it's your mother."

"Oh Lord, does it have to begin already?" Jon took the phone. "Hello?"

"Hi, Jonny, it's me, Sonya, your sister. I've come from Joliet to talk to you. Can we get together tomorrow?"

Jon hesitated; his sister, a Baptist pastor's wife, had no framework to comprehend what he'd been through. "I don't know, Sonny, I've got a lot to do in a short time..."

"Please Jon, I want you to tell me what's going on. I'm not uninitiated about demons. In fact, I recently had a very enlightening discussion with a man who has a ministry casting evil spirits out of Christians."

"Well... would you like to come with me as I close out our apartment."

"You've decided to live on that farm?"

"Betsy and Jay are already there. As soon as I tie up loose ends, I'm joining them."

There was a pause, then she asked, "What time will you pick me up?"

CHAPTER EIGHTEEN

And Laban said to Jacob, What hast thou done, that thou hast stolen
away unawares to me, and carried away my daughters... Genesis 31:26

"Hi Jon," said Sonya, sliding into the passenger seat.

"Hi Sonny," Jon returned, hoping to set a friendly tone by using her nickname. Disagreement was inevitable; but hopefully it would remain civil. Jon pulled onto the main road.

Sonya Kyle, four years Jon's senior, was, strong-minded and persuasive. Early on she'd set the course of her life to either be a missionary or a pastor's wife. Graduating valedictorian from High School and Magna Cum something-or-other from Philadelphia College of the Bible, she was an intimidating force.

Jon, on the other hand, was a junior college dropout, hadn't kept any job for more than a year, and was now involved in "a cult." Sonya could make eloquent arguments from the original Greek as to why speaking in tongues, healing and casting out demons weren't for today, but... there was no denying what Jon had witnessed and experienced since joining the Move.

"Mom and Dad must be pretty upset to drag you out here from Illinois."

"Concerned is more the word," Sonya said. "I don't know what kind of power these people have over you, but you've got to admit that you've made some pretty bizarre decisions lately, even for you."

Jon smiled at her wry humor. "If you had been there, Sonny, and saw what I saw, you'd know why I followed this course."

"Jon, we don't have much time, and I realize that you're anxious to get on the road to Mississippi, but there are a couple of..."

"How did you know it was Mississippi?"

"Oh, your father-in-law had you traced."

"Traced? How?"

"I'm not sure exactly, but he knew you were headed to Mississippi before you got there. He's kept Mom and Dad apprised almost daily. Anyway, I'm not going to try to argue you out of your beliefs about tongues and healing, or even demonic possession."

"That's a relief," Jon grinned.

"In fact, since this business has come up, I've studied First Corinthians 12, 13 and 14 closely, and wonder if maybe those gifts might be for today. I'm just not sure—yet. As for demonic possession, I believe that's a very real possibility—even for Christians."

"So you said on the phone. Why the switch?"

"Lionel and I had an unusual experience not too long ago. A man and his wife visited us and related that Christians can have demons in them. He claimed the Lord had given him a ministry of casting out evil spirits. He further explained that demons could lurk inside people from childhood experiences, and if not dealt with, can remain indefinitely."

"Yeah! That's what Sam Fife teaches, too."

"He also claims to have cast demons out of Pentecostals," Sonya continued. "The most prevalent demon in Pentecostals responds to the name of 'Speaking in Tongues.'"

"I thought you said you believed those gifts were for today?"

"I said I thought maybe; I'm not yet fully convinced. The point is that everything supernatural isn't necessarily from God."

"Oh, I know that," Jon responded. "I've heard demonic tongues."

"You have? How could you tell? Was it during one of their meetings?"

"No... it was Betsy. One night before we went to Mississippi, Minnie and I cast out a spirit. As Minnie began to prepare herself, praying quietly in tongues, Betsy began shouting strange words in a harsh, guttural tone, anger and hatred written all over her face. The glare in her eyes was pure hatred. It certainly wasn't the Holy Spirit."

"I see." Sonya settled back to reconsider. "Have you... ever spoken in tongues?"

"Not exactly. But I've had English words of praise come to mind."

"Like what, may I ask?"

"Sure. Words like: 'Thank You Jesus, You are exalted, You reign on high, You are supreme over all creation and worthy of praise.' Stuff like that."

J.M. MACLEOD

"Well," Sonya said thoughtfully, "... scripture is clear that no one can call Jesus blessed but by the Holy Spirit. Although I envy your newfound devotion, I'm worried that this group is deceptive. But, on the other hand... you may have found a fuller dimension of walking with God than we Baptists like to admit exists. Nevertheless, questionable issues remain."

This was going better than Jon had hoped. "Such as?"

"To name a few: the secretive manner in which you fled to Mississippi; your past rebellion to Mom and Dad; the way you and Betsy conducted yourselves while courting; lying to your in-laws about Betsy's mental condition. Jonny, how can God honor sneakiness by healing Betsy? It would compromise His holiness to reward such activities. Can't you see that?"

Defensive arguments rose in Jon's mind, but died before they found voice. What his sister said was true, to some degree. But, were God's gifts and blessings conditional? If so, who lived such a holy life as to deserve God's grace? "I see what you're saying, Sonny," Jon said, "...and for the most part, you're right. I've behaved immorally and shamefully; but as for going to Mississippi—I have to believe that the Lord led me; not that I haven't had doubts. Believe me, it was the toughest decision I've ever made. I didn't go to Mississippi lightly."

"I believe you, Jon. I'm—we're just very concerned. Cults work the way this 'Move' does. That has us worried. I don't want to judge, but I fear that this group is a cult. Maybe they're okay, but I have a gut feeling that you're doing great harm to your family as well as your own faith."

Might Sonya be right? After all, she was the family's Bible scholar...

That familiar unease rose in the pit of Jon's stomach. If it turned out that the Move was deceptive, he must take Betsy and Jay to a safe place. On the other hand... if the Move was right, and his sister—despite all her education—was wrong, should he needlessly subject himself to more soul-wringing doubt?

The night Sam Fife cast spirits out of Betsy was a vivid memory. What had Baptists ever taught about deliverance? The only group Jon had ever encountered that recognized and dealt with demons was the Move. Betsy was in the best possible hands.

"You've been quiet a long time," Sonya said.

"Just considering... I promise to examine everything in the light of scripture."

"Just remember that cults distort scripture; their doctrines and methods appear to be in line with what the Bible teaches, but in reality, they contradict."

Jon turned into the gravel drive of their Tannersville apartment. "I'll bear that in mind."

Sonya assisted Jon, sorting piles of clothing into those that were suitable for farm life and those that were to be given to charity.

"Why are you putting all Betsy's pant suits and slacks into the pile for the Salvation Army?" Sonya asked. "Isn't she going to need them?"

"Well…" Jon said, noting his sister was wearing a pants suit, "Brother Sam teaches that women wearing pants is a sign of a homosexual spirit."

"Oh, I see." For the first time that morning there was tension between brother and sister. "In other words, they teach that it's okay for a woman to be an elder because in Christ there is no male or female, but she can't wear slacks?"

"I hadn't thought about it like that."

Sonya stopped folding clothes, stared straight into Jon's eyes. "Oh Jonny, can't you see how they've twisted scripture to suit their own ends?"

"It's not like that, Sonya, it isn't. Look, why don't you come and meet Minnie? Then you'll see how special she is, how full of love all these people are."

"No, I don't think so," Sonya declined, turning her eyes back to her work. "I'll confine my comments to you, since you're my brother."

When they finished, Jon settled up with the landlord, who agreed to take the refrigerator in exchange for the last month's rent. Then there was the matter of the borrowed furniture in the apartment. Jon hoped his friends would understand his dilemma of not knowing how to contact them to return their furniture on such short notice.

Jon loaded the car with items to store at his folks' home. On his way back he'd gather what they'd need in Mississippi. After dumping the majority of possessions in the Salvation Army bin, Jon returned Sonya to their parents' house where he also stowed some of their belongings.

Jon spent that night with his folks. The conversation was inconsequential for the most part. Jon's Dad, as usual, went to work in the evening, making an exit shortly after supper. Gertrude McComb, never one to openly confront; just sat with a worried expression as Jon talked with Sonya into the night. Sonya was especially keen to hear the details of Betsy's deliverance.

WEDNESDAY, FEBRUARY 23

Jon went to his employer and drew his last paycheck. He explained that his wife had taken ill and needed special treatment in Mississippi. This explanation received blank stares from unsympathetic bosses.

He then headed to Tannersville and collected the items he and Betsy would need, then turned in the apartment keys.

After cashing his final check and closing out the bank account, Jon headed for Sunbury to face his in-laws.

Charles Rutlidge was outside by the barn working on a piece of farm machinery. The crunch of Jon's tires in the driveway drew his attention. He laid down his wrench and stared as Jon brought the car to a halt.

Jon gulped, breathed a prayer and stepped out. The screen door on the porch creaked open as Minnie Rutlidge, who had been watching since early morning, stepped out and called down from the patio, "Hi Jon."

"Hi," he answered. How she could be so cordial—even friendly, considering the circumstances? Jon turned back to Mr. Rutlidge and said, "Hi Dad."

"Hello boss," Charles Rutlidge responded in his gravelly voice. "How's the car I gave you riding?"

"Fine, fine, holds the road real good."

"Want some coffee and a Danish?" Minnie Rutlidge asked, looking over the railing.

"Uh, no thanks, I want to get as far as I can while there's daylight. I came by to apologize for the sneaky way I took Betsy and Jay to Mississippi. And… for not keeping you informed. I didn't think you'd understand."

"It takes a man to admit when he's wrong," Charles said. "I always say, 'Train up a child in the way he should go, and when he's old he'll not depart from it'. When he is old—not when he is young, but old, the Bible says. You're young; you'll make mistakes; but I know your mother and daddy. I know they raised you right. When you get older you'll get some sense and come back to how you were raised. I'm not too worried about all this."

"Well, I'm not sure that I'm wrong about—."

"Now, as for Betsy," he continued, "...that girl has got to have her lithium. I spent thousands of dollars to find that out. You see to it she gets it, and in a week she'll be right as rain."

"Her problem isn't just a lack of lithium—," Jon said.

"Oh I know; you want her healed. But God works through doctors now. The doctors discovered she needs lithium. That's all there is to it, pure and simple. Now it may be that there's lithium in the plants they grow down in Mississippi, and when she eats her vegetables and greens, she'll begin to feel better. No matter how she gets it, she's got to have lithium, understand?"

"Dad, I've got to do what I feel is right, and—."

"Yes, I know you do. And I'm telling you, lithium is what's right."

It was pointless to argue.

"Now you take good care of her," he said, taking Jon's silence as assent. "I gave her away one day, so she's not my concern any longer. Your daddy wanted me to get the Mississippi State Police over to this town, what's it called? Euphoria?"

"Eupora."

"Right, Europa (sic). I told your Daddy that I wasn't gonna get involved since I gave Betsy away. I told him that when you get older you'll return to your senses, and that he should just believe the Bible and quit worrying."

Jon looked up at his mother-in-law, not knowing what to say.

"Well, you'll be wanting to get on the road, I suspect," Charles said, extending his beefy hand.

Minnie Rutlidge called over the railing, "Keep in touch. Write or phone, and let us know your address."

"I will," Jon promised. "Well, I'd better go now."

"One more thing," Charles said as Jonathan turned toward his car. "Do you need any money?"

"Well, I picked up my last check from Wyandotte, but it was kind of spare. I missed a lot of days."

"This will make sure you get to Euphoria," Charles said, handing Jon two twenties.

Jon had asked the Lord to either make the car run super efficiently or else supply more gas money. God was still providing… "Thanks," Jon said, as he slid behind the wheel.

"See to it she gets her lithium," Betsy's dad called as Jon drove away.

PART THREE

CHAPTER NINETEEN

...his sisters sent unto him saying, 'Lord, he whom thou lovest is sick'... John 11:3

"Brother Jonathan, I believe you ought to come with me to Jackson this afternoon," said Jack Halstead from across the lunch table.

"Sure, but... why?" Jon asked. It was Jon's first full day back on the farm. He looked forward to getting into the routine of farm life. No doubt many others longed for a break from the day-to-day routine and would benefit from a trip to the city. So why was Jack inviting him?

Jack's grin revealed ultra white teeth. "No particular reason. Sister Dixie will be coming along, too. Have you met her yet?"

Jon shook his head.

"No matter; y'all will get along just fi-ine. Come to the Main Trailer around 1:15." Jack rose and headed out the door.

Jon glanced at his watch. He'd been on the farm exactly 24 hours. By now everyone knew his story. He was billeted in an elder's trailer, which gave him little opportunity to mix with others.

Jon had daydreamed about his reunion with Betsy the entire journey from Pennsylvania. Upon arrival, Jon sprinted to the Main Trailer with high hopes. Bunny, Jack's wife, was sorting mail when Jon burst into the addition.

Betsy sat in a rocker wearing headphones, listening to a tape. "Betsy..." Jon intruded, "...it's me, Jonathan."

She opened her eyes for a second, then closed them, ignoring him. Jon's heart sank. Tears welled up. Jon said, "She's no better than when I left."

Bunny looked up. "Brother Jonathan, you must realize that we are not only dealing with powerful deceptive spirits, but Betsy's own will. The Lord will not force her to be delivered against her own will."

"Her own will? Betsy doesn't want to be demon possessed."

Bunny nodded, but added, "She does, however, like some of the deceptions these demons tempt her with. We can cast the demons out, but as long as she clings to their lies they'll have an open doorway to get right back in. We are, however, filling her mind with truth every moment she's awake. We play Brother Sam's tapes over and over. Sister Agnes gives her a test on whatever tape she has been listening to. By the way, have you met Sister Agnes?" Bunny indicated a young, stocky Hispanic woman seated near Betsy. "She's been assigned to watch over your dear wife. Don't you fret none, Brother Jonathan, it won't take long. You just let the Lord do a work of patience in y'all."

That conversation had taken place 24 hours prior. Jon looked at his watch; he had twenty minutes before Jack expected him at the Main Trailer—just enough for a short visit with his son. Hands jammed in his pockets, Jon crossed the field to Jill's trailer. Patience was not one of Jon's strong suits. So be it, the sooner Jon yielded, the sooner the trial would end. He smiled at the absurdity of wanting to obtain patience quickly. Well, at least he wouldn't hinder the process; he would submit and trust to the best of his ability.

"Come in," said Jill just as Jon was about to knock. He entered the Rine's cramped trailer. "I saw you coming." She sat on a kitchen chair, nursing Jon and Betsy's son. Though she was discreetly covered, Jon flushed with embarrassment. "How was your journey?"

"Fine," Jon said, deciding against going into detail. "How's Jay?"

"Well… he still has a cold, though his wheezing is much better. He's feeding well; putting on weight, and generally seems content. My own Jay was jealous when I breast fed, but he's gotten used to the idea now."

Jill's little boy played on the floor with a toy car. He was a genuine towhead, full of the merriment of life.

"Have they told you about your wife?" Jill asked, her head lowered, tending the baby in her arms.

"I keep getting the same answer: 'It's a good report; you just have faith.'"

"They said nothing about the doctor examining her?"

Jon's eyebrows raised. "No. I—I thought… with all the teaching about healing and miracles… that…"

Jill frowned. "Dr. Black came from Eupora and examined both her and Jay." Seeing Jon's confusion, Jill explained, "We sometimes use medicine, though the word of a prophet is sought first. Betsy was examined to make sure she was physically okay, and to start drying up her milk. I'm surprised Brother Jack didn't tell you."

"Maybe he was planning to tell me on the way to Jackson."

"He's taking you to Jackson? That's… interesting." Jill pondered for a moment. "Would you like to burp him?" Jill asked, extending Jay.

Jon took his infant son, gently patting his back.

"Errrp!"

As he cradled his baby, Jon asked about farm life. Jill answered freely.

"It's time to go," Jon said checking his watch and handing his son back. "Thank you for all you're doing."

Jill poked a finger inside Jay's diaper then laid him in the crib. "You're quite welcome, after all, we're all members of the same body."

Jon stepped out into a blustery wind. "I thought Mississippi would be warm," he said to himself, leaning into the frigid blast and heading for the Main Trailer.

Jack was just emerging. Following him was a thin, dark-haired girl. Her lips were set in a grim, straight line; her eyes and nose were red. "Ah, Brother Jonathan," Jack said, "I'd like you to meet Sister Dixie. Like I explained, she'll be coming with us—in fact, her sister is why we're going."

Jon smiled. "Hello."

"First we need to go to Grenada," Jack continued, "…where we'll pick up Brother Patrick. Is that all right?"

"Fine with me," Jon said with a shrug. "I don't even know why I'm going."

"Well, we'd just like to have your company, Brother Jonathan. We're all one, big, happy family, you know."

Jon slid into the Fairlane's rear seat; Dixie sat up front. Brother Jack drove out through a portion of the farm that Jon hadn't yet seen. "Down here is where we do our farming," Jack said, passing an old farmhouse and some outbuildings. "With some remodeling, we'll turn that shed over there into a goat barn. And those fields …" he gestured, "… are where we'll grow corn, potatoes, beans, peas, peppers and such. Do you like snap-beans, Sister Dixie?"

"Sure," she answered noncommittally.

"Go-od," Jack said. "How about you, Brother Jonathan, you like snap-beans, don't you?"

"Can't say as I've ever had them."

"Well, you just take my word for it, you'll like them."

"How many acres does this farm have?" Jon asked.

"Ninety-three acres, give or take," Jack said, glancing at Jon in the rearview mirror. "It looks like more because it's long and narrow. We're driving down through the middle of it. See those trees on the right? That's our border, and the left boundary is about 100 feet into those woods. Brother William tells me it's dark and swampy in there with all manner of snakes and critters."

The Ford passed through the gates and turned onto a macadam road. A signpost read: "Eupora 3 miles". The threesome continued on wordlessly through town.

Dixie stared blankly out the window, sighing occasionally, barely seeing the shacks and shanties as they passed. Finally she turned to Jack and asked, "Will she be alright?"

"I can't rightly say, sister Dixie. All I can do is try to talk to her. If she's awake enough to have faith when we pray, I reckon she'll be alright."

"What happened—if you don't mind my asking?" Jon asked.

Dixie turned around. "My sister was in a bad car accident a couple of days ago. She's been in a coma since. Her spleen is busted, a couple of ribs punctured her lung, her hip is broken and she has a severe concussion. Doctors didn't think she'd last this long." Tears splashed on the seat back. "I heard about all y'all's faith-healing farm and came to see if God could do something."

"You came to the right place," Jon said.

Dixie turned around front again.

Jon's thoughts turned inward as they crossed the wearisome, flat landscape. The farm must be the right place for people in crisis. Surely God would respond to such need. Sometimes it might take a little while… like with Betsy, but, as the Move taught: miracles were soon going to be an everyday occurrence.

Jon followed up, "That's why I brought my wife, because this is the only place that deals with demons instead of just treating mental illness."

Dixie turned around again. "You're Betsy's husband? We both have a lot in common, don't we?"

Jon nodded.

"How did it happen to Betsy? I mean, was it gradual, or all at once?"

Miles passed as Jonathan related their story and how he'd finally made his decision. Jon left out the prophecy about his calling, but told everything else he felt might bolster Dixie's faith.

Jack listened, but said nothing.

"You're quite convinced that it really is demons and not mental illness, then?"

"I was there. Demons spoke through my wife's voice. I saw her gag as they came out. Yes, there's no question."

Jack pulled up to a large gray building. "I'll just go get Brother Patrick. Y'all keep on edifying one another." Jack disappeared behind the hospital's double doors as Dixie told Jon about her sister. With downcast eyes, she said, "The police report said something about drugs and alcohol …"

Several minutes later Jack came down the stairway with a teenager in tow. "Sister Dixie, Brother Jon, this is Brother Patrick."

Patrick nodded shyly and slid into the back seat beside Jon. The teen had blue eyes and close-cropped hair and a friendly but self-conscious smile.

Why had Patrick been in the hospital instead of relying on the elders praying for him?

Jack started the car and headed back out to the main road, asking, "Patrick, did the doctor renew your prescription?"

"Uh, yeah, it's in my pocket," Patrick said, patting his shirt. In answer to Jon's stare he supplied, "Asthma. I get it bad, sometimes."

"Fi-ine. We'll get it filled as soon as we get back from Jackson," Jack said as he pulled onto the four-lane.

"Jackson?" Patrick asked.

"I thought you might like to ride along, Brother Patrick," Jack said. "How was your stay in the hospital? I hope you didn't watch too much of that Babylonian television."

Patrick squirmed. "Well… uh, I sorta did… a little. There isn't much else to do, you know." Patrick's face paled. "There was a World War I movie on called The Blue Max. I saw lots of types and shadows about spiritual warfare," he lamely added.

"Is that right? I'd sure like to hear some of them."

"Well, there were these dogfight scenes—you know, fights between airplanes—and I saw types and shadows of wrestling with demons in that."

"I'd sure like to hear some of those types and shadows; wouldn't you sister Dixie?"

Perspiration broke out on Patrick's brow. "Uh… I saw how the uh, flesh can lead us astray from our goal of winning the war. There was a woman who kept trying to lead the one pilot away from his duties, and how that led to trouble with his commander."

Jack made no further comment.

Jon had enjoyed The Blue Max and movies of that genre. Mercifully, the issue was dropped.

Miles rolled by in silence emphasizing Jack's disdain. Finally, breaking the ominous quiet, Jack asked over his shoulder, "How about a Goo-Goo Cluster?"

"A what?" Jon said, wondering why Jack was offering them baby food.

Jack laughed, saying, "I forgot, y'all are from up north where they don't know about such things as Goo-Goo Clusters. Here, y'all have one. You'll like it." He tossed two chocolate-covered, caramel peanut clusters as large as a fist into the back seat.

Jon unwrapped the candy and took a bite. "Thanks, it's good."

Patrick echoed Jon's sentiments.

Dixie unsuccessfully tried to decline the offer, but Jack insisted. "You're not allergic to chocolate or peanuts, or anything, are you?" he pressed.

"No."

"Well then, come on, have one. Come on, now," he said.

"Okay," she acquiesced. Instead of taking a full bite, Dixie merely nibbled.

Brother Jack embarked on a rambling narration about how the people on the farm moved from Homestead, Florida to Eupora and gradually developed into a deliverance farm.

The farm's history and how they hosted itinerant apostles and prophets fascinated Jon. Jon took the last bite of his candy bar.

"So we loaded up and brought the twelve trailers that now sit on the rim of the hill, and with a caravan of pick-up trucks and cars, we moved the entire encampment from Dade County."

Jon envisioned the logjam of lumbering vehicles blocking two or three miles of the interstate slow lane.

"I see y'all are done with your Goo-Goo Cluster," Jack said, glancing in the rearview mirror. "Here, have another…"

"Oh, no thanks. One was enough. Good, but enough," Jon said.

"Come on now," Jack insisted, "…have another. They're so go-oood."

"No, really, that one quite filled me," Jon said.

"You too, Brother Patrick, have another." Another gray-wrapped candy bar landed in Jon's and Patrick's laps. Patrick shrugged and looked helplessly at Jon. They were so rich, neither could stomach another. Dixie took another tentative nibble, still on her first Goo-Goo Cluster.

"Come on now, you two, eat another." Jack's tone was friendly, but his eyes watching them from the rearview mirror were insistent.

Jon tore open the candy bar, mumbling a polite thank-you. Patrick followed Jon's lead, reluctantly opening the candy on his lap.

Jack continued his monologue of how the trailers were insulated, leveled, and electric and water lines hooked up; he then went into detail about building the Golden Tabernacle. After that people migrated from all over the country to the farm.

Jon dutifully attempted to finish his second Goo-Goo Cluster, nibbling at it as Dixie had wisely chosen to do. Patrick had only taken a bite of his second.

Mississippi rolled past in drab grays and browns. Jon looked resentfully at this second Goo-Goo Cluster. Minnie's insistence on driving up to the Skyline Drive came to mind. Was Jack testing his passengers?

"Brother Sam received a vision of end-time farms spread over the world, sheltering Christians from the Antichrist. How's that Goo-Goo Cluster coming along?"

Jon took a large bite, trying not to gag, then another, and another. A wave of nausea threatened.

"That's what we're accomplishing now," Jack said, smiling as Jon finished the candy bar. "Brother Sam and other apostles fly all over the world, setting up farms—of course not all of them are deliverance farms. Here you go, have another," he said, tossing two more Goo-Goo Clusters into the back seat.

Patrick raised the corner of his lip. He still had half of his second. "Aren't you going to have one," Brother Jack," Patrick asked

"Oh, no-o. Y'all just go ahead and enjoy. I've got lots more up here. How 'bout you, Sister Dixie, ready for another?"

Dixie still had three-fourths of her first.

Jon stared at the Goo-Goo Cluster in his lap. Evidently, it wasn't going to be his last.

"Brother Jon, you're not eating?" Jack said.

"I'm stuffed. Besides, I really shouldn't eat too much candy."

"Oh? Why not?"

Embarrassed at having to point out the obvious, Jon said, "I could stand to lose a few pounds, and all these candy bars won't help."

"Now, don't y'all worry 'bout them Goo-Goo Clusters. Y'all just enjoy." Then, pointing through the windshield, he announced, "Jackson's skyline. That building off to the right must be the hospital."

If Jon ate the third Goo Goo Cluster, he'd get sick. If he didn't eat it, he'd be in rebellion. Appeals were useless; Jack was adamant. Jon unwrapped the Goo-Goo Cluster and broke into a cold sweat.

Jack turned the car into the parking lot.

—·•⋅✄⋅•·—

Patrick and Jon stayed outside the intensive care unit as the swinging doors closed behind Jack and Dixie. White garbed nurses in squeaky, rubber-soled shoes bustled about, engaged in various duties.

"So," Patrick asked, "Why did Brother Jack bring you along?"

Jonathan shrugged. "I don't know. There must be some reason."

"I wonder what's going on in there?" Patrick said. "My guess is that at this very moment Brother Jack is laying hands on Dixie's sister and praying for her healing."

"Wouldn't that shock the doctors if she suddenly sat up, completely healed?" said Jon.

Patrick grinned.

"Hey, even though we're out here, we can join them and claim her healing, too."

"Well… uh, okay." Patrick sheepishly looked at the floor.

"Let's join hands and pray, as it says, 'if any two agree as touching…'" Jon said. "Dear Lord, we join with Brother Jack and ask you to heal Dixie's sister. You have power over injury and death, so we ask for a miracle so that everyone will be amazed and know that You did it. I believe You are healing her. Thank you, Lord."

"Amen," said Patrick, looking shyly around.

"I believe she's well," said Jon.

"Me too."

"Hallelujah!"

"Praise the Lord!"

"I'm so blessed to be in this Move of God where you can actually feel faith," said Jon. "You know, maybe this is why God had me—us—come to Jackson—to pray for Dixie's sister. Maybe Brother Jack needed the extra 'oomph' of our prayer from out here."

The double doors to the ICU swung open; Jack and Dixie returned.

"Is it a good report, Brother Jack?" Jon asked.

Jack gave Jonathan a scrutinizing look. "It's a good report," Jack said; his previous broad smile and light-hearted demeanor gone.

"Well…?" Jon pressed, expecting an account.

Patrick glanced nervously at Jon.

Jack studied Jon for a moment. "One does what one can. The poor girl was hooked up to needles, tubes and bottles—barely breathing. Her spirit was still there, though a spirit of death was also heavily upon her. I rebuked the spirit of death so I could tell her to believe Jesus for healing. That was all I felt led to do."

"Yes, well… she will be healed?" Jon persisted.

Patrick rolled his eyes.

Jack gave Jonathan a long, calculating stare. "Do you believe she will?"

Dixie looked forlornly at Jon through red, swollen eyes.

Jon cautiously answered, "Yes, I believe she'll recover. Patrick and I joined with you in a prayer of faith. In fact, I think that's why the Lord had us come along, to join our faith with yours. Isn't that what Brother Sam teaches—that we should use our faith so it grows."

"Something like that," Jack said guardedly. "We'd best get along now, it's a long ride back. He took Dixie's arm and led down the hallway.

The ride back was quiet; no more Goo-Goo clusters flew into the back seat. About thirty miles out from the farm Jack took a notion to turn up a side road. They bumped and bounced down a country lane and drew up at a farmhouse. The dwelling was dark except for a kerosene lamp lighting a front room and another lantern somewhere in the house's recesses.

His buoyancy returned, Jack said, "We'll just stop here for a bit." Jon and Patrick scrambled out of the cramped back seat.

"Well if it ain't Brother Jack come to call," said a man as a screen door squeaked open. What brings y'all out here this time o' night?"

"Glory, Brother Reggie. We're on our way back from Jackson and thought we might stop in and say 'howdy' for a spell."

"C'mon in then, c'mon in."

They were ushered down a dark hallway into a lantern-lit kitchen warmed by a wood stove. A young, pretty, redheaded woman shoved two logs into the wood stove as the group entered.

"Anastasia, you remember Brother Jack from the Christian farm down by Eupora?" Reggie said.

Anastasia shook wood chips off her apron and smiled. "Of course. Howdy." Her husband's hair was the same bright shade of red. "Praise the Lord. Would y'all like something to et? We're jest about to sit down to supper. It'll only take a second to warm up some stew," she said.

"That would be ni-ice, Sister Anna, if'n y'all are sure there's enough" Jack said.

Anastasia smiled. "Set yourselves down then." She put plates, glasses and silverware on the table. "As you can see Brother Jack," she said, opening a large refrigerator and withdrawing a covered dish, "… we're not totally free of Babylon yet."

Jack introduced Dixie, Patrick and Jon, then related his mission to Jackson.

Reggie, it turned out, was a lawyer in nearby Starkville. He and his wife had purchased a farm near French Camp to revert to a primitive lifestyle so they could learn how to survive the Tribulation. They raised crops and livestock, heated their farmhouse with wood, built their own furniture and even made their own clothing—all while maintaining a successful law practice. "We're almost free of the twentieth century," Reggie said. "Some things still require electricity, however, such as the 'fridge and the tape player—so's we can hear Brother Sam's teachings."

This "pioneer" home deeply impressed Jonathan. Might he and Betsy live like this someday?

CHAPTER TWENTY

... am not I in sport? Proverbs 26:19

WEDNESDAY, MARCH 1

The morning temperature was in the fifties; sunbeams played hide and seek among the clouds, shadows rolled across the bottomland. Jonathan and other "older brothers", as those who had graduated from school were dubbed, waited at the bottom of a hill for the work-oversight elder, William Nobles, to arrive and assign the day's tasks.

David, the young man who'd come to the farm to be a prophet, Danny, Terry and Mickey—three teens from Virginia—waited with Jonathan, leaning against a fence rail. An older man from Texas, Mick O'Shea, stood nearby chewing on a toothpick, watching as Jon's bunkmate, Marvin Fletcher, scurried down the rutted, gravel road. Marvin was newly come from Georgia, and looked the typical ivy leaguer with horn-rimmed glasses and a sandy-brown, JFK style haircut. He was ruggedly handsome despite his bookish glasses.

The elders had assigned Jon and Marvin to a tiny, isolated trailer on the edge of the farm that was owned by one of the Move's traveling apostles.

Mick O'Shea, the lanky, balding Texan, walked just a little slower than he talked. He'd been in the Move for years and had helped claim the Caqueta River farm from the jungle, or so he said. Mick was rambling on about life on the edge of the jungle. "They gots centipedes long as yore finger, spiders and scorpions whut will hide in yore sleeping bags and snakes that has a hankerin' fer human company. Yessir, every mornin' I'd have to shake three inch centipedes outta mah boots," he said, looking around to make sure his audience was impressed. "And ah'd have to do it in sich a way so's the natives didn't see, else they'd a throwed 'em into the breakfast pot. An' ya know the Bible says to et everythin' set in front of ya. If'n we didn't et whut the natives et, they'd git offended an' would quit workin'." He grinned slyly, looked around at his listeners and added, "They don't taste half-bad oncet they's cooked…." He grinned at the groans he received and added, "Y'all will et worse'n thet oncet the Tribulation gits runnin'."

Jon laughed at Mick's outlandish story. If it wasn't for his concern about Betsy, he could thoroughly enjoy being on this "End Time Farm".

Mickey pointed to William Nobles' muscular form trotting down the road. Even at that distance Jon noted the bright gleam of the elder's perpetual smile. William, before moving to the farm, rumor had it, had started out as a shoe salesman and had been so efficient that he wound up owning the store.

"Praise the Lord, Brother William," David greeted.

William light-heartedly said, "Let a hallelujah roll!"

David and Mick O'Shea said, "Hallelujah!"

"I said, 'Let a hallelujah roll!'" repeated William.

All except Jon enthusiastically shouted, "Hallelujah!"

"Is that anything like a bagel?" Jon said.

"Is what anything like a bagel, Brother Jonathan?" asked William, smiling ear to ear, his bright blue eyes sparkling beneath his wavy light brown hair.

"A hallelujah roll!"

A couple of brothers gave an amused groan, but quickly grew silent as William's smile turned into a thin line and his sparkling blue eyes became steely cold. "We do not take holy things, Brother Jonathan, and drag them through the mud of Babylonish humor."

Jon withered.

"Well Glory!" William turned his attention to the others and switched his toothy smile back on, "Let's get down to the farm area and do some work."

Mickey started the tractor and everyone piled on the wagon. Jon silently berated himself for trying to gain acceptance before learning the protocols.

William assigned various tasks to different ones as they bumped along the rutted roadway. Mick O'Shea, David, Danny and Jon were to clean out a decrepit shed that was going to be reborn as a goat barn.

"Oh glory," Mick O'Shea said, "I shore do love goats. Have y'all decided who'll be in charge o' the goats, Brother William?"

"Not yet, Brother Mick," William said, as if to an insistent child. "By the time the goats arrive we'll know whom to appoint."

"Ah've been a-prayin' that it would be me, Brother William. I re-eally believe God gave me a heart fer to love and care fer them goats."

"I know that Brother Mick, I know that. Now, I probably don't need to mention it, but anyone working on a farm needs a pocketknife. Does anyone not have a pocketknife?"

Jon sheepishly raised his hand, the only one to do so. William's toothy smile vanished. He dug into his own pocket and extracted a pearl-handled Barlow knife. He paused, looking at the item in his hand before extending it to Jon, saying, "I want it back at the end of the day."

Jon received the proffered knife, lamenting the two strikes already against him. Jon shuffled toward the shed, jamming the knife into his pocket, hoping he wouldn't need to use it.

While Jon and the others had been at Bible class during the morning, George, a Vietnam veteran who joined the Move shortly after mustering out of the military, had been at work since breakfast, extracting nails from a pile of used lumber. George was tall and well built. His unmilitary, long hair nearly fell into his eyes.

Jon and David swept cobwebs and dust from rafters and walls, choking the air with dust that floated in the bars of sunlight that streamed through the shed's porous roof. Jon's nose began to run. George offered his handkerchief, which Jon gratefully accepted and wore outlaw style over his nose and mouth as he joined George in salvaging nails.

George reminisced as they worked about his two tours in 'Nam, and that the first thing he did after getting out of the military was to attend a Fife convention. Vietnam had scarred him emotionally, causing nightmares and hallucinations. He joined a local body, and after some deliberation by the elders, was sent to the farm for deliverance.

"And... did they cast out any spirits?" Jon asked.

"Nah! They just put me to work all day and meetings all night; by lights out, I'm bushed. Haven't been bothered by dreams nor hallucinations anymore, though."

"How long have you been here?"

"'Bout three months."

"When you're ready, will you return home, or stay here?"

George stopped tugging on a nail and said, "I got a word from a prophetess that I'm to learn wilderness survival. When I'm ready, I'll go to Peace River in Canada."

"Peace River? Is that what the Move calls it, or its real name?"

"I think it's called that. Anyway, that's where I'm headed. How about you? Once Betsy gets delivered, will you stay or go back to Pennsylvania?"

"I'm not sure," Jon said, bending over to pull a sixteen-penny nail out of an oak board. "Brother Sam hinted that we might go to the Caqueta River. But, hearing Brother Mick describe it, I'm not so sure that's where I want to raise a family."

"Mick O'Shea? Don't pay any attention to him. He just likes to hear himself talk. For as long as he's been in the Move he hasn't been given responsibility for anything. Whatever he told you was made up."

Jon's back ached and sweat ran into his eyes despite the morning chill; he took a moment to stretch. George attacked the bent nails still in the planks. Jon closed his eyes and for an instant leaned against a post. A shadow fell across the doorway. Jon opened his eyes and saw William watching the work crew. Jon instantly jerked upright. William shook his head and left.

George wasn't even aware that William had been there. "Let's take a break and get a drink," George suggested. The others happily agreed. They went out into clear air and bright sunshine. A jet of cool, sparkling water cascaded from the pump to the splashboard, splattering their dusty shoes. Jon guzzled freely, enjoying the fresh water springing from the ground.

"Jest like takin' a sip o' the River o' Life, ain't it, Brother Jonathan?" said David, wiping his chin.

"Ah praise the Lord fer this here water," Mick said. "God musta knowed we was gonna be livin' here an' made the water extra special jest fer us."

George scowled and stalked away. Jon relinquished the spigot to the next in line, wondering what had caused the bad blood between Mick and George.

The singing was, as Brother Chester put it, "truly anointed". It had been energetic, at any rate. The assembly had been on their feet, clapping and singing for more than an hour. Jon had been exhausted even before the meeting; now the worship service had drained his last ounce of stamina; he almost slept where he stood. After several minutes of waiting for a prophecy, it became obvious that no one felt inspired. Finally Chester intoned for all to be seated.

A hand touched Jon's shoulder and Jack Halstead whispered in his ear, "I'd like to see y'all after the meeting tonight, alright?" Jon nodded. Jack winked then proceeded forward to take the podium. It was abundantly clear to anyone who'd spent more than twenty-four hours on the farm that Jack and Bunny Halstead were in charge. Whatever they "suggested" got done. David had let it slip that Jack was an apostle and was revered in the Move almost as much as Sam Fife.

Jack addressed the assembly in his down-home, humorous style about the farm's inhabitants professing freedom from Babylon. "I've seen how y'all act in town," he said through smiling lips. "Oh sure, y'all ride through the streets of Eupora lookin' out the van windows at the hippies standing 'round on the corners, and y'all cluck yer tongues, saying, tch tch..." Jack switched to falsetto, "alas Babylon."

Giggles broke out across the room.

"Then," Jack resumed, "... as soon as you get out of the van, you go running into those Babylonian stores and buy fingernail polish and Coca-Cola and all manner of fancy doo-dads to put in your hair so's people will think you have naturally curly hair. And you try on them frilly dresses and fancy shoes that everybody knows will fall apart in a good Mississippi rain, and then bring all that stuff back out to the van, and sit there lookin' out the window, and say to everyone in earshot, 'Alas Babylon!'"

Jon laughed along with everyone else. Jack continued, reminding them that people in the Move were called to perfection, and perfection would never be reached until Christians quit dabbling in the loves and ways of this world.

The meeting ended after one last song about laying burdens at the cross and going on to perfection. Then someone spoke in tongues for thirty-seconds, prompting David to launch into a ten-minute interpretation. Somewhere during the interpretation, Jon's mind wandered. Then the meeting was over.

Jon went looking for Jack, hoping their conversation wouldn't take long, he was ready for bed.

"He went back to the Main Trailer right after speaking," said a girl. Jon jogged the narrow, pebble pathway to the Main Trailer.

As he ascended the steps Jon heard a muffled but heated discussion as he knocked. Marie opened the door. "Oh, Brother Jonathan, Brother Jack is waiting for you. Come in."

Jack Halstead and William Nobles stopped their discussion as Jon entered. Agnes Caliano, Betsy's companion, was also present. "Brother Jonathan, I believe you know Sister Agnes?" said Jack.

Jon nodded. "Hi."

"And of course, you know Brother William. I believe you're in his farm crew? How is the goat barn coming?"

"We start replacing rotten planks tomorrow," Jon said.

"Fi-ine, fine. We had an idea that you might help us train some of the younger brothers to the glory of work, but, more about that later. We've been talking to Dr. Black," he continued, "Have you met him yet?"

"I've seen him from a distance."

"Yes, well, he's a born-again believer—Southern Baptist, I believe," Jack looked to William for confirmation. "We've shared your wife's situation with him. He made some calls and got hold of the psychiatrist who helped her before..."

"Dr. Hotchkiss?" Jon blurted.

"Yes, that's the name. Anyway, Dr. Black thinks it would be a good idea to give lithium to your wife. What is your opinion?"

Jon gasped as if he'd been sucker-punched. Why had he come to Mississippi if God's will was for Betsy to take lithium? She could have gotten lithium back in Pennsylvania? Did Betsy need deliverance or did she need lithium?

"I... I don't know what to say. I... I just want the Lord's will," Jon said, trying to sort out his confusion.

Jack and William exchanged glances.

Could it be that they—elders in the Move of God—were stumped? Were they falling back on medicine? Or... were they looking to vindicate themselves, saying, "What could we do, it was what her husband wanted?"

Jon's pulse pounded in his ears. Didn't they understand that he was in danger of losing his will to see the trial through? "Whatever God's will is," Jon said, locking eyes with Jack.

Jack frowned. "God's will! God's will! Everybody says they want God's will. You're supposed to know God's will. So tell us, what do you want us to do with Betsy? Should we give her lithium, or not?"

"I don't know what to say. You should know what to do. I want whatever God wants. I came here because I was told you could deliver Betsy. I could've given her lithium back in Stroudsburg, but I knew lithium wouldn't cast demons out."

William eyed Jon keenly, "Are you saying you don't want us to give her lithium?"

"I didn't say that. I don't know. You're the elders, do what God shows you. My family is in your hands; you decide what God wants. I don't know enough about healing and living by faith to make that decision. All I know is that God led me to bring Betsy here."

"She hasn't improved since the day you brought her," said Agnes rising from her seat. "I've been with her since the first night. I don't know much about healing and all that either, but I know she needs something more than deliverance."

"Brother Jonathan," Jack said, "…she's your wife. Don't you care enough about her to make a decision?"

Jon bit his lip; he had endured sleeplessness, fasting, family rejection and untold personal anguish, not to mention traveling a thousand miles just so his wife could be set free from demons; of course he loved her and wanted what was best for her. Coming to Mississippi had been the most gut-wrenching decision he'd ever made; and now they wanted him to let them off the hook because they hadn't gotten anywhere?

Jon smoldered. "Yes, I love her very much. That's why she's under your care. If she needs lithium, then give it to her." Before they could respond, Jon turned and went out the door.

He barely felt the cold night air as he stormed past the after-meeting strumming of guitars, singing, sharing of revelations and visions still going on at the Golden Tabernacle. Jon lowered his head, not wanting others to see the tears in his eyes.

It was… the Virginia Skyline Drive and Goo-Goo Clusters all over again. If Goo Goo Clusters had been a test to see how compliant he was… well, now they knew that when the chips were down he wouldn't be forced into any decisions against his convictions. But… what were his convictions?

At his tiny trailer Jon closed the door behind him, glad Marvin had been detained on clean-up duty. He knelt to pray, but found no words. Hadn't he left this at God's throne a thousand times already? Jon sobbed and buried his head in the pillow.

CHAPTER TWENTY-ONE

...as cold waters to a thirsty soul, so is good news from a far country. Proverbs 25:25

SUNDAY, MARCH 5

Dear Mom, Dad and Danny,

I'm sorry I didn't call. I just never got around to it. I trust you're all doing well. I love you and miss you so much, especially since my visit home and the time we spent together.

I suppose I'd better tell you first about my journey. Sonya suggested that I use the two days traveling time to seek God's will, when I would be alone and not be pressured from either side. Remember how we all prayed around the table that the Lord would reveal His will to me without outside interference?

After I left the Rutlidge's I prayed, I sought, I asked, I knocked, and the Lord answered me when I stopped trying to use my own wisdom.

> *Trust in the Lord with all thine heart;*
> *and lean not on thine own understanding.*

This verse came to mind and I realized that no matter how much I prayed, I'd never be able to make this decision in my own wisdom. I realized the only thing to do was to trust my every step to the Lord each day.

I now know beyond any shadow of doubt that Jesus led me here. I've met many wonderful brothers and sisters in Christ. You probably feel that I'm deceived, but I know that He is able to keep that which I've committed... and that God seeks to have a unified Body—not many denominations. Those are the work of Satan. When God creates, He does things singularly, it is the Devil that does things pluralistically. Anywhere you look in the Bible you'll find this is true. God created a garden, a man and a woman. Satan deceived mankind, and made man his slaves. Then through mankind, Satan made many cities. Cities are spiritual deserts as far as God is concerned.

Well, enough teaching. Betsy is doing well. She is much better now than when I first arrived. The very atmosphere here is one of God's love manifested through His people. People worse than Betsy have been helped here. The elders are considering whether or not Betsy should take lithium. Please add your prayers to ours for wisdom in this matter.

Jay is doing fine. He's grown so much! I'll take some pictures and send them. The doctor suggested that Betsy's milk should be dried up since she isn't capable of nursing him. One of the other nursing mothers volunteered to nurse Jay until Betsy is herself again. I watched Betsy bottle-feed Jay today. She loved him so much, cooing to him—I'm sure God is doing a great work in her. I am praying for you, as I am sure that you are also praying for us.

Oh yes, read the second chapter of Joel, for I feel that we are on the threshold of that day—The Day of the Lord! Don't fall asleep and think that things are no worse off than they ever were.

Well, may Jesus Christ, the Bishop of our souls, reward us according to His purpose,

In love,
Jonathan, and for Betsy and Jay

P.S. Would you please send me some income tax forms, my cassette recorder, and if you can find them, Betsy's and my Bibles? They should be in the Baby basket in the basement. I forgot I placed them there when I left. Thank-you, I love 'y'all' very much.

Jon

Jonathan re-read his letter. How was he to speak his heart without sounding preachy? This was the toned down version, as evidenced by the crumpled letters littering the floor. Chester had taught powerfully from Joel in the morning session. Denominations—well intentioned as they were—were asleep, not aware of God's purposes.

Fundamentalists, so sure that gifts of the Spirit weren't for today, so confident that the Church would be zapped up to heaven all of a sudden, were so unprepared.

"Oh Lord, open my family's eyes," Jon prayed as he stamped the envelope.

MONDAY, MARCH 6

"Arise, sons of God. It's time for God's children to put off their slumber," Karen Nobles' familiar voice chirped through the loudspeaker system. Jon groaned and rolled over.

The loudspeakers twanged with guitar music and two teenaged girls, Karen and Geraldine sang:

> Wake up O Zion wake up!
> Wake up and trim your lamps,
> When the stars of heaven shall fall,
> And the moon will turn into blood,
> Then the sons of God shall awake, Zion awake!

"Come on, Brother Jonathan, on your feet," Marvin said, standing bare-foot on the frigid floor. "Get up, or the Lord will have them sing it again just for you."

"Ooh, Marvin." Jon snuggled under the covers.

Right on cue, Karen and Geraldine sang it again.

"What did I tell you?" Marvin chided as he pulled on his jeans. "We'll have to hurry if we don't want to be the last ones at the prayer circle."

Jon grimaced as his feet touched the icy-cold linoleum floor. "I hope they soon give us a wood stove."

"Brother Jonathan, you know as well as I that the Lord wants to harden us for wilderness living," Marvin said, tying his work boots.

"I'm going to South America, where it's warm," Jon said, pulling on socks and jeans.

"Well, wherever He sends you, this is the training you need." Marvin grinned.

"Oh Lord, I don't want to go to Canada."

"I'll see you out there, Brother Jonathan," Marvin said, closing the door behind him.

Jonathan finished dressing and stepped into the frosty early morning. The morning prayer circle was Chester's idea to engender unity among the men and boys. Attendance was voluntary, but any brother not showing up was considered to be under spiritual attack.

Jon hurried across the field, relieved to see that only half the brothers were milling around talking to each other in in low tones. Even from a distance Jon recognized George's ramrod-straight posture.

"Praise the Lord, Brother George," Jon said. "You sure look happy this morning."

"I am happy, Brother Jonathan," George said with a bright smile, "… there's something—."

"Well, ain't Jesus good?" said David, the "seer," as he was becoming known.

George scowled and turned away. George didn't get along well with David either; according to him, David was just trying to impress the elders with his visions and prophecies.

Chester said in his New England twang, "Aire we all heah?"

"Wait! Wa—it! I'm a comin'!" called Mick O'Shea, coat flying behind as he raced over the frozen yard. He drew up huffing, pulling his coat closed and kneeling to tie his shoelaces. Mick O'Shea was the one who usually taunted latecomers, saying, "Nice of y'all to join us, brother. Has the Devil got y'all more concerned with restin' yore body than risin' up in the Spirit?" Then, sometime later in the day Mick would sneak up on the tardy brother and politely inquire as to whether he'd like to stop work for a while and take a brief nap so he could get up on time tomorrow. Now he was the tardy brother.

"What's the matter, Brother Mick," mockingly scolded George, relishing the moment, "… your bed more important than prayer with your brothers?"

Mick looked as if he was going to have a seizure. Regaining his composure, he said through gritted teeth, "I fergot 'twas mah turn to sweep down the trailer till it was too late to git here on time."

George smirked.

At Chester's leading, each one took the hand of the man on either side and bowed his head.

Several brothers prayed for a blessing on the day, some lifted up personal or family needs.

Then Mick O'Shea prayed, "Lord, Ah want to thank Ya for mah brother George, hee-yah. I know he loves Ya, Lord, and that he wants to git perfected, so please send some fiery tribulations his way so he kin git perfected."

George's eyes bored into Mick, but Mick was blissfully unaware as he stood swaying slightly, eyes closed. No one else prayed, so Chester closed in prayer and dismissed the gathering.

"George," Jon whispered lowly, "… you shouldn't provoke Brother Mick like that."

"Ah, he likes to dish it out, but he can't take it. He needed somebody to show him what it's like to be on the receiving end. Maybe now he'll quit annoying everybody."

Jon and George joined the breakfast queue in the Golden Tabernacle. Girls served from behind tables as men and boys passed by and loaded their trays with eggs, grits, jelly, toast, coffee, milk and orange juice. Lunches and suppers were delivered by waitresses, but since people had varied morning schedules, breakfast was served cafeteria style.

"George, you were about to tell me something earlier?" Jon said.

A smile lit George's face. "Well, I don't know if I ought to share it yet, Brother Jon. Leastways till the other person involved knows."

"C'mon, what?"

"Nope," George said, sticking out his square jaw. "I'm not gonna say till the time is ripe."

"Brother Jonathan," interrupted William Nobles. "I'd like to see you after breakfast."

"Is everything... okay?"

"Fine, just fine. It's not about your wife, but a work detail. By the way, that baby of yours is just the cutest little fella."

"Thanks."

"Are you spending enough time with him?"

"I try." Farm chores all day and spending what little free time he had before supper with Betsy didn't leave Jon much time for Jay, especially since the evening meeting followed so soon after supper. By that time Jay was asleep.

After breakfast, Jon dumped his dirty dishes in the receptacle and reluctantly sought out William.

William Nobles was by the tool shed behind the Main Trailer talking with Don Wilson. Don, the youngest and newest elder on the farm, was a lanky young man with gentle eyes and a more-red-than-blond shock of hair. He was a gentle, caring soul—like Jill Rine.

"Ah, Brother Jonathan," William said, "... the elders have been discussing you, and some feel that you'd be a good leader for the younger brothers—you know, the little guys 5 to 8 years old that run loose after classes."

Jon glanced over at the three trailers and other small buildings behind the Main Trailer that comprised a makeshift campus where adults with teaching certificates mixed Bible lessons with language arts, history, and math. In fact, the outer community thought of the farm as some sort of private religious school. There were about twenty junior and senior high school-age girls and nearly as many boys; but just a handful of boys fell into the five to eight-year-old range.

William continued, "We'd like these 'little brothers' to service the trailers not yet hooked to septic tanks. Their job will be to empty the sewage into a collection barrel. You can drive a tractor, can't you?"

Jon nodded.

"Good. You'll drive the tractor and wagon with the collection barrel, and they'll empty pails from each trailer. Any questions?"

It seemed odd that such a distasteful chore was assigned to young boys, but who was Jon to question an eldership decision? "When do I start?"

"Glory!" William beamed. "Classes let out at eleven. Meet them by the Main Trailer. You'll need a firm hand; some of these youngsters resist authority... and this is a job they'll not like. All they know is that they're to report to you; the tractor will be at your disposal when you come up from morning chores."

Jon heard himself say, "Fine," as he turned and headed toward the farm area, wondering what he'd just gotten into.

--- · ⚬ · ---

The tractor idled rhythmically as Jonathan waited for the six boys assigned to the "Bucket Brigade," without a doubt the most disgusting duty on the farm.

Finally the door opened and several teens burst free of the confines of school. Some of these youths were sent by judicial systems that had been persuaded that the farm was sort of a religious reformatory for petty criminals. Others had been sent by their parents or a local Move body for deliverance. Still others were on the farm because their parents were traveling elders. Despite Minnie Eastman's rhapsodizing, Jon discovered that only a few teens, such as David, actually wanted to be on the farm.

Six younger boys cautiously approached Jon. The only one who didn't regard Jon suspiciously was little Billy Thompson, the son of elders Bill and Lisa, who carried himself like a little prince.

"Boys," Jonathan said, "I'm Brother Jon." Ten wary eyes studied Jon from top to bottom. Billy's eyes investigated the wagon. "We've been given a job that will bless the whole camp—a job no one likes, but as sons of God, we'll learn to deny ourselves and do even nasty jobs for the glory of the Lord, right?"

Twelve hostile eyes stared silently up at Jon.

"Right. Let's start with names. Billy, I know you already, so who are you three brothers."

"I'm Tommy."

"I'm Jimmy."

"I'm Robby."

"That's more like it," Jon said, hoping to dissipate the hostility. "And who are you two?"

"Jackie Caliano."

"Agnes' brother?" Jon asked.

"She's my mom." The others giggled.

"Oh, well, glad to meet you, Jackie. And you?" Jon looked to the last one.

"I'm Buddy, and I ain't gonna carry no poop buckets."

"H-how did you know your job was to carry—er—poop buckets?"

"Billy told us," Jackie said. "He heard his mom and dad talking. They said the elders want us to quit running around wild after school."

"Well, little brothers, I—"

"We don't like being called 'little brothers' either," Billy saucily said as he climbed on the wagon. "And since I'm an elder's son, I'll ride in the wagon and work the lid."

"You'll take whatever job I give you, young man. And I don't care who your parents are. You'll take turns working the lid. Tommy, you work the lid today."

"Yeah, and all you do is drive. You don't have to carry them buckets," accused Buddy.

"That's enough," Jon said sternly. "We have a job to do, and it's not going to go away, so we had better get the proper attitude. If we praise the Lord we might even find that it's fun."

"Yuck!"

Jon whirled around. "Who said that?" Silent, angry faces stared at him. Jon wondered afresh what he'd gotten into.

Buckets were handed out, and after a brief explanation, the boys were sent to gather each trailer's human waste. They grudgingly obeyed. The trailer-keepers kept close watch to make sure the youngsters cleaned up anything that sloshed over the rim. Of course, this only intensified the potty crew's disgust.

Later, after dumping the collection barrel, Jon dismissed his crew and wracked his brain for a way to make the job more agreeable. It was obvious that the little brothers had been assigned this task because the teens would absolutely rebel.

On the second day the potty crew showed more resistance. They'd had twenty-four hours to invent ways to get out of their task. Buddy occupied the tailgate the entire time, refusing to budge. No amount of coaxing or threatening shifted him. His attitude soon infected the entire crew. They whispered among themselves as they approached the trailers, careful to not let Jon overhear. Halfway through the detail they mustered their courage and mutinied, standing with arms folded, refusing to carry any more "Poop-Pails." Only when Jon switched off the tractor, dismounted and said he was going to fetch Brother William did they reluctantly pick up their buckets and resume their task, casting dirty glances backward.

Jon determined to give it one more day before consulting someone—anyone but William—about the potential insurrection confronting him. Jon didn't blame them; it was a disgusting job, especially just before lunch. Jon got a good whiff of the effulgence every time the lid was opened and nearly gagged. How much worse would it reek in the heat of summer?

WEDNESDAY, MARCH 8

Jonathan emerged from the Golden Tabernacle after a breakfast of Rice Crispies, toast, and orange juice when William approached, accompanied by elders Bill Thompson and Chester Ludwig. Jon smiled in greeting, intending to pass by.

"Well, glory! There he is now," William said. "Brother Jonathan, it doesn't look like things are working out so well with you and the little brothers, does it?"

"Not yet... but I—."

"Well," William said, looking down over the meadow, "I think we'd better make a change. From now on, you stay in the fields. We'll give that responsibility to someone else." Chester and Bill avoided Jon's eyes.

"I...I think in a few more days things will go smoother," Jon said, not wanting to give William any more reason to think him incompetent. "We're still getting used to each other... they'll catch on..."

William turned steely eyes on Jon. "I said, we'll give that responsibility to someone else."

Jon nodded, dropped his eyes and continued to the farm side. He wanted so badly to redeem himself in William's eyes. But at least he was free of that loathsome chore and the mutinous "little brothers."

As Jon passed the Main Trailer, Dixie, whose sister had been the reason for the trip to Jackson, came out the door and ran down the steps, crying into a handkerchief.

"Sister Dixie," Jon said, "... what's the matter?"

It took Dixie a moment to recognize Jon. "My sister," she said, "... died early this morning." She sobbed again.

"But..." Jon said, "...we prayed... I believed..."

Dixie rushed down the gravel pathway and disappeared into her trailer.

Jon stood rooted to the ground. He'd been so certain… Jackie's recovery would've been such a faith-builder, such a vindication of the Move…

Doubts inundated Jon afresh: Betsy wasn't any better, despite what he'd written his folks. And why was Barry the epileptic given medication? Why did Patrick still use an inhaler?

THURSDAY, MARCH 9

"Galoree halle-loo-yah!" Mick O'Shea shouted as he emerged from the Noble's trailer. The sky was still overcast from the previous night's storm. As a result of the night's heavy rain, puddles swamped the farmland, so there was no work in the fields. William tried to conjure up busy-work for the older brothers lest they be idle. The work crew loitered outside William's trailer waiting for assignments.

"Ah've got mah goats, Ah've got mah goats!" Mick celebrated. "They're gonna let me take keer of the goats. They're comin' hee-yah today. Ah'd best git down to the barn and make sure everythin' is ready." Mick swaggered around the corner, skipped down the rain-rutted roadway hollering, "Thank you, Jee-sus! Well, galorree!"

Those without assignments resumed small talk as William desperately sought for ways to keep them all busy.

"George," Jon asked, "… you still haven't told me what made you so happy the other day."

George smiled. "Not yet, Brother Jon, not yet. But… soon."

"C'mon George," Jon said, but his urging was cut short by William coming out on his deck where he stood overlooking his workers like Caesar reviewing his troops.

"Brothers, y'all may as well get ready for Bible class in the Golden Tabernacle this morning. The fields are too muddy. You have about half an hour, so go get your Bibles and notebooks. Brother Jack is teaching this morning. Maybe we'll get into the fields this afternoon."

Jon looked around for Marvin. Earlier that day they'd mentioned feeling a need for more Bible teaching. Marvin flashed a quick smile and whispered, "If y'all hurry, you've got enough time to visit Sister Betsy. I'll git your notebook."

"Right," Jon said, and was off at a gallop.

Betsy bobbed back and forth in a rocking chair, headphones clamped over her ears, her fingers forming mystic symbols. By her fluttering eyelids, Jonathan doubted that she even heard the tape. He nodded at Agnes who was doing some mending. Jon angled around front of Betsy where she couldn't help but see him if she opened her eyes.

"Hi Betts," Jon ventured. "I said, Hello Betsy," Jon repeated louder. "It's me, your husband, remember me?"

Betsy opened her eyes, stared icily and droned, "I am married to Christ," then closed her eyes again.

"Now, Betsy," Agnes broke in, "… this is your husband, Jonathan. Remember last night you told me all about your husband Jonathan and your baby, Jay?"

Betsy was unresponsive.

Agnes looked apologetic, explaining, "Well, last night she told me all about your apartment in Tannersville, and Jay, and your friend Bob who lived with you."

"Bob? No one named Bob lived with us—oh, she meant Bop, our dog."

Agnes laughed. "That would explain some of the weird things she said Bob—er—Bop did."

"She was lucid?"

"Well, sort of. She knew your baby at first when we took her to Sister Jill's. But then she kept insisting that Jill's two-year-old was her Jay. When we told her that the little baby was hers, she started telling us how you left her at someone named Minnie's(?) and went to work and didn't come back. Then she wondered who was feeding Bop. She was afraid he might bite someone, which now doesn't seem so strange."

"Well, isn't that an improvement?"

"There were a few times when the real Betsy came out, but she immediately returned to this manifestation. What was she like before the demons took over?"

"Well… she was smart, and witty. We punned and laughed at each other's jokes. She's very caring, and gets emotionally involved with needy people… and she loves God. She has a lot of faith, in fact, it was through her arguing for the truth that I got baptized in the Holy Spirit."

"No wonder Satan wants her so confused." Agnes looked directly at Betsy and said, "You devils think you're in control, but we're gonna get every last one of you out. Do you hear me? Every last one."

"Every last one," Betsy sneered back. "That's right, that's right, every last one!"

Jon ached for Betsy to be herself, to sing, and laugh and love Jay and him, for the three of them to live together, for everything to return to normal. Why was God taking so long?

"Why hello, Brother Jonathan," Bunny Halstead said, coming into the room. "I didn't know you were here. Aren't you working this morning?"

"Brother William said the fields are too muddy, and that we should all go to Bible study. I wanted to spend some time with Betsy before class started."

"Well isn't that ni-ice? Sister Betsy, yore husband has come by for a visit. Isn't that nice?"

Betsy ignored Bunny.

"By the way, Brother Jonathan," Bunny continued, "… has my husband told you that the elders have decided to give lithium to Betsy?"

Jon sat up. "When was that decided?"

"Yesterday. They want to experiment and see if there is any change. I do hope that is all right with you?"

"Yes, fine, but, but…" Jon tried to verbalize the questions burning in his mind.

"But what?"

"But what about the demons?"

"Oh, we'll still deal with them, don't you worry none about that. We'll make sure she's all healed and delivered."

There was no pressing the issue. Despite everything, Jon was glad Betsy was going to get lithium, even if it meant he couldn't tell his folks that the Lord had set Betsy free from mental illness without medicine.

It was nearly time for Bible class; Jon stood and said, "Betsy, honey, I have to go now. I love you."

She looked up and smiled briefly, but then a dark look crossed her face and she made a mystical finger design.

CHAPTER TWENTY-TWO

… go thy way; the Devil is gone out of thy daughter…Mark 7:29

MONDAY, MARCH 13

Dear Mom, Dad, and Danny,

Oh how I miss 'you-all'. Things here are wonderful. Betsy is much improved, and I know it's not just the lithium. She's only been on it for a couple of days—not long enough for the medicine to have had any real effect—but by God's power she's beginning to come forth as herself. When she was in Philhaven, it took several weeks for lithium to work, and that was at a much higher dosage. Then they gave her six capsules daily, but here they're giving her only three, so you see, the Lord's hand is in this more than the medicine.

The Lord is doing a work in me too! Would you believe that on Saturday I was on my hands and knees all day, planting potato spuds and loving every minute of it? We had such a great time in the field, sharing God's love as we dug and planted. God's love just flows over everybody down here. It's so great— you'll never know how great it is unless you come see for yourselves.

I'll try to write in more detail later about what's going on down here, but I thought I'd drop a quick note to let you know that things are improving.

I do hope 'y'all' can come to the farm, then you'll see for yourself why I love it here. Beyond any shadow of a doubt, this is the place Jesus wants me to be. Even after Betsy gets better we'll likely stay; there's so much to learn. I have a feeling that Betsy will be well soon. Jay is doing fine, he had a cold, but it's breaking up.

Psalm 144 has been a real source of encouragement to me whenever I feel depressed.

Oh, by the way, this is not a 'faith-healing center' as I had said earlier, but a 'faith-building center.'

Well, all praise to Jesus Christ our Lord, for all things are in His hands...

I love you all so very much and long to see you.

In Him and in love, your son,

Jonathan

Jon sat on a log beside the fire pit outside the Golden Tabernacle checking his letter. He'd finished lunch early and went outside to write.

"Brother Jonathan McComb, please come to the Main Trailer," crackled the camp loudspeakers. Jon jumped to his feet. The message was repeated, but he was already racing across the field.

"Package for you, Brother Jonathan, Marie said matter-of-factly as he entered the add-on. On the desktop was a brown paper package addressed to him.

It had to be his Bible and other things he'd requested. His folks hadn't rejected him, as often happened to those who joined the Move. Betsy and Jon's folks loved the Lord, in their own, denominational way, but eventually they'd forsake their religious platitudes and join the Move.

"Hi, Hon," said a familiar voice from behind.

"Betsy!" The transformation even since the previous night was stunning. He had seen small changes over the past few days, but nothing had prepared him for this. "You—you look—so good." Indeed, some blush and mascara had been artfully applied, making her look as beautiful as he remembered.

Betsy blushed and darted shy glances. Though traces of confusion remained, there was no doubt; Betsy was more herself.

"She saw you coming and hurried to get dressed to look nice for you," Agnes said, standing slightly behind Betsy. "Doesn't she look good? See how much weight she's lost?"

For a brief instant Jon caught a furtive look in Betsy's eye, but then her rightful demeanor returned. "You're beautiful! You've lost weight, huh?"

"She doesn't hardly eat," Agnes said, hovering like a mother hen.

J.M. MACLEOD

"I'd like to see my baby." Betsy looked to Agnes, then Jon, imploring, "Will you take me?"

Jon raised his eyebrows and looked hopefully to Agnes, who said, "Let's ask Bunny." She disappeared behind the hallway curtain.

Jon suddenly felt awkward; his baleful expression prompted Betsy to ask, "Have they been treating you badly, too? My poor, poor Jon."

"No Betts, they haven't been treating me badly at all. I love it here. In fact, if you were well, I'd be about the happiest man on earth."

"Oh, I thought maybe they were keeping you locked up."

Agnes emerged from behind the curtain. "Sister Bunny thinks it would be a good idea for the two of you to began doing things together."

Jon had expected to be reunited with Betsy as soon as she was lucid, but it now became clear that the elders were only going to permit them to date. Jon buried his feelings. "Uh, good. Yes, that would be ... good. Well, let's go see our son, shall we?"

"Yes, we shall," Betsy said a bit airily.

As soon as Jon and Betsy were away from the Main Trailer Betsy confided, "I'm so glad to be away from them. All of them."

"Why Betts?"

"You don't know? They're false prophets. They force me to listen to tapes of false teachers. They're always telling me I've got demons, they don't let you, me and Jay live together. Why don't they let us live together as a family?"

"Betsy, listen to me," Jon said, "… they're not false prophets. I know they're of God. And you do need to be delivered of some remaining demons."

Betsy halted. "Oh, no I don't! Sam Fife cast them out at Minnie's house, remember?" She looked around at the circled trailers. "How did we get here, anyway? I remember... staying at Minnie's house, then all of a sudden I'm in the middle of a bunch of people screaming 'come out in Jesus' name'. Jon, what are we doing here?"

Aware that they were under observation, Jon resumed walking to Jill's trailer, explaining how Minnie and Mary had accompanied them to Mississippi and why Jill was taking care of Jay and why the elders thought it best that Jon stay elsewhere till she was completely recovered.

Betsy paused again, stating, "They really are false prophets, Jon. We should leave."

"Betts, Hon, you'll see things differently when your mind clears more." Jon knocked on the aluminum screen door. Jill invited them in.

"I just changed him and put him down for his nap, but I'm sure he's not asleep," Jill said. "I'll get him. It's good to see you doing better, Sister Betsy." She retrieved and handed their son to Betsy.

"Why... he's got pimples all over his face." Betsy said.

Jill smiled. "They're just milk bumps. Lots of babies get them." Betsy was reassured and cooed to Jay who sighed and hiccuped sleepily. "I'm so glad they've given you medication, Betsy. All along I felt it wasn't right to withhold it. You're so much better already."

Jon's eyes teared as Betsy cuddled their baby.

"He's so big," Betsy said. "I've missed part of his life. I remember thinking that your Jay was my Jay; I couldn't believe he'd grown so much. I'm glad I didn't lose a couple of years."

"Now don't you worry none. He's a good baby; so easy to care for, it's just a joy."

"I'm tired. I think I should go back," Betsy said, handing Jay back to Jill. Jon rose and followed.

"Thank you, Jill," Jon said. Jill was the only elder with whom he was comfortable enough to drop the "Sister" title. She was also the only elder he fully trusted. She looked at things practically, which, Jon gathered, was sometimes a cause for friction among the other elders.

Jon clutched Betsy's hand as they walked to the Main Trailer where she turned and said, "You don't need to come in. I'm just going to lay down."

"Uh, I need to get my package," Jon said, perplexed that she wanted to be rid of him so quickly. "Oh, your Bible came, too."

"Okay." Her tone was unenthusiastic.

Though disappointed, Jon would be patient; a work was being done, not as quickly as he'd like, but it was being done.

Jon tucked his bundle under his arm and crossed the field humming a worship tune. He glanced at his watch he knew he'd missed the teaching.

"Hey, Brother Jon, aren't you joining us for another glorious afternoon of work in the fields of the Lord?" David said as he and Marvin passed going the other way.

"Can't wait. I'll be there as soon as I stash these things."

"Glory, Brother Jon," Marvin said, "... isn't it marvelous what the Lord has done for Sister Betsy the last couple of days? Soon the three of y'all will be back together." His smile and sparkling eyes indicated he wasn't too unhappy about losing his roommate. "Well, you know what Brother William says about being late for work. If we wait for you, he'd surely be displeased."

Jon knew all too well.

"I'll tell him why you're late, if you like? I'm sure he'll understand."

Jon was late, twenty minutes late, and Brother William did understand, though he kept a close eye on Jon the rest of the afternoon, sending him to the lower end of the farm where Daniel, David and Marvin planted potato quarters.

David expounded on types and shadows as they planted. "Someday brothers, the workers will be in the field just like this, planting quarters, and the harvesters will follow right behind, diggin' up full-growed spuds as fast as the planters put 'em in the ground."

"What?" Danny said, taking a moment to stretch.

"He's right, Brother Daniel," Marvin said from another row over. "I heard that on Brother Sam's tape just the other day: The plowman shall overtake the reaper."

"That doesn't make sense," Danny said.

Marvin formed another mound, explaining, "That means... the day is coming... when there will be... continuous productivity. Y'all haven't heard that tape yet?"

Jon said, "I thought that was type and shadow of those who were witnessing about Jesus, and as soon as some became believers they'd immediately mature in the faith and bring new converts with them."

"Oh, it couldn't mean that," David said.

"Why not?"

"Because, we aren't supposed to keep bringing spiritual babies into the kingdom."

"That's absurd," Jon said. "We're supposed to keep winning the lost until Jesus comes. Everybody knows that." Jon looked to Marvin for support; but Marvin declined comment, fervently attacking the soil with his hoe.

"Brother Jonathan," David said in a patronizing tone, "... can't you see that Jesus can't return until we're all mature in Christ?"

"Well, yeah, I know that."

"Then don't you see," David continued, "... that we can't be perfect as long as there are spiritual babies running around doing all sorts of things in the flesh? Evangelism must come to a stop or we'll never reach perfection. If we get the spiritual babies and children who are already in the Church mature, without bringing in any more, it could happen in a matter of a few years. But as long as there are new believers constantly being added—who also have to attain maturity—Jesus' coming will be put off indefinitely."

"It can't mean that," Jon said. "Not with all the people in the world who still haven't heard the gospel. I think what it really means is that newborn Christians will be as mature as those who've been walking with the Lord for years. Remember what Jesus said about the first being last and the last being first, and the vineyard workers who worked a full day, some a half day, some only an hour—but all received the same wage. I believe evangelism will continue until Jesus returns."

"I agree with Jonathan," Danny said. "If Ephesians validates apostles until Jesus comes back, why not evangelists, too?"

Danny and Jon stopped digging and waited for David's rebuttal.

David sighed. "Well, Praise the Lord! I see y'all have unsaved family members, so you're not willing to accept this truth." He socked a spud into the ground and covered it.

"David is right," Marvin said, "... about evangelism coming to a stop. Apostle Buddy Cobb brought forth the same word and had it confirmed by Sam Fife."

"Well, just because an elder says so doesn't mean..." Jon stopped arguing his point when he spied Brother William strutting across the rows of potato mounds. The last thing he needed was for William to hear him arguing against the Move's elders.

David added, "It's not as if evangelists aren't necessary to the five-fold ministry anymore. But they should concentrate where the gospel hasn't been preached, not in America where there's a church on every corner."

"So, what's the Move doing about evangelism in those countries?" Danny asked.

"I don't know," David said, "... but there's so much confusion just getting the American Church in apostolic order that there hasn't been much time to ordain evangelists."

"Well... Marvin interrupted, "... Brother Sam and other apostles have been going to Africa, Australia, England, the Philippines—all over the world, establishing bodies and farms."

"Hallelujah!" David said. "I'm sure God must have some other purpose for evangelists than bringing more spiritual babies into the Move."

Jon wanted to ask, "What about China, Russia and Eastern Bloc countries?" but William was within earshot, so he just buried another spud.

"Glory," William said. "It sure is a blessing to see you brothers hard at work and giving glory to God at the same time," "It's almost clean up time before supper, so plan starting new rows accordingly."

Jon and Betsy sat together in the evening meeting. Bunny thought it would be good for Betsy to sit in on the "high praises," so Jon was on one and Agnes on the other side of her.

Jon stood to worship, but a vague uneasy feeling that his family wouldn't be reunited any time soon gnawed at him. Jon pushed aside such doubts and raised his hands, forcing himself to sing along:

> In the name of Jesus, In the name of Jesus,
> We have the victory, glory glory glory!
> In the name of Jesus, In the name of Jesus,
> Demons will have to flee.

A few rows ahead Mick O'Shea broke into a "Holy Ghost Shuffle." The accordion, piano and guitars pounded out the lively gospel song as elder Bill Thompson led the singing, working himself into a lather, waving his arms and prancing around the platform. From time to time he'd stop and exhort the body to rise up yet more in the Spirit and drive all the Devils out of Sapa:

> When we stand in the name of Jesus,
> Tell me who can stand before us?
> In the name, the name of Jesus,
> We have the victory.

The chorus was repeated ten, twenty, thirty times; people clapping and singing until they were caught up in a euphoria of praise.

Jon, however, was not caught up in the euphoria, but was plagued with doubts about Betsy's recovery.

> In the name of Jesus, In the name of Jesus,
> We have the victory, glory glory glory!

Jon peeked at Betsy, who glared at Mick O'Shea's animated dancing.

"Betsy, Hon, join in the praises, get set free," Jon whispered.

Betsy looked up, anger in her eyes.

The song finally ended and Bill declared, "Now that's praisin'! Sister Lisa, my wife, will give us the Word tonight, but I believe Sister Bunny will be taking some of you out for a class. Is that right, Sister Bunny?"

Bunny made her way to the platform and said, "Amen, Brother Bill, we're going to have a tape on overcoming the enemy. The following brothers and sisters will come with me: Tony, Mitch, Mickey, Les, Rob, Fred, Marvin, Jonathan, Danny, George, David, Harold, Terri-Lee, Geraldine, Karen, Alice, Diane and Dolly. Follow me to the trailer classroom."

Jon was reluctant to leave Betsy, but Agnes whispered, "It's all right, I'm taking her back to the Main Trailer anyway."

Jon nodded, and bid Betsy good night.

CHAPTER TWENTY-THREE

Who hath believed our report... Isaiah 53:1

WEDNESDAY, MARCH 15

"Ah, Brother Jonathan, I was just about to have Marie page you," Jack Halstead said as Jonathan McComb entered the Main Trailer. "I'd like to talk to you about your wife's medication."

"Yes?"

"Come back to my quarters," Jack said, leading past the girls' rooms. Jack and Bunny occupied a cramped room at the very back of the trailer. The room's condition was surprising in light of Bunny persistently needling the trailer's inhabitants to keep their living space orderly. The bed was unmade and dirty clothes were draped over a chair... but then, Jack and Bunny didn't live in luxuriant privacy and the spacious comfort of their own trailer like other elders.

"Have a seat." Jack waved toward the laundry-draped chair. His smile was subdued. "I've talked with Dr. Black about your wife's medicine. He's read up on it." Jack held a medical journal open before Jon. "There seems to be a divided opinion about just how safe this drug is."

"Dr. Hotchkiss mentioned that fact before we were married, but said the drug wouldn't hurt anyone who needed it."

Jack eyed Jon, then continued, "Well, this... er, medical report lists side effects, some of them very serious."

Jon tried to focus on the page held in front of him.

"We believe God does things in accordance with our faith, Brother Jonathan," Jack said, taking on an authoritative tone. "We believe prolonged exposure to lithium could cause Betsy problems later in life, therefore, continuing to give her lithium probably isn't God's will, since, in time, it'll cause physical damage."

"But... but if she needs it, it won't harm her... her body will absorb and use it so it won't harm her."

"The medical community is divided on that point, I'm afraid. There seems to be more evidence of harm as opposed to what little good it does. And since her main problem is spiritual rather than chemical, we've decided to stop giving her lithium and trust God for healing. She's doing so well, she may not need lithium anymore. We'll start deliverance sessions again if demons manifest."

"I see," Jon said. They were so sure that it was God's will to use lithium a week ago, and now they were just as sure it wasn't. "No, I don't see," Jon said, sitting forward. "I'm confused."

"God is not the author of confusion, but of peace," Jack said. "If you are confused Brother, you need to sort it out with the Lord. Haven't you committed her to the Lord's keeping?"

"Yes, of course I have."

"Then you need to excrcise faith that He's taking care of it."

"But... I am. That's why I brought Betsy here on Brother Sam's recommendation. Brother Jack, I know the Lord led me here... to be under your oversight. I'm submitted to you, but... I'm confused. First you say 'the Lord says no medication', then you say the Lord says, 'give her medicine', and now you say the Lord says 'no medicine' again.'"

"Are you questioning whether we have the Lord on this?"

That question was a touchstone to determine whether a person was under a rebellious spirit. Jon chose his words carefully. "It's just that Betsy has been so much better lately. I don't want her stability go downhill."

"Oh, if that's all that's bothering you," Jack said, his wide, toothy grin returning to full glory, "... we are certain of her complete deliverance. Her healing is just a short time away. We're confident she's made real gains since the lithium has cleared her mind; those gains won't be lost just because we take lithium away. We have the Lord on it."

The interview was over. Jon rose to go; a familiar, gnawing doubt nagged at him. How often could Betsy flip between dementia and sanity without permanent damage? Jon's instincts clamored against this newest decision; yet, should he not follow the path of faith rather than instinct?

Or… could this inner alarm be from God?

"Betsy is in full agreement," Jack said, following Jon down the hall. "She believes the Lord will heal her."

"She never did like taking it."

"No? Well, considering the consequences, that's understandable. Have faith. You'll see great and marvelous things, only have faith."

Jon, dazed and confused, continued down the hall to the addition where Marie sat at the front desk. "Do you know where Betsy is?" he asked.

"She and Agnes went for a walk. I can page her over the P.A. if you'd like."

"No, don't bother." Jon went out and descended the stairs questioning whether his faith was in the Lord, or in medicine? If he resisted Jack's assessment, was he not trusting medicine more than God? He'd brought her to the farm to be set free from demons without the aid of lithium, tranquilizers and psychoanalysis. But then… why were others, such as Patrick, getting prescriptions filled? And why did Dixie's sister die?

Deliverance sessions had accomplished nothing as far as Jon could see, so the elders resorted to lithium, throwing Jon into a tailspin. But he had made the mental adjustments and went along. Betsy improved; Jon gladly accommodated the results. Now once again, Jon stood in front of the Main Trailer, bewildered. Who could give him wise counsel? Of course—Jill, being an elder, must have been in on the decision and could help him understand this abrupt change.

"Come in," Jill invited at Jon's knock. Jon entered the tiny living quarters where, no matter where you happened to be, table, chairs, sink were all just a short reach away. "Come to see your little boy?" she asked.

"Well, yes, and to sort things out. I hope you don't mind; I feel I can talk freely with you."

Her eyes narrowed. "No, I don't mind at all. What do you need to sort out?"

Jon picked his son up. "He's getting so big."

"Uh-huh. He's about six weeks old now, isn't he?"

"Six weeks? Is that all the longer it's been since this nightmare began? It feels like years."

"You've been through a lot."

"I don't think it's over." Jon described his conversation with Jack.

Jill's brow furrowed and there was a smoldering fire in her eyes.

"Did I say something wrong?" Jon asked, startled at the transformation in his son's caretaker.

"You were told that all the elders took part in this decision?"

"Uh... I don't remember if he said all the elders or not. But, that was the impression I got."

She turned away. "I can't believe they actually went through with it, and to say it so matter-of-factly that all were in agreement!"

"What?"

"Will you stay here and watch our boys? I've got to go out."

"Sure. Is something wrong?"

"Jonathan, understand me, you did nothing wrong, nor is your confusion your fault. Goodness knows I'd feel at least that much confusion in your shoes. I'd better say nothing more." She slipped into her coat and paused half way out the door, saying, "I want you to know, I wasn't in agreement with their decision."

"Oh? Oh! Now I am confused."

"I don't wonder," Jill said and went out. Jon watched through the window as she stalked toward the Main Trailer.

Jon jounced Jay on his lap, playing with him and talking to Jill's little boy who was playing on the floor with a hapless beetle that had crawled from under a cabinet. Jon prayed for knowledge and strength to obey God's will—whatever that might be.

Jill returned forty-five minutes later, her jaw set, her brows furrowed. Jon looked up as she hung her coat in the closet. She turned and said, "Jonathan, I'm truly sorry."

"For?"

"For the way you and Betsy have been treated like guinea pigs. I'm sorry that I haven't been more out-spoken for what was right."

"Jill... the Lord led me here... I have to believe that. It can't all be a... a mistake. I trust God to work through the elders. Whatever they decide, I'll go along."

"You need to know..." Jill said, sitting down across the table from Jonathan, "... that several days ago, I, as a prophetess, was asked to seek a word from the Lord. Two other prophets were also asked to seek a word on the same subject. I wasn't told what the topic was, and had no idea who or what the word they sought was about. That night I had a vision of Betsy with a hypodermic needle in her arm," Jill indicated the inside of her elbow. "She was smiling, walking about and taking care of her baby. Then a hand pulled the hypodermic out. Immediately a black cloud formed around Betsy's head and she fell over unconscious. Jon, I had no idea that the elders were seeking a word about Betsy until I saw that vision."

Jon went numb. "It... it seems pretty clear .... Are you violating a trust by telling me this?"

Jill made no reply.

J.M. MACLEOD

"Why didn't they follow the word you gave?"

"They thought I'd guessed who the subject was, and since I was sympathetic to you and Betsy—and since I'm taking care of your baby—they felt I had a bias, therefore the word I received was unreliable."

"Are you sure you weren't biased?"

"Absolutely. I didn't even think about the subject as I prayed. But, when I received that vision, I knew. I told them plainly that I knew they were seeking a word about whether Betsy should be on medication, and that the Lord had shown me she should stay on it or demons would again gain control. One of the other prophets received no word, and the word the other one received was vague, but was interpreted to mean, 'Go ahead with the plan.'"

"Even after you explained your vision, they ignored you?"

Jill nodded.

"What should I do?"

"I... I don't know, Jonathan. It's wrong to resist the elders, even when they're wrong. You must trust the Lord. That's all I can say. God won't fail you."

Tears blurred his vision. "I'd better go. Pray for me." Jon returned his son to Jill's arms, bundled up and stepped out into a frigid March wind.

CHAPTER TWENTY-FOUR

In a dream... He openeth the ears of men, and sealeth their instruction. Job 33:15-16

TUESDAY, MARCH 21

It was getting dark; Jon was lost in the forest, he needed to scale the mountain and get his bearings. Trees were thick, branches reached high overhead. Was he headed the right way?

He attained the crest, but to his dismay he was still hemmed in by foliage. He became aware of eyes peering at him from behind trees. A dog's head ducked quickly out of sight behind an oak. There was something odd about the dog. It reappeared and Jon knew what was so odd—it was yellow! Not a Labrador Retriever yellow, but bright yellow, like a lemon. Other animals in bright hues of blue, green, red, even pink appeared from behind other tree trunks. There were farm animals; cows, pigs, goats, sheep; and exotic animals, elephants, bears, zebra and rhinoceros, all playfully frolicking by their own trees, paying little attention as Jon passed by.

Then Jon passed a tree that had a vicious Doberman chained to it. The dog leapt at Jon, jaws slavering. Jon was too slow in getting out of harm's way, but fortunately, the dog's chain snagged; the canine's jaws snapped mere inches from Jon's throat.

Jon backed away, searching the ground for a club. He found a four-foot long metal pipe. Holding it like a baseball bat, Jon warily made his way past the Doberman.

Other savage creatures appeared, mixed amongst the playful, brightly colored ones. Large, black bears roamed unfettered. Jon feared that they might see him and attack.

"Is this all?" Jill looked up from the handwritten page.

"All that I can remember," Jon said. "There might have been more, but I don't recall. Is it from the Lord? Does it have a meaning?"

Jill studied the dream again. "I see definite symbolism. Trees stand for Christians, like it says in Jeremiah, 'those who hope in the Lord will be like trees planted by the waters.' Animals stand for beastly natures—the Antichrist is called the Beast—in other words, evil spirits clinging to the flesh nature. I don't see why some were friendly but others were dangerous. Nor do I understand why you were wandering around. Yes... I do think it's of the Lord, but I'm not sure what He's saying. Perhaps He wants to teach you to understand dreams and visions for yourself. Or … take it to another elder."

"Well, thanks anyway."

"Betsy isn't doing well, is she?" Jill changed the subject.

"She was..." Jon dropped his gaze, "nearly herself," he said, trying to swallow the lump in his throat. "Why did God allow this setback? I still believe, but... is it another test? Or, is He punishing us? Jon wiped at the tears in his eyes.

Jill's eyes glistened too; she quickly looked away.

"I'd better go," Jon said, handing his son over.

"I'm praying for you and Betsy, Jon."

Jon nodded and left.

He passed the Main Trailer willing his tears to stop; moping would be interpreted as not being victorious. The last thing Jon needed was someone descending with a hearty, "Well praise the Lord, Brother, don't you know Jesus is the Victor?"

Thankfully, he encountered no one. Instead, the distinctive sounds of "battle" poured through the thin walls of the trailer. "Battles" usually occurred in the Main Trailer's addition where it could accommodate over a dozen "prayer warriors." Sometimes Betsy was the subject; other times it was one of the other main trailer residents. Rarely were brothers subjected to deliverance. Sessions lasted hours. Often the farm population was unaware that deliverance sessions were taking place because they were concurrent with the evening worship. Several elders being absent from the meeting was often the only clue that a deliverance session was taking place.

But now, in the middle of the afternoon a session was taking place. Muffled but understandable voices came through the walls of the trailer. "In the name of Jesus, Devil, tell me who you are."

"Come out you filthy thing, you have no right in her."

"The blood of Jee-sus! The blood of Jee-sus!"

Jon stood rooted, wrestling with his desire to see Betsy free, yet not wanting her to be the focus of such emotional trauma.

"Oh Lord, make it right. This hurts so much. Please, Jesus, when will You make an end?" The Agony and the Ecstasy crossed Jon's mind again. Jon sighed, jammed his fists in his pockets and walked on.

The shouts suddenly took on a different tenor.

"Hallelujah!"

"Thank You, Jee-sus!"

"Pah-raise the Lord!"

"That's it, that's it, you come out of her, too."

The battlers had broken through. Demons were being evicted!

"Oh Lord, let it be Betsy." Jon contemplated bursting in on the deliverance session.

The shouts turned angry again.

"Come out, in the name of Jee-sus!"

"Tell me your name, I command you, in Jesus' name!"

Jon stood with one foot on the steps, ready to ascend.

The door suddenly opened and David, the youthful seer, stepped outside. His smile grew even wider upon seeing Jon. He said, "Well, galoree, Brother Jonathan."

"David—is Betsy …?"

David descended the stairs. "No, Brother Jonathan, not this time I'm afraid. It's Sister Diane Lee. She's been acting up, and the elders wanted to see if evil spirits were causing her rebellious attitude. They asked me to help pray, to see if I'd get any words from the Lord. I did too. The Lord showed me the demons as they surfaced. I identified them to Brother Jack. In fact, I had to leave just now because I saw that she has a demon of lust for me that won't release until I leave the battle."

"Oh," Jon said. "I had hoped they were making some headway with Betsy."

"She has fallen right back under the enemy's dominion, hasn't she, Brother Jon? So quickly too. But don't you worry none, I was praying for you both last night, and the Lord showed me a vision of Sister Betsy."

"Betsy? My Betsy?"

"The same. She was all alone at the bottom of a deep pit. Then a bright light shone down from heaven and she woke up as if from a trance. She began climbing up the beam of light and got out of the pit. She was then in a beautiful garden filled with delicious fruit."

"Really?"

David nodded. The two walked on toward the Golden Tabernacle.

"That interpretation seems plain. Have you checked it out with one of the elders?" I asked.

"Yep. Brother Jack said, 'It's a good report.'"

WEDNESDAY, MARCH 22

"Good morning sons of God, time to rise and start the day."

Rain drummed on the roof. Jon looked over at Marvin who was still asleep.

Jon smiled. Marvin always slept through the morning call when it rained. "Oh Marrrrrrvin," Jon whispered softly, stealing out of bed, crossing the chilly floor, putting his lips next to Marvin's ear. "Marrrrrrvin."

"Umm?" Marvin murmured.

"Marrrrvin..." Jon whispered, then shouted, "Come forth!"

Marvin sat bolt upright, eyes wide, chattering, "Hallelujah! Hallelujah!"

Jon giggled and fell back on his bunk, begging, "Forgive me brother, I just wanted to practice raising the dead."

"Oh," Marvin said, "Did I miss the wake up call again?"

"Uh-huh. Let's get down to the Golden Tabernacle for breakfast. There won't be any prayer circle."

"Why, hello brothers," Mick O'Shea greeted as Jon and Marvin entered the Golden Tabernacle. "Shore is a Texas-style rainstorm out there. Whachya gonna be doin' fer chores this mornin'?"

"We'll probably attend Bible class. How about you?" Marvin asked.

Mick puffed out his chest and said, "Ah'm gonna be tendin' mah goats. By the way, has either of y'all ever had goats milk?"

Marvin wrinkled his nose. "Nope, don't think I have."

Jon shook his head.

Mick's wide smile revealed a gold tooth and not a few gaps as he said, "Well, yore shore 'nuff gonna git some today! They're all outta cow's milk, and the only milk for cereal is from my—er, the Lord's goats."

"Well Praise the Lord, Brother Mick!" Marvin said, always up for an end-time challenge, "… I've been waiting for a good reason to try goat's milk, and now it seems, I have it."

Jon smiled. Knowingly or unknowingly Marvin had disarmed Mick's ploy.

"Y'all seem pretty happy, Brother Jonathan, considerin' yore trial has come back on you, an' all."

Jon cringed inside, but outwardly copied Marvin's tactic, knowing that Mick was only trying to get a reaction. "Hallelujah, Brother Mick, I'm learning to be an overcomer. Besides, you might say I've heard an encouraging word."

"Oh?"

"Well, I don't want to say too much, but somebody had a vision of Betsy being in her right mind."

Mick's eyes grew round. "Praise the Lord! Kin I ask who had the word?"

"I don't know if I should... you know, so only the Lord gets the glory and all?"

"Y'all don't have to tell me... I jest wanted to know who it was, cause they's some folks what gets dreams an' visions and such truck, but it ain't o' the Lord, ya know? An' I only wants to spare ya from bein' deceived."

"Brother Jack thought it was of the Lord."

Mick blinked twice. He knew better than to meddle in an elder's—especially Brother Jack's—affairs. "Well, it oughta be all right then."

Jon smiled; Mick's unscratched itch would chafe all day.

"Y'all will tell me how ya like goat's milk, won't ya?"

"Brother Mick," Marvin said with the fervor of a convert, "… I'll tell you right now, by faith, that I like goat's milk,"

Mick quickly covered his disappointment, saying, "Now that's the kind of talk I likes to hear. Y'all have a blessed day, now. Oh! There's David. I'd better tell him about the goat's milk." He scurried away.

Heavy rain continued through morning Bible class and into the lunch hour. Several field hands sat around talking about the morning's teaching on types and shadows, trying to come up with additional insights. Then the conversation turned to whether or not they'd spend the remainder of the afternoon working in some musty shed.

George entered the Golden Tabernacle, striding military style straight to the field workers. "Brother William sent me to tell Mickey and Tony to go to the goat shed and help Mick O'Shea build milking stanchions. The rest of you are to do something edifying with your time, like listen to a tape." He looked around to make sure they'd heard, then did an about face and left.

Tony checked his watch, commenting, "It's almost one o'clock, Mickey. We'd better get down there."

Mickey grunted in agreement. The two lanky Virginians donned their slickers and headed for the farm side.

Marvin said to Jon, "I'm going to the tape library and get a Donald Gray Barnhouse tape. Want to come?"

"Well," Jon stalled, "This would be a good time to go into town and get some things I need, like a pocketknife. Besides, my car hasn't been run since the day I got here. A run will do it good."

"Can I come?" asked Danny. "I haven't been off the farm since January."

"I guess so. You do reckon it'll be edifying to go to town, don't you?"

"Oh Amen! Amen!" Danny grinned. "It'll be good to see how corrupt Babylon has gotten. That way I'll be happier here."

Laughing, they both stood to leave.

"Better check with an elder before y'all leave," David somberly advised.

"Right," Jon said, remembering that no one was to leave the farm without permission.

"Let's ask Sister Wanda," Danny said. "She usually goes along with whatever someone wants to do."

CHAPTER TWENTY-FIVE

...for these things I weep; mine eye, mine eye runneth down with water, because the comforter that should relieve my soul is far from me, my children are desolate because the enemy prevailed... Lamentations 1:16

The rain had slowed to a drizzle. There was a shortage of elders at the moment. Droplets formed on their outer jackets as Jon and Danny looked up and down the pebble path for Sister Wanda. She wasn't in the Main Trailer, or her residence, or the schoolroom, or the kitchen area. Nor were there any other elders available to ask permission for a venture into "Babylon."

"It's like this, Danny," Jon said, "I need a pocketknife, and Brother William said that we should all have our own tools. I know he doesn't like me using his knife all the time, so..."

"I agree," Danny said. "Let's go before anyone who'll say 'no' appears."

They trotted toward the parking lot.

"You do have money?" Danny asked as they swished through knee-high grass.

"Yep." Jon patted his wallet. "And my car keys. For some reason I grabbed them as I left the trailer this morning."

"I have some money, though most of it's in the Main Trailer bank."

"I didn't know there was such a thing."

"Yeah," Danny said, "... I'm surprised they let you keep your money. Most people are told to put their money in Sister Wanda's accounts."

"Why?"

"Some of the kids here have criminal records and the elders want to remove temptation. There are some who don't especially want to be here, you know. You and Marvin are here of your own choice and have each other's trust."

Jon unlocked the car door. "I hope the battery isn't dead." He stretched across the seat, unlocking Danny's door. "Smells musty."

Danny crinkled his nose. "Not as bad as Brother Mick with his goats."

The engine chugged for a moment, then roared to life. A cloud of blue smoke billowed from the tailpipe. After letting it run a few minutes Jon put it in gear and they bumped across the grassy field, avoiding the partially hidden stumps and rocks. Danny gripped the dashboard with both hands to prevent being tossed around. He looked over his shoulder, saying, "So far so good." They grinned sheepishly at each other; it felt like a jailbreak.

Moments later they passed the farm's mailbox and headed toward Eupora.

Downtown Eupora was a collection of bars, a gas station, a grocery store, a general/hardware/feed store, a church, and twenty or thirty houses.

"There's darkness in their eyes," Danny said, looking out the window at people they passed.

"They have no idea that the world's about to come to an end, do they?"

"Living their lives as if it's gonna last forever, eating and drinking, marrying and giving in marriage..."

"There's a parking spot ahead... by the hardware store," Jon said.

They entered the depression-era store, self-conscious of their Yankee accents. They walked around examining the store's merchandise; Jon selected some bandannas and a pocketknife.

Several farmers were clumped in a corner, chewing tobacco and talking in a soft, southern drawl; Jon surmised that but for the soaking rain, they'd be out working their fields.

The lady proprietor at the register smiled, asking as she rang up the items, " Are y'all with the school out they-ah in Sapa?"

Jon blinked uncomprehendingly. "School?"

"Uh-huh. That they-ah school fer the delinquent boys from up north."

"I don't know of any school..."

The lady's eyes narrowed. "Are y'all sure you ain't with thet school? Y'all gots the same look in yore eyes as they gots."

Jon responded "No ma'am, we're from the Move, not any school."

"Well, y'all look like them from the church school thing, especially yore eyes." She handed Jon his change. "Are you sure you ain't with thet school?"

The idle farmers over in the corner had stopped talking amongst themselves and closely watched the two Yankees.

Danny wordlessly paid for his purchases. As Jon and Danny headed for the door, the lady commented for all to hear, "Now why do ya suppose they lied 'bout bein' with thet church school?"

"Man, that lady gave me the creeps," Danny said as soon as they were outside. "She told those farmers that we lied to her?"

"Yeah. She thought we were with some church school. I don't know who she was thinking of. Do you?"

"Don't look at me. I just hope those farmers don't take a notion to come after the lyin' 'Yankees'. Hey, do you suppose she meant our school for the kids."

"Of course, that's it! No wonder she didn't believe me. I never thought of the farm as a school. That must be what the townsfolk think." Jon said. "Imagine what they'd have thought if I'd said, 'No Ma'am, we're from a demon-chasing deliverance farm.'"

Danny slid into the passenger seat. "Yeah, imagine that. Are we going back already? It seems like we ought to enjoy our freedom a little longer, I mean, we've been cooped up in camp for so long..."

Jon studied the foreboding sky. "Well, we won't be able to work as long as it's raining. What else should we do?"

"I dunno. There ought to be something… let's walk around town for a while. At least it's a change of scenery."

"Okay, but only a little while. I don't want Brother William on our backs. We had a good excuse for coming to town, as long as we don't abuse it."

"Sure. Hey, there's a candy store."

They got out of the car and headed toward the newsstand. They barely glanced at the covers of the magazines, whispering, "Alas Babylon." They wandered around the store, purchased some candy bars and just as they left, the sun broke through the clouds.

"Uh-oh! Brother William will be looking for us now," Jon said, scampering toward the car. Danny was right behind him.

"Want a piece of my Goo-Goo cluster?" Danny asked.

Jon's stomach lurched. "Ugh, no thanks."

"I love 'em. So does Brother Jack."

"I know, I know."

Jon missed the turnoff to the farm. Several miles down the road they realized their mistake and headed back.

"Man, we're really gonna be late now," Danny moaned.

"I know," Jon said. "I forgot what the road looked like; I didn't think that little trail was our turnoff."

"Well it was, and now we've lost more time backtracking."

Jon gritted his teeth. Their little outing had become an impending disaster.

Jon navigated a turn as fast as he dare over the rutted roadway and steered into the little lane at the mailbox, like teens sneaking home after curfew.

"Let me out here," Danny said. "I'll see if we've been missed."

"Right."

Danny trotted up the pebbled pathway.

Jon crossed the field and parked. He got out of the Chevy and jogged uphill when he saw Danny's slouched silhouette against the clearing sky. "Uh-oh." He slowed his pace; no sense hurrying just to get rebuked.

"Brother William is waiting for us in the Golden Tabernacle."

Like naughty boys sent to the principal's office, Jon and Danny approached William who was on the platform fiddling with microphone wires.

"Where have y'all been?"

"Uh," Jon said, "… we went to town to get some tools for work. We figured since it was raining, and we couldn't work in the fields, that—. "

"Tools? What kind of tools? Where are they?"

Jon fished in his pocket and brought out his pocketknife. "And some bandannas, you know to keep the sweat out of my eyes."

"Who told you could go?"

"We looked for an elder to ask, but no one was around."

"So we figured," Danny said, "… that since we were going to get tools, and we wouldn't be gone long, it was alright."

"It doesn't take two hours to go to Eupora and buy pocketknives. All the elders were in a meeting down on the farm side."

"Well, we sort of got lost coming back," Jon said, "…after all, we haven't hardly been off the farm enough to know the roads that well."

William's nostrils flared.

Why was it always William? Why not Jack, or Don, someone who'd give them the benefit of the doubt?

"Y'all going to town has put the work crew at a serious disadvantage. We didn't know what became of you… spent a lot of time searching the trailers and woods for you—and y'all were in Eupora enjoying yourselves." He shook his head and turned back to his wiring project. "See if you can make yourselves useful for the rest of the day. Your selfish actions have cheated your brothers who have been working for the glory of the Kingdom, providing for your needs, while you two just went to town for a good time. I want you to think about that."

"But—," Danny said, "… it's not like that, we—."

"Come on Danny," Jon cut in, tugging Danny's arm and heading toward the door, "… let's go to work." He then whispered, "The more we defend ourselves the guiltier we'll look."

Jon and Danny took the short cut down the sloping meadow. They arrived on the farm side and followed the banging noise coming from the goat barn. Inside was Mick O'Shea. A Texas-sized smile spread across his face as he announced, "Boy, are you two in bi-ig trubble. Brother William is lookin' fer y'all."

"We just spoke to him," Jon said nonchalantly.

"Ya did! Well…?"

"We just explained we were on business, and he understood."

Danny nodded. Mick, unable to tell if they were in trouble or not, bent back to sawing, the wind taken out of his gloating.

Marvin entered the shed, exclaiming, "Well, galoree! I sure am pleased to see you brothers are all right. What happened?"

"I'll explain later. Right now, do you need any help?" Jon said.

"Well Brother Jonathan, we're waiting on Brother William to come down and show us how to safely work a chain saw. We really haven't been doing much else, jest standing 'round talking, waiting on Brother William."

"You mean you haven't done any work yet?" asked Danny.

"I been the onlyest one a-workin' 'round he-ah," said Mick between rips of his saw.

"Well I'll be… Brother William sounded as if—."

William's shadow fell across the threshold. He said, "Are y'all ready?"

Mick looked from William to Jon and Danny, then scowling, turned back to his work.

William winked at Jon as he led outside to a stack of logs. Jonathan smiled back, confused at the change in William's attitude.

"Now," William began, "… the most important thing is safety, which y'all were told to study. The second thing y'all have to realize is that dirt is the enemy of your blade.

Never let the blade run into the ground, or soon you'll be doing 'smileys', and having a hard time getting the saw to cut. Here, Brother Marvin, have a go at this log." He handed the purring Homelite to Jon's bunkmate.

Marvin gripped the handle and revved the trigger, grinning appreciatively. His jaw firm, he attacked, pushing the Homelite back and forth. William stepped in, touching him lightly on the arm, laughing and shouting, "No, no, you just rest the blade, the weight of the saw will cut for you. Don't force it."

Marvin nodded, gave an embarrassed grin and re-assaulted the log. Each brother took a turn, getting used to the feel of the chainsaw.

"Well, that's enough for today, I guess." William picked up the saw. "Somebody grab the oil and gas and come with me. The rest of you..." he looked at his wristwatch, "... find something to do for the next half hour till dinner."

"Brother Jonathan," Marvin said, "... I believe I am going to go up to our trailer and write my Dad a letter. Coming?"

"I don't know, Marvin, I thought I'd look for something to do. If Brother William catches me goldbricking—."

"Rest assured, Brother Jonathan, that I believe you, whatever you tell me, I believe you had the highest intentions."

"Thanks Marvin, I wish Brother William shared your opinion."

"I'm sure that he doesn't despise you, though that is what some of the brothers think. I know that he is an elder of God, and whatever his reasons for being stricter with you, they are from the Lord."

"You don't suppose he could make a mistake?"

"Elders are appointed by God in this Move, 'suh'," he said with a mock salute.

"But don't you suppose that Brother William could have gotten the wrong impression of me, and has never changed his mind?"

"He's an elder, and elders do not go by first impressions or personal feelings. That's what makes this Move so different. No one gets appointed to eldership that is still making mistakes."

Jon fell in beside Marvin as they trudged up the hill. "But you just said you'd believe me if I said I had a good reason."

"That's right. 'Cause I know you Brother Jonathan."

"And you'd believe Brother William too, if he said I didn't have a good reason?"

"That's right, 'cause he's an elder."

"Well, we can't both be right at the same time if I say I had a good reason, and he says I didn't have a good reason."

J.M. MACLEOD

"That's right too."

"Marvin, listen to me, don't you think elders can make mistakes?"

He stopped, turned and looked directly at Jon. "Did y'all have a good reason for leaving the farm today?"

"Sort of."

"That implies a 'sort-of-not', too. And that is what Brother William is reacting to. Don't you see Brother Jon, that it's the duty of the elders to help us become what we are called to be? If they let us get away with little things, we might never mature spiritually and our future ministry would suffer, and the whole body of Christ worldwide would be impeded from reaching perfection."

"Well, if that's the way you want to look at it..."

"It's the way we have to look at it. Otherwise we'll be caught up in petty squabbles and personality clashes like so many churches. In this Move of God, Brother Jonathan, we will rise above those foolish things that hold the rest of the body back."

"I know... but I still think elders can make mistakes, just like any of us."

"Well, perhaps, but I'd have to have convincing evidence."

They topped the hill and rounded the bend and soon entered the small trailer that was left on the farm by traveling apostles Harold Michaels and his wife, Michelle. Jon flopped on his bed to wait for the supper call. Marvin, true to his word, set about searching for paper and pen to write his Dad. Marvin longed for his Dad to get saved, water baptized, and join the Move. "Do you know if there's any writing paper around, Brother Jonathan?"

"I'm fresh out. But the Michael's might have some in one of those bureau drawers. I'll check. I don't think they'd mind." Jon opened a drawer. A prescription bottle rolled out. Jon picked it up and read: Michelle Michaels, Valium 30mg; take twice daily, AM and PM.

"Hey Marvin, what do you suppose this is all about?" Jon held up the bottle. "It's a prescription."

"Valium! Potent stuff."

"What's it for?"

"It's a tranquilizer—you know, for bad nerves and stuff."

"Now why would an apostle's wife need a tranquilizer?" Jon said.

Marvin looked Jon eye to eye. "I understand your confusion Brother Jonathan, but you mustn't let that interfere with what the Lord is doing in Betsy's life."

"But Marvin, don't you see? They're preaching one thing and practicing another when it comes to their own."

"No, I don't see that at all. I see that they seek the Lord, and if He says 'get medicine', they get medicine, and if He says 'not to get medicine', they don't get medicine. Why do you suppose that bottle was left here? Probably because she doesn't need it."

"Or maybe the Lord arranged it so I'd see they have a double standard."

"You can't allow yourself to think like that Brother Jonathan. You know the miraculous events that led you here better than I do, and now, because of a little pill bottle, you want to turn back?"

Jon sat on his bunk cradling his head, wishing with all his heart that he hadn't found that bottle. He knew the elders weren't infallible from the way William regarded him. But now... evidence that apostles used valium for depression! "I... I don't know what to think, Marvin."

The loudspeakers crackled to life as Karen and Terri-lee sang a chorus then announced that supper would be ready in fifteen minutes.

"You know what to think, Brother Jon, but you must have the courage to face it. Just because some may use medicine doesn't mean the Lord wants you to."

"Maybe you're right, Marvin, but... it doesn't seem fair to withhold lithium from Betsy while they freely allow an apostle's wife to take valium. Betsy was doing so well… when they took it away she immediately went downhill. Doesn't that say anything?"

Marvin sat beside Jon and put an arm around his shoulders. "I know it's hard Brother Jonathan, but this is how the Lord is making a man of God out of you. You have to be like Isaac, letting his father tie him up for the sacrifice. Come, we'd better hurry and get in line for dinner."

CHAPTER TWENTY-SIX

...foolishness is bound in the heart of a child, but the rod of correction shall drive it far from him... Proverbs 22:15

Jon went to visit his son. Claude, Jill's deaf husband, babysat the boys. One of the Main Trailer girls had been acting up and the elders needed Jill's prophetic gift. Claude assured Jon that Betsy wasn't the subject. Jon coddled and cooed to Jay, wiping his drool as he looked about with wide, wonder-filled eyes.

Half an hour later the loudspeakers announced the start of the evening meeting; Jon kissed his son and bade farewell to Claude. He hurried past the Main Trailer and wondered who was sitting under the sea of glaring faces chanting, "Come out in the name of Jesus," and "The blood of Jesus is against you."

He shuddered, remembering the hateful stare from Betsy's eyes when he himself had been admitted to one of Betsy's deliverance sessions. "I command you spirit of insanity, in Jesus' name, come out of my wife." Had it been a demon staring hatefully at him, or was it Betsy, confused, psychotic and angrily wondering why her own husband was taking part in torturing her?

Jonathan forced the memory from his mind as he entered the Golden Tabernacle. Worship dragged on and on as Jon, nagged by the doubt that these people might be deceivers, had difficulty entering into worship.

"Lord, please show me the truth."

"Tonight," Bunny said after the singing, "... we'll have another of Brother Sam's tapes entitled The Law of Faith, There was a general murmur of approval; Sam's teachings were held on a par with scripture. "I know many of you have heard this one," Bunny continued, "… but the more you hear it, the more you glean from it. You will be tested." So saying, she bent the microphone down to the tape player that was on a stool and jabbed the play button.

"Hallelujah!" Sam Fife's raspy voice erupted across the room, "… in tonight's study I'm going to share with you one of the Lord's most important teachings. I will read from Mark eleven, and then go back as the Spirit of God leads."

He read from Mark eleven, bringing special emphasis to verses twenty-three and twenty-four:

"For verily I say unto you, That whosoever shall say unto this mountain, Be thou removed, and be thou cast into the sea; and shall not doubt in his heart, but shall believe that those things which he saith shall come to pass; he shall have whatsoever he saith.

"Therefore I say unto you, What things soever ye desire, when ye pray, believe that ye receive them, and ye shall have them.

"Hallelujah!" (*Excerpts taken from a Sam Fife booklet of the same title, transcripted from the tape) "The first thing that we want to see, is the reason Jesus cursed this fig tree. It certainly was not because he was angry with it. Our Lord never foolishly lost His temper like that. Besides, the Bible says the time of figs was not yet.

"When I was a young seminarian, I was presented another view of why Jesus cursed the fig tree that seemed very plausible, and for some years, made me miss the real truth that is here. That is the view that the fig tree was barren, and therefore a type of the nation of Israel. Jesus, they told me, put a curse on it because God had put a curse on Israel. I accepted that at the time, but later I went back and studied the context of the Scripture. Then I discovered that Jesus cursing this fig tree had more to do with His teaching His disciples about the Law of Faith! Hallelujah! I discovered that He did it just to show His disciples what faith can do. He knew it would be recorded in the Bible for saints down through the ages to read and learn about the Law of Faith, so He was doing it as the Spirit led Him, to show all generations what faith can do. He did it so that He might show His disciples, by example, that there is a power that operates through faith that can cause a fig tree to die simply by one who has the faith speaking the word of faith. He was going to begin teaching them about the power of words, and the faith behind those words that causes things to happen."

Jon listened as Sam taught that the tree didn't die immediately, but in Jesus' heart the deed was done, so it was received by Jesus as being done, though the eyes of the disciples didn't see it as done.

"This is God's definition of faith: believing you have received something before you have received it. It does not take faith to believe it after you have received it.

"Thirdly, look how simplistic Jesus' faith was when He spoke to the tree. He looked at the fig tree and talked to it as though He were talking to a person. In simple, childlike faith He said in effect: "You will die." Here we see a little bit of the secret of the way to use this powerful word of faith. Now if someone were to be seen talking to a fig tree, right away they would call the paddy wagon. That is because this thing called childlike simplicity has fallen into disrepute in our sophisticated world today. Sophistication has become the god of humanity. Not until we become converted and be like little children will we see the power of God again in our churches."

Jon crossed his legs, seeing a correlation in Sam's teaching to his present situation. Was Betsy's deliverance delayed because he didn't have enough faith? Maybe he didn't receive because he was in perpetual doubt.

Sam's voice cut in on Jon's reverie. "If I were to say to you that it is possible for you to speak to a mountain, and command it to be moved, and rise up and float into the sea, and if you did not doubt in your heart that it will come to pass and see it done, everything within you would probably cry out, 'Oh, not me!' But you would be wrong, because Jesus, the Son of God said, 'Whosoever!' You see, Jesus took the biggest thing He could think of, a mountain, and said, 'This is what faith can do'. Then in His next words He gives us the key: when He says '...and not doubt in his heart that what he says shall come to pass.' The key is 'doubting not' in your heart, in our inner being, in that part of our being which psychiatrists call our subconscious mind. When we speak the word of faith, whether it be for the moving of a mountain or just for the moving of mountains in our personal lives, and doubt not in our hearts, Jesus said: 'IT SHALL COME TO PASS!'

"Now, 'come to pass' does not necessarily denote right now. This is the problem with so many people. They pray, and if their prayer is not answered immediately, they begin to doubt in their heart. Then they get discouraged and give up. They are tempted to think there is something wrong with God or His word. But you see, "shall come to pass," can denote one minute from now, or one week from now. We are to leave the time element in God's hands; and the believing element in our hands. Beloved we have only to believe that there is a power that emanates forth from the nature of God that operates when we believe. We don't have to have anything else, just believe and not doubt in our heart."

Sam illustrated with a personal example: a pastor had told him he ought to have prayed 'if it be God's will', whereupon Sam replied, "'Jesus did not tell me to pray if it be His will, but He told me that when I pray, to believe I received it!' Then he said to me very wisely, 'Oh, but you are not moving any mountains.' I replied, 'No, that's true, I'm not moving any mountains, neither did Jesus go around moving mountains. But He got a lot of sick people healed.

"Jesus did not give us this teaching so we would go around moving mountains. He did it to show us what faith can do. Though you may not have that kind of faith right now, if you will make that your goal, and strive toward that kind of faith, you'll move a lot of little mountains out of your life on the way to that goal. There is no sickness so great that the same power Jesus used to kill that fig tree, by the speaking of the word of faith, cannot heal it. I had stomach ulcers for fifteen years—not the usual type of ulcers that some people get and can get over by watching their diets. No, I had 'roll on the floor and groan' type ulcers every night before going to bed. Then one day I was sitting in the sanctuary and came across these verses again, and the Spirit of God spoke to me. First He said that 'all things' certainly included stomach ulcers, and the second thing He showed me was that when I finished praying—believe I had received it. I had never seen that before. So I knelt down, laid my hands on my stomach and prayed, 'Lord, from this moment forth I believe these stomach ulcers are healed.' I rose up believing it was done.

"It certainly did not appear to be done however, for I had the same pains every night for the next month, even worse. The worse they got the more I realized the Devil was only trying to make me doubt in my heart. But at the same time the Spirit of God reminded me more and more of the truth of Jesus' statement, and I believed it more. Then one night, a month later, I went to bed and had no pains the whole night through, for the first time in fifteen years. I was healed of those stomach ulcers, and I have never had a pain from them since."

Jon sighed. He must believe that Betsy was free of demons and psychosis because he'd asked. And even though it wasn't seen, he must believe, regardless of how Betsy acted, even if an apostle's wife took valium. Sam's tape had revived his hope. It was the very thing he needed to hear. Jon could again trust that this was the Move of God.

Rustling paper reminded Jon that a test was coming, but he little cared. He'd heard what he needed.

That night as Marvin and Jonathan bedded down, a knock came on their door. Marvin was out of bed in a flash, greeting their visitor, "Well, Galoree."

Danny, snug in his winter coat against the night chill breathed out a stream of vapor. "Come in, come in," Marvin said. "Don't stand there letting the cold in.".

"I can't; gotta get back soon as possible. The elders want you—both of you—to come help."

Jon was already out of bed, pulling on his jeans. "Help do what?" Was it about Betsy? Was this finally her deliverance? Jon had been encouraged by Sam's faith teaching. Was God now going to reward his faith?

But Danny was already gone.

Marvin and Jon headed across the campground between the parked trailers. A small group was gathered outside the Main Trailer. Three people jogged around the near end of the field; the middle one supported—or dragged—by the outer ones. The trio turned, heading for Marvin and Jon.

"Marvin, what's going on?" Jon said.

Marvin's breath was visible under the flood lamps in the crisp night air as he said, "I don't know, Brother Jonathan, but we'll surely be told in a few moments."

They trotted over to the Main Trailer where Brother Jack closely observed the trio as they continued running around the perimeter of the field. Rob and Tony, two of the Virginia boys, were supporting a girl between them.

"Brothers Jonathan and Marvin," Jack said, keeping his eyes on the runners "... how nice of y'all to come help us encourage our sister Debbie to repent."

Debbie, a teenaged occupant of the Main Trailer with close-cropped blond hair and a cute, pixyish face was the girl being towed in the middle. She had had bouts of biting her arms and digging fingernails into her flesh, but most of the time she was friendly and polite, giving no hint of demonic troubles.

Rob and Tony half-dragged Debbie to the assembled group in front of the Main Trailer.

"Hold up a minute, boys," Jack said.

Tony and Rob, breathing heavily, stopped. Debbie, dripping with perspiration despite the night's chill, bent over double, laboring for breath.

"Now Sister Debbie," Jack said, "... have you had enough? Are you ready to apologize to Sister Bunny, and the others you offended?"

Debbie wavered, gulping in huge draughts of air, head hanging down, unable to respond.

"Debbie?" Jack persisted.

"Come on, Sister Debbie," drawled Mick, stepping out of the shadows. "Y'all can't keep runnin' much longer."

"That'll do, Brother Mick," Jack said, lifting Debbie's face. "I still see that spirit of rebellion in there, sister. I'm afraid you haven't run enough of that rebellious energy out yet. Brothers Jonathan and Marvin, would you help Sister Debbie use up some of her extra energy?"

"I guess so," Jon answered. "What do we do?"

"I thought you might be glad to help out. Just escort Sister Debbie around the field, making sure she keeps running."

"Yessir, Brother Jack, we'd be glad to help our sister realize the error of her ways," Marvin said, taking one of Debbie's arms and motioning for Jon to do likewise.

Jon took Debbie by the elbow and the three started off at a slow trot.

Debbie whimpered.

"If y'all would just quit your rebellion, Sister Debbie," Marvin said between breaths, "… this wouldn't be necessary. Don't try to make us feel sorry for ya, we know how the Devil tries to play on our sympathies. We are going to do our duty for your sake, sister. Right, Brother Jonathan?"

"Right," Jon said. "You've got to see how deserving you must be of this discipline. Remember—no chastening for the moment is enjoyable—but afterwards it yields the fruit of peaceableness to those who are exercised by it."

Without realizing, Marvin and Jon had quickened the pace. Debbie's feet scraped the ground and she rasped for breath.

"Slow down, Brother Jonathan, she can't sustain this rate," Marvin said. They had reached the far end of the field and began to loop back toward the Main Trailer. "Brother Jonathan is right about the chastening of the Lord, Sister Debbie. Please repent and apologize to whoever you offended."

"But… I… didn't do… anything," Debby gasped.

"Come now, Sister Debbie, Brother Jack wouldn't discipline someone for nothing," Jon said. They unintentionally increased their pace again.

"Brother Jonathan is right, Sister Debbie. You must have rebellion in your heart if Brother Jack tells you that you do. If he were to tell me I had rebellion in my heart, I would instantly receive it by faith, even though I might not think it's there. We have to trust the elders, even when we don't understand."

They drew near the starting point; Jack stepped in front of them with his hand up, indicating a halt. "Take her pulse," he instructed Sister Ally, who served as the farm's nurse. "You boys had her going a might fast out there," he said matter-of-factly. "She's been running for some time and I'm not sure that pace was good for her. I appreciate your zeal in helping out, though. Y'all can go back to your trailer. Someone else will take over."

Later, as Jon settled into bed, he felt ashamed of his role in Debbie's punishment. In his zeal he had nearly brought harm to the poor girl.

Was Betsy being treated like that too?

CHAPTER TWENTY-SEVEN

… a foolish son is the heaviness of his mother. Proverbs 10:1

FRIDAY, MARCH 31

Jon opened the envelope and read:

March 29, Wednesday, 10:00PM

Dear Jonathan,

After talking to you on the phone tonight, I've been sitting here thinking, and I feel you are not being quite honest with us. Maybe you are happy there, but I'm sure if Betsy had any say in the matter, she would want to be where she could get better quicker than she is. If she were in her right mind, do you think she would want other people taking care of her baby? I think perhaps your father is right—that you have found a haven from the world. You don't have to think, everyone is taking care of you and your family. You don't have to work for a living, no decisions. I told you once before in a letter that your actions do not affect only you. You already know about Barney and Andrea, how they were tormented by someone calling them with lewd suggestions, claiming to be you. You may claim you had nothing to do with that, but if your actions were not questionable, they never would have thought it was you calling.

In the first place, you are to blame for Betsy's condition. If you had any sense, you would have made her take her lithium. You would not have allowed her to go to those highly emotional meetings in her weakened condition, in a partial post-partum psychosis.

Not only have you upset our whole family, because if Dad does not have another heart attack or me a nervous breakdown before this is all over, I'll be surprised. Not to mention the Rutlidges and all their friends and relatives. Lydia Bonser, my co-worker, is terribly upset over what has happened and asks me every week how you are and when I have nothing to report, she sighs, and goes away.

I think you are deluding yourself that Betsy is getting better. Maybe she does have her lucid moments, and just happened to have one when her father called her, but if these people could help her, I'm sure it would have been done in less than six weeks.

You talk of love, which I am sure is only to keep me from arguing with you. Oh Jonathan, Jonathan, what has happened to you? This house is a house of mourning. I feel that we have lost you, and not only you, but Betsy and dear little Jay too. People are afraid to ask me how my grandson is because they feel it will upset me. And it does, though I try not to let it show.

If this letter hurts your feelings, I'm sorry, but you have hurt us deeply. You are making me a bitter, old woman. When I think of the audacity of those people taking you all the way down to Mississippi, my blood boils. That action was criminal. Christians? Spare me such Christianity! They had their little fun and games and no one was going to spoil their game of casting out demons. Don't you see how they wanted to glory in your flesh? I wonder what they think about it all now? I'm sure they feel that it is not their fault, but it is! Theirs, and yours, for letting them do it.

If you love your wife, take her back to Philhaven, where they know about her condition and can give her proper care. Then when she is better and you still want to go back to Eupora, I'll not argue with you. But see that Betsy gets proper care. Remember, you were wrong about her condition before. Don't add more insult to injury. How long are you going to let this condition go on? And by proper care, I don't mean people talking mumbo jumbo over her like witch doctors! I mean somebody who knows what they're doing. Those people might be doing more harm than good.

I'm ashamed to face the Rutlidges, knowing what you have done to their daughter,

Goodbye, MOM

P.S. I think it is plain selfishness on your part to stay there and not get Betsy competent care. If you really loved her, you would want her to get better the fastest way possible. The Rutlidges report that after talking to Betsy's former psychiatrist, to fully recover, she would need more than lithium now.

Jon sighed. His parents didn't know the self-doubt, torment and longing for his wife and child that he was already going through.

Jon and his mother had talked just the other night. He tried to get her to understand how the Lord works through trials. She had said little then, but it was obvious from this letter that she hadn't agreed with him. There was some truth in her accusations: Jon wasn't being totally honest. Jack had sat beside him during the phone conversation, advising Jon in whispers to say that Betsy was doing much better, and that it was just a matter of time until she and Jon and Jay were back together.

"I can't lie to my Mom," Jon had protested, cupping his hand over the phone.

Jack's eyebrows went up and his lips pursed, then he said, "Well, y'all don't have to tell them everything, either."

Jon told his mom that things were progressing, even though they weren't. Why should she be more distressed than she already was? Instead, following Brother Jack's instructions, Jon emphasized how much of the Bible he was learning, that he had a better grasp of doctrines such as the vicarious blood atonement of Christ, salvation by grace through faith, spiritual gifts and Christian love.

"Mom, you and Dad should visit and see for yourself. This isn't just a deliverance farm; it's a glorious place where we put Jesus' teaching into action, loving and serving each other. You can't learn community like this in a denominational church."

"Well, I don't think you know what love is to treat your family this way."

"Ah, Mom, don't take it like that. I have to do what the Lord has called me to do. Look it says in the Bible that God is love, right?"

Silence.

Jon continued, "I'm confessing to you that all through my rebellious teenage years I wasn't a good son. But here I've learned what true love is; I'm ashamed of my rebellion and attitude. I love you and Dad, Sonya and Danny too. I never really knew what love was. But, I also have to obey God and do what He has called me to do."

Jack smiled and nodded his head. The conversation ended shortly after.

That night Jon returned to his trailer more miserable than ever, looking more and more a fool in his family's eyes; and perhaps, in his own.

Jon re-read his mother's letter. It was true, he hadn't been totally honest, but how could he tell his folks what was actually happening?

'… you have found a haven from the world. You don't have to think;, everyone is taking care of you and your family. You don't have to work for a living, no decisions…'

Haven? Jon mused looking at his callused hands. Blisters and backaches were mementos of this "haven." Yesterday he'd hoed for ten hours, then, he spent another three hours in the nightly meeting. He'd much rather have a regular life, a job, attend church, live with his family, play with his son—rather than live in some tiny trailer in a hayfield on this muddy, rain soaked, mosquito infested, backwater township of Sapa, Mississippi.

Jonathan lay back on his cot. Every night for the next week Marvin would be at the Golden Tabernacle, sweeping and setting up tables after meeting in preparation for the morrow's breakfast. Mick O'Shea was scandalized that Jon hadn't yet been appointed for this duty. Every newcomer got assigned that duty almost immediately. For some reason though, Jon had been skipped.

Jon rolled over and tried praying, but how could he trust God when He could, but wouldn't, stop Betsy's torment? Those thoughts were wrong, but he failed to find fault in the logic. Faith insisted that God was love, and that He was doing what was best—but it didn't seem best.

Jon tossed on his cot. The door opened and Marvin entered, dripping wet. The temperature was in the fifties—normal for early spring. "Brother Jonathan, y'all still awake?"

"Can't sleep."

"The farm is under heavy attack again tonight."

"How' that?"

"They're praying for somebody down at the Main Trailer, and there was a fight in one of the boys trailers, and Sister Debbie—the one we had to 'run' a few nights ago—is sitting on a stool, outside, in the rain, wearing only her short-sleeved dress. Seems like the ol' Devil is having at us again."

"Debbie is in the rain without a raincoat, or any coat?"

"Brother Jack and Sister Bunny decided to put her outside to cool off. In fact, they dumped a bucket of water over her."

"That poor girl!"

"Now don't you go feeling sorry for her, Brother Jonathan. She's got to quit letting them demons dominate her. The elders know what they're doing."

"She'll catch pneumonia!"

"Don't you think the elders considered that? The Lord will make sure she doesn't get pneumonia if that's what it takes to break her rebellion."

"I hope you're right."

"Being out here on your lonesome so long isn't good for you. I can see ya getting full of doubts again."

"I have to admit that, I guess."

"Well, let me minister to ya." He placed his hand on Jon's head saying, "I command you, spirit of depression, leave Jonathan, in Jesus' name."

Jon just sat.

"Is it gone?" Marvin asked.

"Well..."

"Brother Jon, you've got to resist, too."

"Did it ever occur to you that maybe I'm depressed because there's a lot of depressing things going on in my life? Everything doesn't have to be a spirit, you know."

"That sounds like the Devil trying to talk me out of delivering you, Brother Jon."

"Look Marvin, if I punched you in the nose, and your nose started to bleed, would that be a demon of bloody nose, or just a bloody nose?"

"That would be a demon that made you punch me, Brother Jonathan. But I'd forgive you."

"And I forgive you for being insensitive."

"You don't think your depression is a demon?"

"No! I think I'm under a lot of stress, and depression is a natural result. It's not a demon. You don't understand my pain."

Marvin sat on his cot and sang, "Nobody knows de trubble Jon seen..."

Jon stood. "That's right! You don't know the trouble I've seen. Do you have a demented wife, a son living with another couple, and family and friends sure you're in a cult? Sure you bear the work of the farm, incessant meetings, kowtowing to the elders, living in an unheated trailer, taking cold showers, and working the live-long day on this cursed, red clay. I have all that plus my own grief, more than anyone else on this farm can lay claim to, so don't tell me I'm possessed by a spirit of depression until you've known my grief."

Marvin stared at Jon through his rain-speckled glasses.

"I'm going for a walk." Jon grabbed his slicker and stepped out into the chilly rain. He wandered down to the pebble pathway—the only place he could walk without mud clumping on his feet. He yearned to be alone where he could scream out his rage… Instead, he hunched over and plodded along the pathway toward the Main Trailer, walking off his anger.

He paused in front of the Golden Tabernacle. Fifty yards away in the glare of the Main Trailer's floodlights was a pitiful, shivering figure sitting on a stool. The curtains at the window parted—Bunny's silhouette appeared, checking on her disobedient charge. Jon wondered if Debbie's parents—apostles roaming somewhere in the world—would approve of this treatment of their daughter.

Yet who was Jon to accuse? He had nearly run the poor girl into cardiac arrest just a few nights ago.

Jonathan turned, and slowly made his way back to the trailer he shared with Marvin.

CHAPTER TWENTY-EIGHT

He... gave them power and authority over all devils, and to cure diseases. Luke 9:1

SATURDAY, APRIL 1

Jon rolled over and stared at the ceiling. It had been hours since lunch; heavy rain made fieldwork impossible. Being Saturday, there had been no Bible study in the Golden Tabernacle; Jon's options were open.

He considered spending time with his son, but was too depressed; he'd only break down and cry. Jill didn't need that. She had enough troubles dealing with other elders over the way they treated Jon and Betsy.

Visiting Betsy wasn't an option either; she reacted violently at the very sight of him. So, sleep became Jon's refuge.

But sleep evaded him. There was a guitar leaning in the corner.; one of the brothers had left it there earlier. Jon hefted the instrument and strummed an A minor, then improvised a progression and hummed along. Jon's Bible lay open to Psalms. He scanned Psalm sixty-nine; verses thirty, thirty-two & thirty-four fit his melody. Was the Lord was giving him a song?

> I will praise the name of God with a song,
> And will magnify Him with thanksgiving,
> The humble will see this and be glad,
> And your heart will live that seek God.
> Let the heavens and earth praise Him,

The seas and everything that moveth therein.

Jonathan sang it again, his parched soul absorbing its message like a fresh spring rain. This was what Jon needed, praising God despite his woes.

The camp's loudspeakers interrupted Jon's vespers with an announcement. "Attention, all available elders, report to the Main Trailer immediately." Jonathan listened for a hint of who might be undergoing deliverance. He felt somewhat renewed; able to face people again. He donned his coat and headed toward the Main Trailer.

He passed by the trailers of brothers and sisters doing housekeeping: sweeping, taking out trash, shaking out blankets or rugs... Jon looked around and saw elders streaming from all areas toward the Main Trailer. Jon slowed his pace, not sure he'd be admitted. Three elders ascended the steps of the addition and as they opened the door, Betsy and Agnes came out.

Agnes invited, "Hi Jonathan. We're on our way to the Golden Tabernacle for some coffee. Like to join us?"

Jon turned to Betsy. She avoided looking at him.

"I—I don't think so, Agnes. She might become difficult to handle..."

"Oh pooh! Sister Betsy, you want your husband—Jonathan, you remember him don't you—do you want him to have a cup of coffee with us?"

"I am married to Christ, not Jonathan. And if I was married to him," she eyed Jon disdainfully, "I wouldn't want his corrupting company. He's dead, you know?"

Agnes laughed and said, "Dead! Why, he's standing right here talking to us. He's going to have a cup of coffee with us. Isn't that nice?"

Betsy glanced at Jonathan, her eyelids fluttering. Finally she said, "I don't care what he does."

"Well, good then, he's coming. You be nice to him. He's been through a lot of grief for you."

The three filled the pathway on their way to the dining hall.

Betsy laughed heartily at some inner joke which Agnes and Jon could only guess at. "That'll be a surprise, won't it? Ha ha ha ha."

"What are you laughing at, Betsy?" Agnes asked.

Betsy immediately sobered. "Nothing you'd understand." She tossed her head.

Agnes and Jon helped themselves to the coffee urn. Betsy seated herself at a table, mumbling under her breath.

"I thought maybe... perhaps... they were praying for Betsy," Jon said.

Agnes glanced about the open room, lowered her voice, and said, "I'm not supposed to tell, but... a girl, a woman actually, is who they're praying for. She's from a body up north somewhere—and... she's an elder!"

"An elder?"

Agnes nodded. "That's right, and the wife of an elder."

"An elder got demon possessed?" Jon asked.

Agnes sat back. "She just had a baby. Demons got in under the guise of post-partum depression. Her husband sent her here for deliverance."

If an elder of the Move was subject to demonic possession, how could they help Betsy?

Agnes and Jon joined Betsy at the table. Agnes took a sip of coffee and made a face. "Ugh! What is wrong with this coffee?"

"It was brewed in HELL," Betsy said, whirling around.

"It tastes like it, Sister Betsy," Agnes said with a laugh.

"It's the milk," Jon said. "Mick O'Shea told me they're using goat's milk for coffee and breakfast cereal."

"Oh Lord," Agnes said, "...do we have to go through the Tribulation drinking goat's milk?"

"How bad is she, the elder, I mean?"

"Her name is Rhonda Meeks, or Meeker, or something like that. She's as bad as Betsy was the first day she came, only... Rhonda is a kicker. Got demons of violence in her. Jack and Bunny thought I'd better take Betsy out before some of Rhonda's demons got in Betsy."

"Yeah, that's right. We gotta keep them out," Betsy said.

"Amen, Sister Betsy, amen."

Jon's vision blurred. His sweet Betsy, once so smart, loving, sensible and tender, was now reduced to a mimicking lunatic without social poise or any sense of propriety; and... she hated the very sight of him.

"Jon, I know this is hard," Agnes said. "Don't take anything she says or does seriously. This manifestation isn't your wife. Remember that."

Jon nodded and dabbed at his eyes.

"What was Betsy like before? I mean, I'm sure she wasn't like this when you married her."

Jon swallowed the lump in his throat. "She was witty, sweet, and sensitive. We'd talk for hours, just being romantic, planning our life together. She was fun loving and zany.

When I took her home to meet my parents, my dad teased her and she threw a glass of water on him."

"Betsy, did you do that?" Agnes asked. "Did you really throw a glass of water on your future father-in-law?"

Betsy responded hilariously, "Yessiree-bob! Just threw a glass of water on him."

"Calm down, Sister Betsy," Agnes gripped Betsy's forearm. "It wasn't that funny."

Betsy pulled away from Agnes' hand, an angry glare in her eye.

Street-wise and tough from growing up in Brooklyn, Agnes was more than a match for Betsy.

Betsy stared out the window, ignoring the coffee Jon had prepared for her.

Agnes rose, saying, "I'm gonna see if they don't have some real milk in the kitchen. I can't drink coffee with goat's milk in it."

When Agnes was out of hearing range, Betsy said flatly, "They beat me."

"Beat you? Who, the demons?"

"She does. And so do Jack and Bunny."

"Oh Betsy, I don't believe that. These are godly people. They wouldn't do that."

"With a belt. It stings." Betsy turned and, ignoring Jon, gazed out the window.

Was it true? Jon had seen how they'd dealt with Debbie, but Debbie, though rebellious at times, wasn't psychotic, but responsible for her choices. Betsy was out of her mind; harsh discipline would be counterproductive.

"Betsy, you must be mistaken. Don't you mean they were spanking someone else?"

Betsy snarled in reply, "They beat me! They beat me—and you let them do it! Why don't you take me away from this awful place? Don't you know they're false prophets?"

"Betsy, calm down. They don't beat you, and they're not false prophets."

Betsy rose and slammed her fist on the tabletop, sloshing coffee from the Styrofoam cups. Her eyes flashed as she shouted, "False prophets, all of them! Including you, Jonathan McComb, son of Satan!"

Her outburst convinced Jon that Betsy had confused what she'd observed as if it had been happening to her.

Agnes came running from behind the partition. "What's going on? Betsy, sit down and drink your coffee. What did you say to her, Jonathan?"

Betsy flopped down and drank the steaming coffee in one gulp.

"She said you—we—we're all false prophets, and..." Jon pondered mentioning Betsy's claim about being beaten.

But Agnes was preoccupied with Betsy who was flapping her arms like wings, as if she could escape by flying. "Maybe you should leave. I think your presence is causing this. The demons don't want you around her. She never acts like this in the Main Trailer."

"Yeah." Jon stood to leave. "I'll visit our son."

"Well, hallelujah! It's about time," Betsy said.

"I'm sorry about this Jonathan," Agnes said. "It won't always be like this. Keep trusting God."

Jonathan nodded and left. Distressing images filled his mind. Were they beating Betsy? Who knew what went on in the Main Trailer other than those who lived there?

As he passed the Main Trailer Jon heard the familiar shouting of warfare. Would Rhonda get better results than most of the Main Trailer's occupants?

Jon spent an hour at the Rine's, talking to Jill and taking pictures of his son.

The session with Rhonda lasted through the late afternoon, dinner, and on into the night. The elders took shifts, refusing to give the demons any quarter.

During that night's meeting a shift of elders traipsed in from the battle, haggard, deep creases lining their foreheads and puffy circles under their eyes. If the elders coming from the fray were this worn out, how was Rhonda, having recently given birth, faring?

The meeting was subdued, both in praise and teaching. Blind Loretta led worship with her accordion, but without the presence of an elder, the song service didn't last long. The teaching was a tape by one of the Move's apostles, but few paid attention. Instead, everyone in the building watched the changing of the guard as one bunch of weary elders trudged in and another group left to take their place.

Jon skipped the snack after the meeting, going straight to his trailer. He flopped on his bunk and sobbed, begging for Betsy's deliverance.

The next thing Jon knew, Marvin was standing over him in his pajamas, shivering. He gently nudged Jon. It was Sunday morning.

After breakfast and morning chores Jon took his seat with the elder brothers as the meeting began. Instead of dispersing throughout the congregation as usual, the elders huddled near the front. A woman with deep circles under her eyes and a dazed stare sat in their midst. Her brown hair was tied back in a ponytail. She was about five feet two and no more than a hundred pounds. She looked rather ordinary except for her glazed eyes. William and Chester sat on either side of her.

Jon searched for Betsy and Agnes, but they were nowhere to be seen. One of the girls from the Main Trailer caught Jon's eye, came over and whispered, "Betsy and Agnes are sleeping in this morning. They didn't get much sleep last night."

"Thanks Marie," Jon said. From the hollows under her eyes, Jon guessed that she hadn't slept much either.

The microphone screeched as musicians took their places on the platform; the meeting was about to begin. Bill Thompson stepped up to the mike shouting, "There is victory in the camp."

There was a half-hearted response of "Hallelujah!" and "Praise the Lord!"

Exhausted, but grinning ear to ear, Bill Thompson shouted again, "There is victory in the camp."

The same response rose from the congregation. Jon joined in, not wanting to appear disgruntled that they'd gone all day and all night with this new comer just because she was an elder.

Once more Bill bent down to the mike shouting, "There is victory in the camp."

Then the musicians launched into a song proclaiming the enemy has been overcome. Jon watched Rhonda Meeker and the elders on either side, forcibly holding her up, trying to make her sing and raise her hands. They only succeeded in keeping her from sitting down, and that was a struggle. Despite their claim, this was certainly not the "victory" Bill wanted everyone to cheer about.

"Glory!" someone near Jon shouted. Clapping and "Holy Ghost shuffling" broke out all over the Golden Tabernacle.

Jon went along outwardly, but within thought that for all their efforts they hadn't achieved any more success than they had with Betsy—or any of the other girls in the Main Trailer.

An hour or so later the music wound down and a contingent of elders escorted Rhonda back to the Main Trailer for more "prayer." Those in the meeting would hear one of Brother Sam's teaching tapes. But before the tape, Don Wilson, the youngest and newest elder, made some announcements.

"And here's an item that will bring cheer. Brother Sam's sister and brother are coming to the farm with their families for a few days of ministry."

Excited chatter swept through the crowd. Sam's whole family was anointed to apostleship. Even his sister, who had been delivered of demons, was now an apostle. Were they as anointed as Sam? If so, maybe they'd cut Betsy's deliverance debacle short and show these ineffective elders how it was done.

MONDAY, APRIL 3

"Brothers Marvin, Tony, Mick O'Shea, and Jonathan McComb will report to Brother Chester after Bible study," announced the loudspeaker.

Jon stood next to Mick O'Shea in the breakfast line. "What's that all about?"

"Why Brother Jon, we gots us a special service to do for our brothers and sisters," Mick said. He spooned grits into a bowl and moved on to the next station for toast and eggs.

Jon followed, filling his tray, waiting for Mick to spill what he knew, but Mick kept it to himself.

"Ah, he don't know nuttin'," said George, a few places behind. "He's just pretending, so he has sumthin' to hold over you."

Mick eyed his accuser, then, deciding not to rile the hand to hand combat expert, turned back to the array of food on the counter.

"I do too know what we're gonna be doin," he stated lowly so George wouldn't hear.

"What?" Jon asked.

Mick smiled, revealing toothy gaps as he said, "Outhouse holes."

Spaced throughout the circle of trailers were seven outhouses: five close to the trailers and one at each entrance to the farm.

"Outhouse holes?"

"Yep. All this rain has filled up the outhouse holes so they need to be covered over and new ones dug. Galoree, it's a smelly, disgusting job, and I shore am grateful they chose me to do it. I gets to suffer fer my brothers and sisters. And so do you, Brother Jon."

"How do you know this?" Jon asked.

"Heered Brother Chester and Brother William talkin' this mornin'. Eat hearty, 'cause you'll not likely want much lunch."

Mick and Marvin were assigned to remove the existing outhouses and fill in the septic pits; Tony and Jon were to start new latrine pits. Jon broke ground with a mattock, taking the first shift. Tony, nearly a foot taller and able to climb out of a deeper hole, would do the deeper delving.

As the outhouse crews went to work, an airplane flew over waggling its wings. A cry went up from Mick, "Galoree! That'll be Brother Sam's sister and brother."

The plane buzzed the farm again, then flew off towards the Greenville airstrip. Tony said, "The apostles do that so we'll know to send a car."

Moments later one of the yellow and white vans rattled out the upper road to retrieve the apostolic Fife siblings.

Jon showered after work, barely cognizant of the showerhead's frigid payload. He was excited about talking to the Fifes, beseeching them to pray with Betsy. Jonathan shut off the water, lathered up, then turned the water on again to rinse. Shouts of "Yow!" and "Galoree!" erupted from nearby shower stalls as workers washed off the day's grime.

Jonathan hurriedly toweled dry and dressed, wanting time to pray. Betsy's torment must end. All the flip-flopping of giving, then not giving lithium had been a test. Surely the Lord would answer with deliverance this time.

CHAPTER TWENTY-NINE

But truly I am full of power by the Spirit of the Lord, and of judgment, and of might, to declare unto Jacob his transgression, and to Israel his sin... Micah 3:8

Sam Fife's sister, indeed, all the Fife siblings, were not what Jon had expected. They looked like a bunch of backwoods hillbillies: overweight; slovenly dressed; dull eyed. They sat in the front row with arms crossed while the congregation stood in worship. Well, God has chosen the foolish things of the world to confound the wise, Jon thought. They were Sam's family; they had Sam's and Jack's approval. Jon would take it by faith that Sister Fife's word was the very thing he needed to hear.

Loretta laid her accordion aside and took a seat. A hush settled on the Golden Tabernacle. Sam Fife's daughter, also a resident of the Main Trailer, sat among her relatives looking out of place. Finally Eunice, Sam's apostle sister, the one who had been delivered of demons, waddled to the microphone and for a full minute glared at the assembly. The fat of her cheeks nearly squeezed her eyes shut. This was an apostle? A messenger of truth? A bringer of deliverance? Jon prayed for more faith.

"I have noticed," Eunice said in a low, hoarse voice, "... that the ways of Babylon have crept in even here, where saints are supposed to be manifesting as sons of God." She stared disdainfully at the crowd. Her husband and her brother nodded in agreement. "I see make-up—even in my own family," Eunice glanced at Dolly, "... jewelry, fancy-schmancy hair-dos, finger-nail polish...."

Dolly, guilty of all the above, shrank down. If Dolly received such open contempt, what mercy could other girls expect? Bunny Halstead often encouraged girls to apply cosmetics so as to "look nice"; in fact, most of the elders' wives took great pains with their appearance for their husbands' sake, sporting coifed hair, jewelry, nail polish and make-up.

"Even among elders," Eunice said, her voice rising theatrically, "… have I beheld Babylon's temptations taking hold. Some even let their children play with Babylon's toys. There is no surer way to condemn your children than by letting them taste the lusts of Babylon. Dolls, toy cars, baseballs and footballs. The children in this Move of God need no such amusements."

Jon looked around to see how the elders were receiving this word. Usually Bill Thompson's grin was as wide as his face, but both Bill and Lisa, little Billy's parents, sat stone-faced.

The crowd was still as a graveyard under Eunice's harangue—all except Jill, who hoping to enjoy an edifying word, had left the boys in her husband's care. Jill rose out of her seat and went out the back door. Onlookers assumed she was going to nurse one or the other of her charges, but Jon caught her scowl as she brushed past. His heart sank. He trusted Jill. She had taken on the burdens of his family, whereas other elders only pontificated over Jon's situation, involving themselves only in fruitless deliverance sessions. By seeing Jill's reaction to Eunice Fife's teaching, Jon despaired of finding help for Betsy from Sam's siblings. In fact, Jon hadn't needed Jill's opinion to know that he didn't want these Fifes near Betsy.

A newcomer to the farm, a Chinese brother named Terry Soo sat on the end of Jon's row. Jon had heard that Terry had been in underground church meetings with disciples of Nee To Sheng, better known as Watchman Nee. Jon saw Terry sadly shake his head as Eunice Fife prated on.

The entire meeting became surreal, as if Jon were standing on a high cliff above a turbulent sea with winds whipping around him and waves crashing higher and higher, eroding the ground away on which he stood. How could someone so disgusting have become elevated to such high authority in this Move of God? Yet no one challenged her. Most sat expressionless, caught off guard by her blitzkrieg of accusations.

Gradually zealots in the crowd began punctuating the diatribe with, "Well, glory!" and "Hallelujah!"

A smile crossed Eunice's face. Supporters encouraged her to rant on for another hour, breathing condemnation on Babylon and rebuking everyone in sight for letting Babylon take root like mold in their midst.

"You've got to beat the desires of the world out of them children. Don't tell me to spare the newborns; they need to be spanked right from the womb. That's when training begins. Their little fleshly desires will control you if you let them. If you wait a month to chastise them, you've given the Devil a month's foothold. Don't let them cry and get their way and control your life; teach them early what it means to be a child of obedience. And don't let them have those rattles and baby plugs—toys! That's where idolatry begins."

Perspiration rolled from her forehead as she strutted back and forth, jabbing her finger at various individuals in the audience, her voice carrying without aid of the microphone.

Jon wanted to trust Jack and Bunny, but if they approved of Eunice Fife's teaching…

Eunice went on and on proclaiming an angry, vengeful, God who wanted people to only read the Bible and pray. If Eunice Fife was truly an apostle, Jon no longer wanted any part of this Move of God. Yet, if this was the true Move of God—and he'd had so many confirmations, how could he just walk away? The cliff beneath his feet crumbled; Jon plunged toward a dark, tempestuous ocean of doubt and despair.

The meeting closed; everyone stood to their feet, murmuring a pretense of embracing the hard word. Lisa Thompson took over and led the final song.

Jon stumbled out of the Golden Tabernacle gasping for breath, loath to chat with anyone. Not only had hopes for Betsy's deliverance been dashed, but his confidence in the Move was once again severely shaken. Where could he turn? What counsel could he seek? He glanced toward Claude and Jill's trailer; their lights were out.

Grief and doubt washed over him.

MONDAY, APRIL 10

A gully-running downpour continued all night and on into the morning. Even the pebble pathway was no haven from the ubiquitous red mud. No one could walk out of doors without tracking mud wherever they went.

A week had passed since Eunice Fife had strafed the farm. Toys disappeared and children were scarcely seen while she remained in camp. An hour after she and her retinue overflew the farm to spread misery to other bodies, Billy Thompson rolled his Tonka dump truck out into the yard of his folk's trailer. Soon other children and toys reappeared, and nothing more was said about such Babylonian encroachments.

"Hi George," Jon said sliding in beside his friend. "I didn't expect to see you here in Bible class."

"Ah, there's nothing to do on the farm side, at least until this rain stops. I hear it's supposed to rain all week. So, here I am for class."

"We—ell, if it ain't Brother George," Mick drawled from behind. "Come to git some edifyin', are ya?"

George ignored him.

"Ah shore am glad to see ya here. By the way, did y'all heah thet we're gonna git a new elder teachin' us this mornin'? Brother Ronnie Meeker came all the way from Ohio to be with Rhonda, his wife, and their baby. He's an elder up in Ohio, but is movin' here 'til his wife gits delivered."

"You just make it your business to know everything, don't you?" George said over his shoulder.

"Seems yore a might put out at sumthin'. Could it be 'cause Brother William tole ya that ya had to come to Bible class?"

George's neck sinews bulged.

Jon intervened. "Meeker? Do you mean the woman they prayed with for twenty-four hours straight? Her husband is going to be our teacher?"

"That's right." Mick grinned as he strolled out of harm's way to another table.

"That busybody!" George said. "Someday just me an' him is gonna be down on the farm side alone and he's gonna shoot off his Texas mouth once too often…"

"He's harmless, George, just don't let him get under your skin."

Suddenly George smiled. "Listen, remember when I told you I had a secret?"

Jon nodded.

"Well, I can tell you now, only you've got to promise that you'll tell no one else—especially Mick. Okay?"

"Promise," Jon said as he mock crossed his heart and spat in his hand.

"Do you know Diane that lives in Sister Bobbie's trailer?"

"The cute one with a reddish-blonde Dutch Boy cut?"

George's smile revealed pearly white teeth. "We're gonna get hitched."

Jon did a double take. "Married?"

"Hush. Not so loud."

"How…when…? Does she…? I mean, I never see the two of you together…"

"I got it confirmed by one of the prophets."

"That's it? You just get a word from a prophet—no dating, no courtship, no getting to know each other?"

"According to Brother Jack, dating is Babylonish. This is how it's done in the Move of God. I sought a prophetic word; it got approved by Brother Jack and Sister Bunny, who then asked Diane… and she agreed."

Jon was incredulous. "When will you…?"

"We're still waiting word on that, but I believe it'll be soon."

Ronnie Meeker arrived and class began. Jon found him to be a lively teacher, creatively and humorously interlacing the basics of Christianity with the more spiritually advanced concepts of the Move.

The next week passed slowly for Jon; fieldwork was hampered by the weeklong, daily deluges. The only notable event occurred on Thursday night during dinner when Jack announced George and Diane's engagement. A spontaneous, joyous outburst greeted this surprise from all except Mick O'Shea, who sputtered over the fact that a secret that large had eluded him.

The same night that George and Diane's engagement was announced, one of the men in Brother Chester's trailer opened the flue on their wood stove all the way to drive out the chill, then forgot to dampen it back. The stovepipe venting through the trailer wall, turned cherry-red. Smoke poured into the cramped living quarters. A bucket brigade quickly extinguished the smoldering wall before any severe damage was done, but a burnt smell lingered in the trailer for weeks. No one owned up to having left the flue wide open, but Jon noticed that Mick O'Shea was uncharacteristically subdued for several days.

The week of rain frazzled everyone's nerves; tension was high and fights broke out in the boys' trailers and nasty arguments erupted in the girls' trailers; elders were constantly on guard, admonishing their charges to stay in the Spirit. The Main Trailer was in a constant state of battle; teams of elders came and went all times of the day. Even William lost his effervescence as his farm projects were continually delayed.

Jon slept most afternoons. There was no use visiting Betsy; either she wouldn't see him or a deliverance session was in progress. He spent time with his son when he could, but with no work anywhere on the grounds, and with both Jill and Claude and their child in the tiny trailer, Jon's presence (not to mention the mud he inadvertently brought in) overwhelmed the tiny living space.

After Friday night's meeting the rain stopped.

CHAPTER THIRTY

I watch, and am as a sparrow alone... Psalms 102:7

MONDAY, APRIL 17

"Brother Jonathan, wake up. I have something to tell you."

Jon's eyes opened. Marvin hovered overhead.

"I'm going home today. My father, remember I told you about him, needs me. He's close to becoming a Christian.... Anyway, I need to go home for a couple of weeks."

"Oh... well... it'll be a good time for me to pray without distractions." Jon swung his feet over the edge of the bed.

Marvin's face fell. "I surely didn't mean to be a distraction to your praying, Brother Jon. I wish you had told me—."

"That's not what I meant... I just mean that I'll have no excuse for not praying more. When are you leaving?"

"Brother Jack is driving me into town this afternoon to catch a bus. I'll pray for you and Sister Betsy every day."

Jon dressed hurriedly in the morning chill. A momentary queasiness hit him.

Marvin caught the slight quiver. "Are you all right?"

Jon belched, then grinned reassuringly. "I'm fine, just gas, I guess."

"You ought to get on to breakfast, then. I have packing to do."

Jon stepped out into a foggy morning. He'd missed the morning prayer circle; in fact, he'd even slept through the wake-up call. No doubt Mick O' Shea would be laying for him. The aroma of buttered toast, eggs and bacon wafted from the Golden Tabernacle's rear exhaust fans. That usually whetted Jon's appetite, but instead, Jonathan felt another wave of queasiness. Confident it would pass, Jon entered and ate a hearty breakfast.

Lunchtime came, but Jon had no appetite. This time he respected the warning, choosing instead to go to the trailer and take a nap.

A loud knock on the door roused him. "Jonathan? Brother Jonathan, are you in there?" It was Danny. Glancing at his watch Jon saw with dismay that he'd overslept the lunch hour. No doubt Brother William would think he was shirking.

"Yeah, I'm here. I fell asleep."

Danny poked his head inside. "Brother William sent me to look for—say! Are you all right? You look pale as a sheet."

Convulsions seized Jonathan's bowels. He brushed past Danny, heading for the outhouse, calling over his shoulder, "Tell Brother William that I don't feel so good."

Jon made the outhouse just in time, thankful it wasn't in use. He broke out in a cold sweat. He went back to the trailer and lay down, but a few minutes later he again was running to the outhouse.

Jon visited the outhouse every couple of hours the rest of the afternoon and throughout the night. When Jon wasn't rushing to the outhouse he crawled back on his cot and fell immediately asleep.

The next day was a blur of sleeping and heading for the privy. He took no nourishment and drank sparingly; nevertheless the diarrhea continued.

Thursday mid-morning, a light knock came on the trailer door. "Brother Jonathan, are you in there?"

Jon blinked and rolled over.

The knock came again.

"Come in," Jon muttered.

Brother Chester entered. He took one look at Jon and sat on Marvin's cot, saying, "I hear you aren't feeling well."

"I keep having diarrhea," Jon said in a whisper.

"How long?"

"Two days, I think."

Chester bowed his head, then stretched out a hand touching Jon's forehead. He prayed in tongues, then commanded, "Spirit of infirmity, I bind you in Jesus' name."

Jon felt something move in his abdomen and his right leg began shaking.

"Satan trembles when confronted by the Anointing," Chester intoned. "I command you to release this young man, in Jesus' name, and come out of him."

The pressure in Jon's abdomen dispelled in a prolonged release of flatulence; Jon felt instantly well—and hungry.

Chester suppressed a smile and said, "A fitting method for that foul spirit to leave. I understand Brother Marvin has gone home for a while?"

Jon sat up. "Yes, that's right."

"And you're out here all alone?"

"I don't mind. In fact, I've been looking forward to—."

Chester waved his hand, silencing Jon's comment. "You'd better move into my trailer for the time being."

Refusal wasn't an option. Jon looked around, gathered needed things and followed the elder.

"This'll be your bunk," Chester pointed to a lower berth, "... and your chore will be to sweep the floor every morning."

Jon settled his gear onto the bed. "Who bunks above me?"

Chester thought for a moment then replied, "I believe that belongs to Brother Mick O'Shea."

Jonathan groaned.

Chester smiled and said, "When Brother Marvin returns you may go back to your little trailer. Are you hungry?"

"Famished."

"It's still a couple of hours 'til lunch, but I think the kitchen staff will fix you something."

Jon mumbled thanks and headed for the Golden Tabernacle. The days of diarrhea had left him dehydrated and pounds lighter.

Dolly Fife looked up from stacking dishes and remarked, "Why Brother Jonathan, we've all been quite concerned for you. Are you alright?"

"Brother Chester just prayed for me... I feel much better. In fact I'm really hungry now."

"You've lost weight. I think there are some scrambled eggs and toast left over from breakfast."

"That would be great. You, uh... you still live in the Main Trailer, don't you?"

Dolly nodded as she shoveled cold eggs onto a plate and added toast and a jelly packet.

"Is Betsy...?"

Dolly looked up. "Not much change, I'm afraid. But your little boy is growing so fast, and he's so cute."

Jon retreated to a table, musing how odd it was for Sam Fife's daughter to be a resident of the Main Trailer and not an elder, or at least a helper, like Agnes.

Residing in Chester's trailer did little for Jon's depression. He'd gotten used to Marvin's snoring and mutterings, but the cacophony of twenty snorers made for sleepless nights. That, coupled with the fact that he couldn't bear his grief openly and cry aloud for Betsy's deliverance without bringing a Job's comforter down on him, made Jon yearn for Marvin's return.

MONDAY, APRIL 24

Jon fought back tears. He was alone in the trailer, sweeping the floor; the others were heading for school, Bible class or various work details.

In bitterness of soul Jon silently cried, "Oh Lord, have mercy on Betsy, if not me. She's tormented day and night… our little baby won't know his mother… I miss my wife and child..." He stabbed at the pile of dust on the floor with the broom, angrily demanding, "I want it to end. I've had enough."

He brushed tears from his eyes. He spied a desk near the doorway that had two Bibles lying side by side; one a King James and the other a Chinese translation. They belonged to Terry Soo, the Chinese believer. Curious, Jon studied the vertical markings of the Chinese Bible, making no sense of the figures. He then turned to the King James Bible to see what Terry had been comparing. Jon's eyes were drawn to: And so, after he had patiently endured, he obtained the promise, (Hebrews 6:15.)

Had the Lord drawn his eyes to that verse? Jon shoulders heaved as he leaned on the desk and wept. God hadn't forgotten his family.

Mindful that this solitude could be interrupted at any moment, Jon took a deep breath and finished his chore. His heart still ached, but it wasn't a hopeless, angry ache anymore; rather, it was a willingness to endure yet a while longer for the godly results it would produce.

J.M. MACLEOD

CHAPTER THIRTY-ONE

Know ye not this parable? and how then will ye know all parables? Mark 4:13

FRIDAY, APRIL 28

Morning Bible classes were cancelled; it was planting time. Jon and the elder brothers along with the senior-high boys, were assigned to plant various crops: corn, beans and potatoes in the fields; and in the garden: okra, radishes, peas, peppers, cucumbers, various melons, spices and whatever else the elders thought might grow. Despite the poor soil, the elders believed, because of the farm's growing population, that God would miraculously bless the harvest. Whatever resources the elders drew from to pay the weekly grocery bill was, no doubt, getting strained.

Jon looked at his callused hands then plunged his fingers into the yielding earth as he continued planting the quarter-mile cornrow. Mickey from Virginia, in the next row over, stood to straighten his back; he was the only worker on the farm with any real agricultural experience. Jon sank to a knee letting David and Danny on either side catch up.

"Crows," Mickey said with disdain, observing a flock skimming the end of the field.

"They won't do any harm now that we've covered the seed, will they?" Jon asked.

"Those black-feathered thieves will walk along the row, tug the germinating two-inch stalk out of the ground with their beaks and swallow the seed, root and all. I hate crows."

"Sounds like a type and shadow to me," David, the would-be prophet, said. "Like when Jesus said that the birds of the air swoop down and snatch away the seed from the wayside. Even after it sprouts it's still vulnerable, just like believers who get born again and start to grow in their spiritual life. Then Satan swoops down and—."

"Are you guys gonna take all day?" shouted George from the end of a row. He had out-paced everyone, even Mickey.

They all bent back to the task. It wouldn't do for William to suddenly show up and see the bunch of them standing around talking, especially with George was so far ahead.

The elders soon expected to have a viable farm. A gift of nanny goats and a rambunctious billy from another body swelled the herd to nearly twenty. With only a day's advance warning pigs were added to the livestock, causing feverish construction of a hog pen. A chicken house was also in the planning. A couple of feeder calves and two milk cows were promised, generating need for a larger shed.

Weeks of day-long work continued under a hot spring sun; weeding and cultivating followed planting, then second plantings, followed by more weeding and cultivating—all done primitively by hand.

The elders' wives demanded that the billy goat, Solomon, be separated from the nannies; his odor corrupted the taste of the milk. Mick O'Shea fretted about Solomon being isolated from his harem, but the elders' wives remained adamant. They could barely abide goat's milk as it was, let alone Solomon's overpowering "fragrance" which crinkled even Mick's nose. Another pen had to be built at the furthest extremity of the lower farm, anything closer and the billy would still befoul the odor of the milk. The distance between pens added to Mick's workload, but he had desired the responsibility of the goats—all the goats—and that meant carrying water, hay, grain and any ovulating nannies all the way to the billy's solitary confinement. And he made sure everyone knew the sacrifice he was making.

The billy didn't take kindly to being separated from his harem. From the first day he was banished to the far side of the farm he began continuously battering the weakest post in his pen. William kept assigning work crews to repair each night's damage.

Marvin returned at the end of two weeks, and Jon moved back into the little trailer, greatly relieved to no longer be under Chester's domain. Chester turned out to be as austere and humorless as his appearance, even if he had spiritual clout against diarrhea.

Marvin's Dad visited the farm for an extended visit, also bringing another "family member"— Major, Marvin's horse, a thoroughbred that had washed out as far as racing, but was a fine animal for riding.

"Glory, Brother Jonathan," said Marvin. "I am so glad to be back among true brothers and sisters where the word of God is preached in power."

"I'm glad you're back," Jon said, helping Marvin tote his luggage. He then filled Marvin in on what he'd missed, starting with his bout with diarrhea.

"Praise the Lord, I knew in my heart it wasn't safe to leave you by your lonesome. But I also knew you'd be in safe hands. My father accepted Jesus into his heart, but still has to get free of Babylon. That's why he came with me, to get detoxed. I cleared it with Brother Jack. He'll be staying with brothers Ernest, Gerald and the others who need to overcome addiction to the demon of alcohol. How is Sister Betsy?"

Jon's eyes lowered. "Since they took lithium away she's reverted to psychosis. She doesn't even know me."

Marvin stopped. "Brother Jonathan, I know this has been hard, and I wish I could have been here, but God knows. Anyway, I'm here now, and I promise to do all I can to get you and your wife reunited."

"Thanks. You're a good friend."

MONDAY, MAY 1

Marvin's and Jon's hammers resounded in staccato bangs as they pounded another temporary fix onto Solomon's pen. Marvin wiped sweat from his brow and said, "Ol' Solomon better appreciate this."

Jon drove a sixteen penny nail flush, then gave it one more whack. "Would you? After all, we're keeping him from his girlfriends," Jon grinned. "And I don't think he's above taking aim at our backsides for it."

The billy shook his horns from side to side.

Both men laughed then Marvin said, "I know something of how he must feel, and you, too, Brother Jonathan."

Jon hefted another plank and tacked it in place. "What do you mean?"

"I'm not unaware of the trial you must be going through, not only emotionally, but physically as well. I know, because I was sexually active before coming to the Lord. I opened up areas of my life that I had no business opening. It was difficult to put away carnal lusts, even though I had no right to indulge them. I can imagine what it costs you to be deprived of conjugal rights on top of all the emotional suffering. I want you to know that I know the price you're paying."

Jon drove home another nail, then another, making no reply. Finally he managed, "That means a lot, what you said. Thanks."

A loud buzzing from overhead drew their attention skyward. It was a Piper Cub, the same model that Sam Fife piloted.

"Glory! That must be Brother Sam!" Marvin said.

"Sam? Coming here?" Jon suddenly went cold. Sam would discern every secret thought and doubt... and every accusation against the Move. On the other hand, Sam also might see how the elders were bungling Betsy's deliverance.

Sam and his wife, along with other members of his apostolic company had indeed arrived, and were sequestered in Wallace and Wanda's trailer—where Jon had spent his first few nights on the farm.

That night in the meeting Jon studied the apostolic company. Everyone expected Sam to get up and lead the meeting, but he never stirred. In fact, he and his companions left before the worship was done.

Maybe tomorrow, after Sam was rested, Jon would approach him. Maybe he wouldn't even have to ask... Sam might see Betsy's condition ... or Jack would surely mention her...

SUNDAY, MAY 7

Sam and company flew out early in the morning, buzzing the farm to say goodbye. Jon watched them go, deriding himself for not directly approaching Sam and insisting that he deliver Betsy. But of course, one never imposes on an apostle, one just trusts that the apostle knows the will of God and will do what needs doing.

Jon sighed and continued on to the meeting in the Golden Tabernacle. Sam had done nothing for Betsy the entire week, nor, as far as Jon knew, for any other Main Trailer resident. He and his entourage toured the farm as if they were royalty but did little to nothing to edify the faithful.

The morning worship lasted only forty-five minutes. Everyone seemed depressed that Sam had come and gone so quickly. Then the Sapa Trio, as they were called, stood to sing. Dolly, Marie, who usually manned the farm office, and Ally, an ex-nun, constituted the "Sapa Trio." To Jon, the blend of their voices was akin to the Andrews Sisters. He was comforted as they stood and sang Jon's Psalm 69 song.

Tears welled in Jon's eyes. He'd shared the song with some brothers, who must have passed it on.

Then the newest elder on the farm stood to preach: Rhonda Meeker! She still resided in the Main Trailer on a rollout bed in the office with her husband, Ronnie. But she was an elder, and as such, could stand and address the meeting.

"We are gonna have the victory!" Rhonda's eyes were glazed and her face bore a hard look. She surveyed the crowd that yelled back, "Glory!" and "Hallelujah!" Then Rhonda launched into a rambling 20-minute repetition of rephrasing the same concept.

If anyone besides Jon thought the performance unusual, it didn't show. Most took it on faith that the Holy Spirit was talking through her. It didn't seem to matter that there was no content in her prating, nor scripture, but only vague phrases about overcoming.

Jon bowed his head. Was he out of step with the Spirit... or was everyone else? How could this woman, barely returned to her senses—if she even was—deliver a meaningful message to the church? Was spiritual discernment at such low ebb that they validated any and everything as of God just because it came from an elder?

Jon turned his eyes upon the elders, who, along with everyone else, grinned and shouted, "Praise the Lord," as if something wonderful was happening, as if Rhonda had been set free from demons and was preaching a good word. But the woman was still clearly disturbed.

Was it all as his Mom's letter had accused, just a game?

CHAPTER THIRTY-TWO

...and she became his wife; and he loved her. Genesis 24:67

SUNDAY, MAY 14

"George and Diane are to be married next Saturday." Jack smiled his best Andy Griffith grin at the rejoicing assembly. He held his hands up for silence and continued, "And it ain't gonna be no Babylonish wedding with fancy-schmancy dresses or tuxedos and an expensive cake and honeymoon."

A new wave of celebration broke out. George, seated next to Jon, was lobster red. Jon searched the crowd for George's intended, Diane, and finally spied her among a bevy of girls; she too, blushed radiantly.

Bunny stepped up beside her husband and took the microphone. "That doesn't mean we won't all be putting on our nicest outfits and getting made up pretty as can be, does it Brother Jack?"

"Well, I should sa-ay not," Jack said. He did a little two-step and sang, "There's going to be a wedding, our joy will soon begin, in the evening when the camel train comes in…"

At that, everyone spontaneously began singing the song based on the story of Eleazar bringing Rebecca to Isaac.

Jonathan was happy for George. He hoped they'd have a blessed marriage, free of trouble and grief. His eyes rested on Betsy next to Agnes in the front row. She was caught up in the excitement, but oblivious to the reason. Jon bit his lip. His personal struggles must not interfere with his friend's joy. This was George's moment; Jon would rejoice with those that rejoiced.

The meeting dismissed. Jon saw Jill and Claude carrying both Jays out the doorway. Jon was about to call out in greeting, but they both averted their eyes, slipping out the door. Jon stood stock still, perplexed. Of everyone on the farm, the Rine's had always exhibited love and concern for his family. An icy hand gripped Jon's heart. They knew something but were unwilling—or unable—to tell him. Bunny came bustling through the mass of people that was clogging the door and Jon pushed his way alongside her, asking, "Sister Bunny, is there something I ought to know?"

Bunny Halstead gave brief instructions to Marie and Ally and sent them on ahead. She then turned to Jon, saying, "Why Brother Jonathan, there is nothing changed that I know about. Rest assured that if there are any changes to be made, you will be the first to know. Meanwhile, you have faith; it's a good report. Your wife is doing just fine."

Jon watched as Bunny made her way up the pebble pathway. He decided to visit his son after the noon meal and see if he could find out what was behind the Rines strange behavior.

Jon was finishing his meal, half listening as David described a vision he'd seen during the morning Bible study. Chester climbed on the platform, turned on the PA and intoned, "There will be an elders meeting immediately following lunch today. It will likely take all afternoon, so adjust your schedules. The following brothers will report for clean-up duty starting tonight, Marvin, Terry, David and Mick."

Jonathan's shoulders sagged. An all afternoon elder's meeting ruled out talking to Jill. He could still play with his son, but talking to Claude without an interpreter was a frustrating endeavor. Claude could read lips expertly, but his enunciation was severely limited. Jon would wait for a better time.

MONDAY, MAY 15
The sun warmed Jon's back as he hoed loose soil into potato hills. The Glory of Work, Sam's teaching, blared over loudspeakers strategically placed on the edges of the field. Had William overheard Jon and others disagree about Move teachings as

they worked and so, decided to remove the temptation to talk as they went about their chores?

Jon rehearsed the previous day's events in his mind. The elder's meeting was not, as Jon had expected, a deliverance session; nevertheless, every elder was required to attend. Main Trailer residents had been temporarily evicted; the topic under discussion remained secret. Betsy and Agnes visited Claude and Jay. Recognizing that Betsy wanted no part of him, Jon left so that Betsy could spend time with their child.

Jon looked up to see one of the vans send a trail of dust into the air as it entered the farm's lower gate. Despite the previous week of rain, the road dried quickly and when stirred by traffic, coated everything nearby with a reddish patina.

"Hey, someone's coming in from the airport," said David from the next row over.

Mitch answered, "Yeah, an apostle, Frank something or other, is coming by on his way back east."

"How do you know?" Lester asked.

"Brother Mick heard Brother Chester tell Brother Don."

"I won't believe it till I see it," George said from three rows over. "I won't believe anything that has its source in Mick O'Shea until my eyes and ears confirm it … and even then I'll question it."

Despite George's misgivings, Frank DeVrona, a Move apostle, had arrived for an overnight stay.

Jon tried not to get his hopes up.

Frank spoke in the meeting that night about coming forth in the miraculous power of the Holy Spirit. Then, gifted as he was with a powerful tenor voice, he sang a stirring rendition of The Highway of Holiness.

Instead of being inspired however, Jon was plagued with despair; his family's trial would never end. Skipping the snack, Jon went to the trailer and sat on his bunk. Would Betsy ever be herself again? Would Jay ever know his own parents? Would Jon grub his whole life away on this farm, never to enjoy his family, never to see his or Betsy's folks again?

WEDNESDAY, MAY 17

"Ah, Brother Jonathan McComb, may I introduce Miss Jane?" William said. A stately, older woman extended her hand. "This is my mother, come to live with us on the farm. Isn't that nice?"

"Good to meet you," Jon said, receiving the lady's hand. Of all the people milling about after lunch, why had William brought her to meet him?

William's eyes twinkled as he said, "Y'all will be seeing more of each other, I'm sure." Then to his mother, he added, "This is the father of that adorable little baby that Sister Jill and her husband are looking after."

"Oh, yes, he's a sweet baby. Very nice to meet you, young man," Miss Jane said.

Jon watched with growing curiosity as William introduced his mother to others. Why had he singled Jon out first? Wryly thinking William had probably told his mother that Jon was the farm's most subversive member, Jon shrugged and went to do his chores.

On his way down the hill Jon noticed that the foundation of cinder blocks around Jill and Claude's trailer had been pulled out. Had their water lines sprung a leak? Jon mused how grateful he was that the Rine's were on the farm; besides Marvin, they were the only ones he felt completely at ease with, freely sharing every pain and doubt.

The beans were ripening; Jon, among others, was sent to gather the "first fruits." The older brothers traipsed into the fields singing all three verses over and over of "My God and I" –one of Sam Fife's favorites. Delight lit up William's face as he watched them go.

The pickings were meager; insufficient for even one farm meal, but it was a beginning. William scanned the puny crop when they reported back, seemingly comparing everyone else's harvest against Jon's. Then he flashed his toothy grin and said, "Well, y'all will do better as more beans ripen." He glanced at his watch and said, "It's a might early, but y'all kin go clean up and have some free time before dinner."

Jon placed his bucket on the tailgate of the pickup and trotted up toward the residential side, anxious to shower, change clothes and visit the Rine's to pump them as to why they'd avoided eye contact the other day. At the top of the gravel road Jon skidded to a halt.

Jill and Claude's trailer was gone! Water pipes stood erect out of the ground and wires lay coiled beside neatly stacked cinder blocks and a pile of two-by-fours. Jon scanned the semi-circle of trailers to see if they had relocated to a different spot. But their little trailer was nowhere to be seen. They were gone!

A chill ran down his spine. Had they absconded with his son? No, of course not. They were too loving, honest and genuinely concerned about Betsy and him to do such a thing. So where was Jay? Jack must have known that they were leaving; William must have... so, that was what lay behind William's sparkling smile.

Jon's alarm turned to anger. He now understood why Jill and Claude had dodged him. Jill had often stood in opposition to the other elders, suggesting a gentler approach in dealing with Betsy and others. And ...Jill had received a clear word to not take Betsy off medication, which was ignored by the elders. Now that the outcome of their decision was obvious, Jill's presence was an embarrassment.

Sounds of an approaching vehicle drew Jon's attention away from the empty trailer space; William drove past in the pick-up with its sparse bean harvest. The elder slowed, flashed a gleaming smile at Jon, then accelerated around the corner.

Bunny met Jonathan as he headed across the field. "Oh, there you are, Brother Jonathan. As you can see, Sister Jill and her family have decided to leave our camp. But don't you worry none, your darling little boy is now in the care of another elder's family. I have to go attend another matter at the moment or I'd tell you more. I'm sure you understand."

Later, Jon lingered in the shower, letting cold water stream over his head and shoulders in the hope that the frigid temperature would cool his temper. He now had no one to turn to, no one to whom he could relate his deepest feelings. Of course there was Marvin, but he didn't need to speak with Marvin to know what he'd say. "Brother Jonathan, the elders are always right; they always do what God wants. Just trust them."

William's teenaged daughter, Karen, met Jon as he entered the Golden Tabernacle for supper. "Umm, Brother Jonathan, my father wonders if y'all would like to come and eat dinner at our family table tonight." Karen Nobles, a pretty and blossoming teen, smiled. Jon felt her awkwardness as she awaited a reply. Now why would William want Jon's company, of all the workers on the farm, at his table?

Jon scanned the hall trying to come up with an excuse for turning down the offer. Then he spotted his son, Jay, being dandled on Miss Jane's lap. William had sent for his mother to come and care for Jay so they could be rid of Jill. This had obviously been in the planning for some time. How long had Jill and Claude known they were to leave? Probably not until the day before they left! Not only was an ally removed, but now Jon's son was "hostage" his to chief antagonist.

"Yes, of course, thank you for asking," Jon heard himself say.

"Sister Betsy will be joining us too, I believe," Karen said. "As you can see, we are now taking care of your little baby. He's so precious. My grandmother just adores him."

Jon sat beside Miss Jane, who offered, "Would y'all like to hold your sweet little boy?"

Jon hugged him close, shutting his eyes to hide the tears.

Agnes sent word that Betsy wasn't coming to supper; an unusual amount of attack had descended upon Main Trailer residents. They would take their meals in to eliminate potential disruptions in the dining hall.

William and his wife arrived shortly before the meal was served. He cordially welcomed Jon to their table. "Please feel free to dine with us any time, Brother Jonathan," he said. To Jon it sounded more like, "Don't impose on my family too often."

As it turned out, Miss Jane rarely came to the Golden Tabernacle for the evening meal. Jon found it better visiting his son during the day. Miss Jane was a good caretaker, and Jon was satisfied, even though Jay was put on formula instead of mother's milk.

Jon kept up a good front over the next several days .

During that rough time Marvin recognized Jon's inner battles and gave him space.

SATURDAY, MAY 20

George and Diane's Wedding Day arrived.

Work was suspended. From the wake-up call through early morning the entire camp was abuzz. The girls' trailers were beehives of activity as single women and teenage girls applied make-up, did their hair and prettied themselves. The elders decorated the Golden Tabernacle for the nuptials. The boys and single men busily polished shoes and "lint-rolled" their suits.

Jon observed all the activity from William's picture window as he played with Jay.

George's family wasn't coming to witness the blessed event; they lived too far away. But Diane's mother and father and three sisters had spent the night in various elders' trailers as visitors. They weren't part of the Move; in fact, a rumor went through the campground like a Mississippi grassfire that they weren't even born-again. They seemed out of place, yet clearly enjoyed the attention they received as family of the bride.

Miss Jane elected to stay home with Jay; Jonathan relinquished his son and made his way to the Golden Tabernacle, aching for his own bride, yet rejoicing in George's good fortune. Diane was a sweet girl with a gentle disposition who had been involved in various duties around the farm from laundry to meal preparation.

Jack, being duly ordained, officiated. The preliminary praises impressed Diane's family; who quickly caught on to the hand clapping. However, they didn't know quite how to handle David letting loose with a prolonged prophecy about the symbolism of a man and woman reflecting the glory of Christ and His Church.

"I now pronounce you… man and wife." Jack concluded the ceremony an hour later.

A shout erupted from the congregation and congratulatory kissing, handshaking and backslapping surrounded the blissful couple. George's eyes uncharacteristically glistened with joy. Diane's face flushed as she received hugs from the well-wishers filing out the door.

A couple of the elders had provided a love nest for the couple by refurbishing an unused building on the lower portion of the farm. The newlyweds were to dwell there until they either procured their own trailer or the Lord led them to another farm.

Jon had entertained hopes that witnessing a wedding might stir Betsy's memories and bring her around to her senses. But it wasn't to be… Agnes hadn't brought Betsy to the affair. He congratulated the couple and made his way outside and sat on a log. All around him girls and boys bustled about in their finery, enjoying the holiday. He stared up the pebble pathway toward the Main Trailer, willing Betsy to emerge, in her right mind, ready to rejoin him in family life.

CHAPTER THIRTY-THREE

... the daughters of Zion are haughty, and walk with stretched forth necks and wanton eyes, walking and mincing as they go... Isaiah 3:16

SUNDAY, MAY 21

"I've seen you girls; rebellious, sinful, mocking the elders," Lisa Thompson rebuked. The evening meeting cowered under the elder's stormy glare. "I've watched you gang together and clap out of time, thinking the elders were unaware. You're fooling no one."

Jon had seldom seen such anger come over the lectern as Sister Lisa now dumped on the unsuspecting assembly.

"Jezebels! Delilahs! Who do you think you're attracting by hiking up your skirts? Who do you think is attracted to your mincing steps and flirty eyes? Do you think your rebellious attitude is attractive to true men of God? No true son of God would want anything to do with a woman who overdoes make-up and acts rebellious."

"Amen," chorused several masculine voices.

The cluster of nearly twenty girls withered under Lisa's diatribe. The group had been sitting together for several weeks, clapping to the backbeat on worship songs, giggling, whispering, passing notes, popping bubble gum and generally being a distraction. But Sister Lisa, a fire in her eyes and sharp words on her tongue, lowered the boom, making them a public example.

"There will be no more," the elder said. "After tonight you will no longer sit together, some of you are being relocated to other trailers. The elders have already decided who is moving where. You will learn to flow in unity with this body, your rebellion will not be allowed; 'rebellion is as the sin of witchcraft, and stubbornness as iniquity and idolatry,'" she quoted. "You will no longer practice witchcraft, do you hear me, you devils? Don't you girls understand the grief your disunity is causing? You're letting Satan gain the upper hand in our deliverance sessions, you're the source of the troubles besieging the camp; you've given the Devil a foothold! Shame on you! Shame on you! I—I…." Her neck veins bulged and her face grew bright red as she slammed her Bible shut and stormed off the platform, down the center row and out the back door.

A hush hung in the air. All eyes were on the cluster of girls who had been the target of Lisa's attack. There had been hard words given from time to time, but never before had such a tongue-lashing come over the pulpit.

Bill Thompson took the stage. "Now think on those things, everyone. Search your own hearts for hidden rebellion. We'll dismiss without any talking or any snack tonight."

MONDAY, MAY 22

Jon and David took a break from planting hot peppers to get a drink from the pump head. Jon surveyed the recent construction on the lower end of the farm as David took a sip from the spigot. Puffy clouds tumbled over each other in a bright blue sky above the pigpen and goat barn; even the billy goat pen was relatively sturdy, foundations for a chicken house were laid out and a farm house where an elderly couple resided was under renovation. Mounded rows of potato hills traversed parallel to the dirt road all the way to the lower gate off in the distance.

Jon bent over to take a drink.

"Looks like Brother Marvin is coming to give us a hand," said David.

Jon finished his drink and looked toward the curve of the road. Sure enough, Marvin ran toward them as fast as his feet could go.

"Brother Jonathan, I've been looking all over for you," Marvin panted as he drew to a halt. "I have good news."

"Betsy?" Jon said, his hopes rising.

"Oh, I am sorry, Brother Jonathan, I should've worded that differently. I should have known that would be foremost on your mind. I'm afraid that my news is not that good, but it is good. The elders have decided to build a bunkhouse in the field by our little trailer. It will hold four of the older brothers—two of whom are you and me."

"Who are the other two?" Jon asked.

Marvin scrunched his brow, "Uh, a new guy from Pennsylvania that came today, name of Rob Manhart, or something like that. I believe Brother Jack said the other brother would be Danny; at least they were considering him. And we're finally going to have a small wood stove. Isn't that great?"

Jon wasn't as elated as Marvin had assumed he'd be. All along he'd felt that his situation was temporary since they were housed in a borrowed trailer; the construction of a bunkhouse implied a more permanent situation—as if Betsy's condition wasn't expected to improve for a long time.

Jon met and talked to Rob Manhart that night. Rob had lived on the outskirts of where Betsy's Dad did livestock business and allowed as he might have met Mr. Rutlidge. Rob was assigned to tend the pigs.

Ronnie Meeker, Rhonda's husband, spoke at that night's meeting. He taught about commitment to the Move, no matter what personal sacrifices were required. Ronnie was usually warm and hopeful, even humorous in his teaching. But tonight he was intense, stern, angry.

During the after-meeting snack Mick O'Shea sidled close and whispered to Jon, "Rhonda left the Move. She done declared her husband was more deceived than all the rest of the nuts here, and that Brother Sam and other apostles were false teachers. I guess they never did get all the devils outta her. She took her newborn and went home to her folks '...until Ronnie comes to his senses,'" Mick quoted. "The ole Devil got her deceived real good and is trying hard to git her husband to forsake his calling as an elder and leave the Move." A hint of a smile played at the corners of his mouth.

"Well then, we'll just have to pray real hard that the Devil doesn't get his way, won't we Brother Mick?" Marvin said, coming alongside. "Thank you for sharing that prayer burden."

Mick blinked, then replied, "Uh, sure, sure. That's why I was sharing that... uh, I'd better go see if Brother Lester knows."

"The Devil always goes for the weakest link," Marvin said after Mick left. "That's why he came to you with that discouraging bit of news, because you keep giving in to doubt, Brother Jon. You've got to stand firm."

Walking to their trailer, Jon and Marvin passed stacks of 4'x 8' sheets of plywood and 2 x 4's and some cinder blocks that soon were to become their bunkhouse. So Marvin was right; the elders were considering putting Jon in a more permanent dwelling situation…Had Rhonda perhaps, done the right thing?

Hi Mom & Dad & Danny,

We miss you all very much. Betsy is coming along. I know that you have probably lost all faith in me, but I know that Rom. 8:28 is still true. More and more the world is spinning around on a dead end course. The Bible says, "Be ye holy, as I AM holy." According to (your) Pastor Norman and the Hebrew language, holy means, "set apart," in the world but not of it. This farm is where the Lord has led me in my walk with Him—set apart from the world in order to come to know Him ever so much more and to be filled with Him more so that Christ in me is the hope of glory. In the farm's atmosphere everything is conducive to spiritual growth so that we may be strong in the Lord and then be able to help others in the world.

My life in the past has been start something, get halfway through, then quit. You know this as well as I. But the Lord is gradually changing me to be more responsible. I just know that His power in my life has been changed immeasurably since I have received "The Baptism in the Holy Spirit." I seldom had success when I tried to lead someone to Christ—in fact in two summers at the Indiana coffeehouse I personally only led a few people to Christ, and their conversions were shaky at that. Meanwhile, the "Glory Barn" coffeehouse down the road in North Webster operated by "Spirit-filled" believers, won many lasting converts. I couldn't understand this until I received "The Baptism of the Holy Spirit." Then I found out that there is a deeper, more precious realization of my Savior as a loving Lord. Well, that's what is beginning to happen in my life.

I trust that it won't be long before Betsy, Jay and I are reunited as a family. I'm sending a few pix of Betts and Jay. I'll send you the negatives later, along with a few scenes of the farm.

Some of the men here are taking up archery in order to supply the farm with meat next hunting season. Since I have experience hunting, would you please send my bow and quiver. There's a shortage of equipment here.

Jay has grown and changed so much (as you can see). I've sent duplicates to Mom & Dad Rutlidge.

I hope you don't feel resentment toward Doug & Sonya Trevor or Minnie Eastman. The Word of God says to straighten out your differences and love your enemies. You really should get to know them, because you'll be spending all eternity with them. I'm sure Alice Dymond would be glad to answer any questions and explain many things to you.

Betsy and Jay and I would love to see you. I know Dad has said that he'd never come down here, but I hope you haven't hardened your hearts against us.

There's lots of room for visitors—actually, as Brother Jack says, there are no visitors (although many come to see what we're all about and end up staying either a short or for longer periods of time) because we all belong to the same spiritual body and family. After all, how can you pass judgment on a place you have never personally been to? Oh please do come down and visit, even if only for a couple of days. I know many of your fears and worries will be cast aside.

I pray for you all unceasingly, knowing that you are going through a hard time. But I am also confident that when you seek the Lord for His peace, He rewards you accordingly.

I LOVE YOU ALL SO MUCH.

Jon, and for Betsy and Jay

Jon laid his pen down. Was he being hypocritical by encouraging his folks to find the peace that proved so elusive to him? And preachy! Did he really need to include snippets of every teaching he'd heard over the last week? Well, he believed every word, even if he didn't feel it. Telling them the truth might be painful, but also might help them see why he'd made the decisions he'd made. Sooner or later his folks must come around.

TUESDAY, MAY 30

Ronnie Meeker taught from the book of Joshua in the morning Bible study. He was standing resolute that Rhonda would return to her senses and come back to the farm to finish her deliverance.

The weather turned chilly despite the nearness of summer. Mississippi summers, Jon was told, were blistering. But a cold front had slipped in, bringing more rain... and mud.

Jonathan stepped out of the Golden Tabernacle into the cool air and was greeted by curious sight: Patrick Simons, the teen who had accompanied Jon, Jack and Dixie to Jackson, was running laps between the Golden Tabernacle and Chester's trailer. He was near exhaustion, spittle dribbled over his chin and flecks of foam burst from his mouth. He tagged the corner of the building and turned to run back.

"Patrick? What are you doing? You'll bring on an asthma attack!" Jon said. Only then did he see Chester standing beside his trailer, keeping an eye on Patrick.

"They... think... I'm... rebelling." Patrick paused to explain, drawing shallow breaths. "So they... are making... me run." He staggered back toward Brother Chester.

Jon knew better than to interfere. What if Jon's or Betsy's folks visited and beheld an asthmatic running his lungs out in the name of discipline? What if they saw a bucket of water dumped over a girl shivering in the rain?

CHAPTER THIRTY-FOUR

If ye shall ask any thing in my name, I will do it. John 14:14

WEDNESDAY, JUNE 7

"Brother Jonathan McComb, please come to the Main Trailer," echoed the camp loudspeakers.

Jon was on his way up the hill from planting an okra patch. Morning Bible classes had been suspended so that "reaping the fat of the land" could begin. He jogged the last fifty yards, rounded the corner and mounted the steps to the Main Trailer's addition.

Inside, Ally, the ex-nun, looked up from her work. "Well, that was fast," she said with a smile. "You have a package, Brother Jon," she pointed toward a corner of the room.

From the package's long, skinny shape, Jon surmised it contained his bow. As he retrieved it a voice from behind said, "Sister Betsy, look who's here, it's your husband, Jonathan."

Agnes and Betsy stood in the entrance of the hallway. "Humph! Thought he was dead," Betsy said as she walked past, glaring at Jon. She then cackled at some inner joke, remarking, "Well, he'll soon get it."

Agnes responded, "Don't talk like that, Betsy." Then to Jonathan, "She doesn't mean what she says; demons are putting wild thoughts into her mind, trying to get everyone upset. Sometimes at night the real Betsy comes out for a while, and she asks about you and your baby. Then she gets confused and thinks we're all false prophets, and is gone again. But… I'm sure there'll be a breakthrough soon."

Jon nodded and left carrying his bow, quiver and target arrows which were in the package, along with a few other personal items.

Jon trotted down the sloping meadow, passing Doug and his disgruntled band of poop-bucketeers finishing a belated round. Doug Counterman had been given the project when Jon had been dismissed, and in time had coerced the little brothers into obedience. Jon restrained a smile as he beheld Doug's usually cheerful face contorted in a scowl as he made sure his charges didn't shirk their duty.

THURSDAY, JUNE 8

"I jest knowed it wouldn't last," Mick O'Shea gloated as Jon entered the Golden Tabernacle for the evening meal. Espying Jonathan, the Texan sauntered over and asked, "Have y'all heard?"

"Heard what?"

"About George and Diane?"

"What? They didn't have an accident did they?" Jon asked in alarm.

Suppressing a sly smile, Mick shook his head. "Naw! Nothin' like thet. They's broke up is whut."

"Broke up? What do you mean, 'broke up?'"

"I mean their marriage is busted. They had a fight, shoutin' and screamin' … A bunch o' elders had to go and separate 'em. Diane is livin' in the Main Trailer now. I knowed it warn't gonna last. Tch tch! Such a shame." The look of glee in Mick's eyes belied his words.

"When did this happen?" Jon asked.

"This mornin' I was down workin' near their apartment an' heard 'em fightin'. I was afeared they might come to blows, so I went an' tole Brother Jack."

"Well, I'm sure they'll work it out. Newly-weds often have spats. Things will work out, you'll see."

"Not this time. Diane called her parents to come and take her home." Without so much as an, "excuse me," Mick trotted off to tell someone else the news.

Burdened for George, Jon scarcely heard a word of the evening teaching. Neither George nor Diane had been at the evening meal, and both were conspicuously absent from the meeting. Jon walked back to his trailer pondering yet again the "infallibility" of eldership decisions.

He entered the darkened trailer and knelt by his bed. Tears flowed as he searched for words. "Lord, I know the elders make mistakes. I'm pleading with You, if Betsy needs lithium, please see that she gets it. I'll do nothing, say nothing to anyone about this; it's between You and me. I trust You, so if the doctor prescribes it, or if it comes unbidden from another source, I'll believe that it's Your will for Betsy to take lithium."

TUESDAY, JUNE 13

Jon looked at the rough calluses on his hands. Some birthday present, he mused, and bent back to breaking up clods of red clay.

"Brother Jonathan," someone called.

Marvin headed straight for him.

"Brother Jonathan," Marvin called again and breathlessly drew up to the garden fence. His horn-rimmed glasses slid down his nose as he said, "Brother Jack wants you and me and a couple of other brothers to knock off work early this afternoon so that we can take part in delivering a new brother who's come to the farm."

"Who?"

"A guy named Richard, from Ohio. You have just enough time to get cleaned up before they start praying. Do you know where I can find David and Mickey?" Jon wordlessly pointed past the barn; Marvin jogged in the direction Jon had indicated.

The frigid water felt good as it washed the sweat and grime of the day's labors off his body. Then Jon dressed and hurried over to the Main Trailer, wondering if he ought to have brought his Bible. He entered into the presence of several elders who smiled benignly, then returned their attention to a young man sitting in their midst on a folding chair.

Jack introduced, "Brother Jonathan, this is Brother Rich. Brother Rich has come to us from Canton, Ohio. He'd like us to pray with him. Would y'all like to be a part of that?"

"Uh, yeah, I guess so, sure."

"Fi—ine. Now we'll just wait a few more minutes for the others to arrive, then we'll begin."

Jon studied the young man anxiously darting his eyes around the room. He was a few years older than Jon, clean cut, muscular, deeply tanned, ruggedly good-looking, but his eyes had that same hunted look that Betsy had when Sam Fife had prayed for her.

The door opened and Marvin entered, followed by David, then Danny and Mickey. Jack made introductions, then added, "We thought you brothers might like to help our brother Rich get set free, and in the process, learn a little bit about spiritual warfare. Shall we get started?"

They all nodded. A babble of speaking in tongues and soft prayers filled the room, then several of the elders laid hands on Rich's head and shoulders. Rich stiffened as he held his breath, his face grew red.

Jack and William knelt on the floor before the young man. Chester bent over and repeatedly traced a cross on Rich's forehead with his finger.

Rich spat on the men kneeling before him.

"Satan vents his rage, but is powerless against the Anointing," Chester intoned.

"We come against you, foul spirits of darkness, in Jesus' name." Brother Jack said. "We command you to reveal your identity."

Rich reared his head as if trying to shake off the hands touching him, shouting, "I am Satan! I am too mighty for you!"

Jack said, "I don't believe that! You are not Satan, and you are certainly not too mighty for the Anointing."

Rich calmed down and said, "Well, would you believe I am Beelzebub, and I'm very strong?"

Jon suppressed a chuckle. It was like something that Maxwell Smart would have said on a Get Smart TV episode.

Jack pressed in, undeterred. "No. I don't believe that either."

"How about… we are several evil spirits that will wear you out?" Rich said.

David whispered into Jack's ear.

Jack drew back and said in an aside, "See how the enemy is trying to disarm us with humor. Stronger demons rely on terrorizing opponents, weaker ones try sympathy or humor." Then to Rich, "We know who you are already. The Anointing has shown us. You are frightened, puny spirits desperately trying to make this man believe there is no God. But Rich has committed his life to Jesus and knows that God loves him."

"No! He doesn't believe that anymore," Rich said, almost in tears. "He can't believe that anymore if…" Rich suddenly fell silent.

"If…?" William took up the challenge. "If… he wants to do something that he knows God won't allow?"

Rich stared sullenly at the floor.

David whispered in Jack's ear again.

Jack Halstead nodded, then stared at Rich. "Richard, I'm talking to you now. Are you thinking of leaving your wife for another woman?"

Rich looked up, his eyes wide, then back at the floor.

Jack smiled at David before saying, "You know that's against God's law, Richard. That's how these demons got in you, by tempting you with adulterous thoughts. They told you that if you denied the existence of God you could have whatever you wanted. That's when your drinking problem started too, isn't it?"

"No! He doesn't—I don't have a drinking problem. I'm not committing adultery. I don't have demons."

"Jesus said to look upon a woman with lust is the same as committing adultery," William said.

"Spirits of lust, adultery, alcoholism and... unbelief, we command you, in Jesus' name, come out," Jack said.

Demons of unbelief? Jon stepped back. How much of this did he, himself, really believe? Then he remembered Chester praying for his diarrhea. "I believe in the Move," Jon resolved, "... with my whole heart."

Rich writhed under the hands pressing on his head. Chester, William and Jack were unrelenting. This struggle continued; half an hour; then an hour—with no visible result. The murmur of tongues rose and receded, like the tide. Rich began sweating; those standing around shifted their weight from one foot to the other, yet there was no sign of the enemy giving in.

Rich suddenly started coughing; the coughing turned into a spasm lasting several minutes.

Then the room became silent as a tomb, waiting on Jack for direction.

Rich looked up, dazed.

"Do you believe in Jesus?" Jack posed.

"Jesus? Yes I believe in Jesus," Rich said.

"Hallelujah!" said those gathered.

Rich looked around the room in confusion, as if trying to remember how he got there.

Jack stood to his feet, saying, "I believe that's enough for now. We've made a breakthrough. I sense there are stronger spirits hiding under those we kicked out, so the battle's not done, is it Brother Rich?"

"Huh? Oh, I suppose not, is it?" Rich said, trying to make sense of what was happening.

Jon pitied him. And he grieved for Betsy, knowing that hers was the same ordeal—and for no fault of her own. Rich had ostensibly invited demons in by wanting forbidden things. But what had Betsy ever done but seek to glorify God?

"Y'all brothers have been a great help to our Brother Rich. Thank you for joining us," said Jack. "It's almost time for the evening meal, so why don't y'all go and get ready for supper?"

Jon filed out with the others; William and Chester stayed behind.

As Jon walked along the roadway toward his trailer he heard car tires crunching on the gravel road. He turned to see who was leaving. Peering out from a back window was Diane, George's wife. Her family had come to fetch her.

FRIDAY, JUNE 16

"Uh-oh!" David said, stopping abruptly inside the gate.

"What's the matter?" Jon asked, nearly bumping into him. They were on their way from the morning Bible class to the farm side to do some gardening.

"Fire ants." David pointed to a three-foot diameter of loose, mounded earth nestled against the fence.

Jon stepped closer to look at the tiny insects crawling towards the central opening at the mound's top. "Fire ants? Is that their real name or—?"

"I don't know," David said. "But they give a wicked bite; stings like a scorpion. Enough bites can kill a grown man. I wouldn't get too close."

"Right." Jon backed away. "We ought to alert Brother William so they can pour gasoline or something on the mound."

"Or..." David thoughtfully said, "... we could curse them."

"Curse them? The Bible teaches us to bless and not curse."

"That means people. But Brother Sam has a teaching about cursing the works of the Devil, and fire ants are a work of the Devil if ever there was one."

"Okay... so what do we do?"

David extended his hand toward the active mound and spoke in tongues. Then he said, "Fire ant colony, we curse you in the name of Jesus! Be gone, die, exist no more on the property of God's children." He turned toward Jon and with a wide grin and said, "That oughtta do it."

The two proceeded to their chores. Jon gave little more thought to the fire ants, thinking David a bit over zealous.

That night Jon spotted newcomers—a family from Greenville, consisting of well-to-do parents and two strikingly beautiful daughters—sitting in on the meeting. The parents sang and clapped along but the teen-aged daughters were less than thrilled to be there. On occasional Friday nights for the last couple of months Jon had accompanied a contingent from the farm that went to Greenville to hold "Hatha" meetings.

From time to time some of the families from Greenville visited the farm to get a fuller taste of body life and worship in the Spirit.

David, seated next to Jon, leaned over and whispered, "That's Luanne, seventeen, and her sister Bonnie, fifteen. Their parents brought them here to live. It seems the older one, Luanne, was getting too intimate with her unsaved boyfriend."

Jon looked curiously at David. "How do you know all that?"

"Brother Jack told me. He wanted me to seek a word about whether a couple of girls should move here."

"He consulted you?"

"Well, he wanted to see if my word matched the words he already got from some other prophets."

The older, dark-haired girl slouched in her seat, scowling as her eyes bored holes into the back of the chair in front. Her younger, blonde sister looked around the room at the teens on their feet, swaying, with eyes closed and hands in the air. Less submissive farm girls jealously glanced at the newcomers with disdain for their jewelry and make-up, while the boys bashfully stole quick glimpses at the new beauties.

"Brother Jack said it was alright to tell their business because we older brothers should be on the lookout; the older girl's boyfriend might try to come and steal her away her."

Bunny taught the meeting that night, making veiled references to ungodly suitors and how wonderful it was to belong to the Move of God. Jon watched the new girls to see if they got the message. They didn't.

"Brother Jonathan," Marie said as she queued behind Jon for the nighttime snack, "I forgot to tell you… a package came in the mail today for you. I was about to call you over the P.A. when we, er, got visitors, and I forgot all about it. I'm sorry. If you like, I'll get it for you."

"I'll walk with you back to the Main Trailer and pick it up myself."

At the Main Trailer Marie retrieved the package and handed it to Jon.

"Thanks," Jon said and retreated out into the night. It was from his in-laws. He paused at one of the patio tables to open the parcel, wondering what was inside. He peeled off the brown wrapping; there was no note or letter. Opening the box he found a bottle of lithium capsules.

CHAPTER THIRTY-FIVE

...and the fruit thereof shall be for meat, and the leaf thereof for medicine. Ezekiel 47:12

Jon bounded up the Main Trailer's stairs and tried the door; it was locked. He banged on the door. All was dark inside. Marie must have immediately gone to her quarters. Jon banged harder.

A light came on. Marie opened the door. "Brother Jonathan?"

"I need to see Brother Jack right away."

"Why? What's the trouble?"

"Something came in the mail... It's about Betsy... please I've got to see him—or Sister Bunny."

"I don't think Sister Bunny is back from the meeting yet, and Brother Jack is in a back room with that new brother, Rich. I don't think he wants to be disturbed."

"This is really important. It can't wait."

"Well... I'll see. Come in and have a seat." With that she went behind the drapery that shielded the living quarters from the office.

Jon paced, tears brimming in his eyes: the Lord had answered his prayer! It was God's will for Betsy to take lithium; Jon no longer cared if his and Betsy's folks admitted that the Move was God's truest church. All that mattered was Betsy getting her medicine.

Unintelligible voices filtered down the hallway, followed by footsteps. The curtain drew aside and a haggard Brother Jack stood before Jon. Down the hall William stood silhouetted in a doorway. Rich must have been giving them a time of it. "Brother Jonathan, Marie said you have something very important to tell me?"

Jon gulped. "Brother Jack, just a few days ago I knelt by my bedside and asked the Lord, that if it was His will for Betsy to take lithium, He would somehow have it appear. I told Him that I wouldn't say anything to anyone about it, or do anything to make it happen, so that if it came, I'd know that it was God's will." Jon held up the bottle of lithium. "This came in today's mail."

Jack took the bottle in hand and examined it. "And you believe this is the Lord's answer to your prayer?"

"What else could it be? I mean… lithium doesn't just show up in the mail every day, does it?"

Jack's head cocked to one side; was Jon's sarcasm rebellion? "No, I'd say that it doesn't."

Just then there was a noise behind Jack; William dodged back into the room.

"I'd better go," Jack said, still holding the bottle. "I'll, uh, take this into consideration. Everything will be fi—ine, you just keep the faith." The curtain dropped back into place and Jack retreated down the hall.

Take it into consideration? Didn't the man recognize an act of God when it was dangled before his very eyes? "Please Lord, don't let them deprive Betsy of the medicine You sent."

"Is there anything else, Brother Jonathan?" asked Marie, coming up the hall and holding the curtain aside.

"Is Betsy awake?"

"No. Everyone has gone to bed early tonight. Everybody under care has been acting up."

"Oh. Well, thanks." Jon went out, wrestling with anger as he descended the steps. If they refused to give Betsy lithium… but he must have faith that they'd recognize God's hand. After all, no progress had been made in Betsy's deliverance since they stopped giving her lithium. Then again, they'd ignored Jill's prophetic word to not take her off medication. Now Jill was gone. There was no one in his and Betsy's corner. The Lord was his only hope.

SATURDAY, JUNE 17

Jon rubbed matter from his eyes as he lined up for breakfast. Heaviness like an anchor weighed on his heart; he felt helpless. Even when God responded to his desperate prayer, there was doubt as to whether the elders would allow God's answer to reach Betsy.

"Good news, Brother Jonathan."

Jon turned. Agnes and Betsy had joined the breakfast queue behind him. Jon stepped out of his place in line and went back to join them. Betsy purposely ignored him, staring out a window.

"They're giving Betsy lithium again." Agnes smiled and turned to Betsy, "Isn't that right Sister Betsy?"

Betsy made a face and returned her gaze out the window.

"In fact, they gave her some this morning. I didn't even know they had any on hand. I thought they'd thrown it all out."

"They didn't have any. A couple of days ago I prayed that if it was God's will, He'd send lithium. It came in yesterday's mail."

Agnes' penciled eyebrows rose. "Oh?"

A smile lit Jon's face. "So, they're giving it to her. After talking with Brother Jack last night, I had the impression they might not."

"Well, what do you know about that? All I know is that Sister Bunny came to our room this morning with two capsules for Betsy. I guess you really do need your medicine, don't you Sister Betsy?"

"And you really need your medicine, too."

Agnes laughed and said, "Yes, I need my medicine too, whatever that may be."

"All men over eighteen years of age report immediately to the Main Trailer."

Jon and Marvin sat up in their beds. "Did you hear that?" Jon asked.

"I was almost asleep; I'm not sure I heard," Marvin said.

Jon glanced at his watch. 11:30 p.m. "I'm not sure I heard right either. I think it said all men over eighteen are to repor—."

"Attention: all men over eighteen years of age are to report immediately to the Main Trailer."

Jon and Marvin hopped out of bed and dressed. They were out the door and running across the field in another minute. "Oh Lord, please don't let it be another fire," Jon prayed.

Others emerged from their trailers in various stages of dress, likewise headed for the Main Trailer. Elders Jack, William and Bill waited under the floodlights with flashlights in their hands.

A crowd of men gathered around the elders. Jack cleared his throat and said, "Brothers, we have called y'all down here tonight to help guard some sisters who have recently joined us. It seems their boyfriends have the notion they can come and spirit them away in the dead of night."

"This is about those girls from Greenville," Mick O'Shea whispered to Jon and Marvin. "I jest knowed those Jezebels was gonna bring trubble."

Jack continued, "… so we are going to patrol the grounds from the lower gate all the way out to the upper mailbox. If you have a flashlight, get it; if you don't have one, see Sister Bunny in the Main Trailer and she'll get you one."

Mickey, the farm hand from Virginia, asked, "Do we know for sure that an attempt is going to be made?"

"The reason we called you out of your beds," William said, "…is because Pappy and Ruth, who live down on the farmside, called and said two cars came down the driveway. So Brother Bill Thompson and I drove down there. We got there just in time to see a bunch of boys jump back in their cars and tear out the gateway. We think it was them, and that they were looking for the trailers on this side of the farm."

Someone asked, "What if we encounter them?"

"It's not likely they'll be back," Jack said. "But just in case they do find the upper entrance, we thought it best to let them know we're patrolling the roads in force. Just seeing that we're on guard ought to deter them. In any case, do not use violence; just let yourselves be seen."

"And if they do actually make it to the Main Trailer, several elders will be on duty," added Bill.

William assigned sections to various pairs. "Marvin, you and Jon, since you live nearest to the mailbox, patrol from the mailbox in to the Golden Tabernacle. Do you both have flashlights?"

"Yessir," Marvin said. "Do we stay up all night, then?"

"We'll let you know," William said.

Jon and Marvin walked their stint, the half-mile between the mailbox and the Golden Tabernacle half a dozen times. The pair had just turned around at the Golden Tabernacle when the faint roar of a motor came from behind the Main Trailer accompanied by headlights shining in the upper branches of trees indicated a vehicle was climbing the hill from the lower side. Two cars barreled around the corner, spewing dust and gravel. Following at some distance was the farm pick-up. Several flashlights from other patrols splayed on the cars as they passed. Jon and Marvin stepped well off the road and flashed their beams into the windshield of the approaching vehicles. The cars sped past Jon and Marvin. A long-haired youth shouted out a back window as they sped out the track, "We're gonna get some of our buddies and come back for our women!" The vehicles then disappeared around the corner in a swirl of dust.

The pick-up pulled up alongside the slightly shaken pair, and William leaned out the passenger window, saying, "Well done, they won't be back anymore tonight."

"They just said they'd be back with some of their buddies." Marvin said.

"Yeah, well, it's a long drive to Greenville. Seeing it's after two in the morning, and the fact that the Greenville police have been alerted, it's not likely we'll see them again, at least not tonight. Y'all can go back to your trailer and get some sleep. Thank you for your assistance."

MONDAY, JUNE 19

Jon yawned as he closed his Bible. Morning class had dismissed early. Ronnie had droned for an hour explaining types and shadows of the Tabernacle, but his topic kept straying to God's wrath upon people who left the Move. Jon guessed that Ronnie missed Rhonda deeply. Of everyone on the farm, Elder Ronnie Meeker shared Jon's pain, but Ronnie's method of dealing with it was to blame his wife. Who could Jon blame?

"Not enough sleep last night Brother Jon?" David said, leaning over Jon's shoulder.

"Huh? Oh, Marvin and I were on patrol last night. We walked from one end of the farm to the other three times."

"Oh, yeah. Billy and I get to patrol Thursday night. I believe it's a good thing the elders instituted a night watch, for it not only protects the camp, but it gives those doing it a chance to pray all night. What time did you get done?"

"Brother William told us to knock-off at 2:00 a.m."

David nodded. "Say, are you going down to the farm side now?"

"Well, since we have a little extra free time until lunch, I thought I'd visit my son."

"Good idea. I think I'll go down and see if I can be of help."

Jon watched him go, then headed toward his trailer. On the way he passed the men building the bunkhouse. Elders Bill, Don and Wallace were nailing down the roof. "Won't be long till you and Marvin can move in, Brother Jonathan," commented Don, the farm's youngest elder.

"Well, the way Betsy is improving, I was hoping she and I could use the Michael's trailer soon," Jon said.

"That may well be, Brother Jon, that may well be," Bill said, grinning widely. "In any case, this bunkhouse, such as it is, will be painted and ready for habitation by this weekend."

Jon studied the box-like structure standing off the ground on cement blocks, its walls rose eight feet in the front and seven in the back. A doorway was cut in the middle of its sixteen-foot width, and had screens with flip up shutters instead of glass windows to keep weather out. The inside was just large enough for two bunk beds, a couple of dressers and not much more. There would be a small wood stove in the middle of the back with a pipe venting out the back wall. Overall, it looked like an over-sized shoebox. Jon desperately hoped that he and Betsy would be together before he was sequestered there.

Movement from the laundry house caught his attention. It was Betsy and Agnes coming across the meadow. Betsy waved vigorously, a smile on her lips. A thrill of joy leapt in Jon's heart and he raced through the high grass to meet them.

"Why Brother Jonathan, I didn't expect to see you here. Is Bible class over for the day?" Agnes asked, nudging Betsy's ribs.

"Hello, Jon," Betsy shyly offered.

"Hi, Betts. Uh, yeah, Bible class finished early today. Were you working down in the laundry?"

"Yes. Now that I'm doing better, Sister Bunny said I should help out with chores. Today we did laundry."

"She tires easily, though. Bunny said she shouldn't over-do. We were just heading for the Golden Tabernacle to get some coffee. Wanna come?" Agnes said.

"Well… okay, but, only for a while. Brother William expects me on the farm side, and I don't want him to think I'm shirking."

"I don't believe I've been down to the farm side," Betsy said. "Would you take me for a walk down there and show me around?"

"Sure. Would it be alright, Agnes?"

"I think it's a wonderful idea. Let's ask Sister Bunny. Besides, I'd like to spend some time with my youngest son, Jackie; I hardly ever get to see him since he lives in Don and Wanda's trailer."

Deciding to skip coffee, the three went straight to the Main Trailer where permission was granted for the expedition. "Now don't keep her out too long, Brother Jonathan, she tires quickly," Bunny said. "When she says she's had enough, bring her back, you hear? It's high time you two got to know each other again."

Like two infatuated teens on a first date, Jon and Betsy fairly skipped down the hill toward the farmside. They slowed at the bottom of the hill to hold hands and talk. "I believe we'll soon be back together, Betts, with Jay, in our own little trailer—the one Marvin and I are using now."

"Jon, why are we even here at all?" Betsy asked, keeping her eyes on the gravel road-way. I'm feeling much better now; can't we just go back to Pennsylvania and be with our family and friends? We could go to Minnie's house for meetings just like we used to."

Jon spoke slowly, "Well, there's much I still need to learn about being an apostle, and—."

"Couldn't you learn it from Minnie and Sonya? I don't trust these people down here. They've done things… cruel things, to some of the girls—and me— for no reason at all. They're all talk about the Manchild, but I see little of the love of Jesus in them. They keep trying to deliver people of demons, but none are ever cast out."

Jon felt he ought to defend the Move, but he also had the same doubts. "We'll talk about this when you're stronger. I don't want you getting overexcited. Let me tell you what I've learned about wilderness living. We've had classes in grafting branches, raising chickens, goats, cows and horses. I've tanned hides; and even castrated piglets. Soon we'll be canning produce, and there's talk of digging a root cellar to store our canned goods underground where it's cool."

"Oh, what's that?" They were crossing through a gate when Betsy spotted the fire ant mound.

"Stand back, Betts. Those are fire ants; very painful, dangerous even, if you get enough bites."

"I don't see any ants."

"Well, they're there, believe me—say, where are they?" Jon jabbed a long stick into the mound. When no activity resulted, he stabbed again, deeper. No ants swarmed in defense of their colony. "How about that? It worked."

"What worked?"

"David put a curse on them, and they all must have died. How about that?"

CHAPTER THIRTY-SIX

For a dream cometh through the multitude of business... Ecclesiastes 5:3

MONDAY, JULY 17

Jon approached Jack's breakfast table. "Brother Jack?"

Jack Halstead looked up. "Yes. Brother Jonathan, what is it?"

"I… uh…had a dream that I thought might be from the Lord. When you get some time…"

"Of course. I'll be finished in a minute. Why don't y'all wait for me in the fire circle? There's something I want to talk to you about, as well. Maybe it's the same thing your dream was about." His bright smile contrasted against the weathered tan of his face.

Jon nodded and went outside to wait. He looked up into a cloudless sky as he sat on one of the logs that served as seating for the Friday night campfires.

"Appears it's gonna be another warm day. No rain in sight, the weathermen say," said Jack seating himself beside Jon. "Tell me about your dream."

"I dreamt I was doing the nightly patrol. It was dark, real dark. The camp dogs were growling and barking, as if fighting something. I walked over to the Main Trailer to see what all the noise was about. The dogs had cornered an opossum. Before I could intervene, the dogs attacked and tore it to pieces."

"Is that it?"

Jon nodded. "Do you think it's a word about a demon trying to invade the camp, but angels will fight him off?"

"Is that what you think?"

"Well, I really don't know, but since it was a wild animal, which Sister Jill once told me could represent evil spirits, so I thought domestic animals might represent angels. Since it all happened near the Main Trailer which—."

"Is where most of the spiritual battles happen," Jack picked up Jon's train of thought. "You may have something there, Brother Jonathan. Sounds like a good report. I'll pray about it." Jack shifted his eyes away from Jon's and gazed down the sloping field. "Now, about what I wanted to tell you… The elders have decided that Sister Betsy no longer needs lithium. We've had a 'word' that the demons lay low when she takes that medication, trying to fool us so that we'll leave them alone."

Jon bit the inside of his lip.

Jack continued, "Now that Betsy is in her right mind, we're confident that she'll fight off psychotic thoughts. With her resisting demons from inside, and the elders charging in from outside, we're sure of the victory." He grinned at Jon.

Jon's stomach churned. Betsy was almost back to being herself—nearly ready to resume being his wife and Jay's mother… How dare they tamper now? How dare they disregard the answer to Jon's prayer?

"Now, don't you worry none," Jack said, putting an arm around Jon's shoulder. "We have a definite word from the Lord on this. You just have faith. Betsy will keep the ground she's gained, and will get even freer than she is now. That bottle of lithium was the catalyst needed to expose the demonic strategy of laying low. Dr. Black advised us that Betsy's recovery was much too quick for the medicine to have taken effect. That's when a prophet got a word about the demons hiding under the supposed effects of lithium. So you see, the medicine arriving in the mail was the Lord's will, not because she needs it, but to expose the demons' ruse."

"What if I don't agree?"

A stern look crossed Jack's face as he stood. "Sister Betsy knows all about the plan and is eager to resist the demons herself. She's of legal age and is able to determine her own course." His bright smile returned as he added, "But I'm sure you also want to see her set totally free from demons. Like I said, you just have faith. Now I've got some matters to attend to. I'll pray about your dream."

Jon sat on the log watching Jack recede into the distance.

"Hi, Hon," a timid voice said from behind.

Jon turned and saw Betsy. He patted the space that had been recently vacated by Jack. Betsy sidled in beside her husband.

"Why so glum?" Betsy asked.

"Brother Jack just told me."

"Oh."

"Betts, you're doing so well, I don't think it's wise to stop the meds."

"Dr. Black explained that over time, lithium could hurt my kidneys and other organs. Besides, Sam Fife cast the spirits out of me, at Minnie's house, remember? There aren't any left, so I won't lose my mind again. Now let's stop this morose talk about mental illness and demons and go find Miss Jane and visit our son."

Jon took Betsy's hand and walked toward the Nobles trailer. It was wrong, very wrong, but by recruiting Betsy to their cause the elders had anticipated and negated any of his objections.

"C'mon, taste one," Mick O'Shea said, standing upright in the garden. He held a collection of slender hot peppers. "I warn you, they're hot. We et hot stuff like this all the time down in South America. I got used to it, so it don't bother me none. But you Yankees take just a little nibble or it'll eat a hole right through yore tongue."

David and Danny took a pepper and gingerly bit near the stem. By their grimaces Jon saw that the peppers were hot. So, he took his bite off the tip, thinking it wouldn't be as potent.

"Oh, Brother Jon, not the bot—!" Mick warned, but it was too late. "The tips are the hottest part."

Liquid fire sizzled on Jon's tongue: sweat popped out on his brow, his face turned bright red and his eyes bulged.

The others, tormented by the milder doses they'd received, couldn't help but double up in laughter.

Jon raced for the pump to flush the cinder that had once been his tongue. His mouth engulfed the spigot and he opened the lever all the way. A blast of cool, subterranean water relieved the flames—until he stopped drinking.

Running up to Jon, Mick chided, "No, Brother Jon, no! Water only makes it worse."

Tears streamed down Jon's face as he sucked air over the roasted member. The fire had spread to his whole mouth.

Mick laughed, even as he tried to give Jon helpful advice. "It'll pass, brother, it'll pass. It'll take some time, but it'll pass. Too bad we don't have any milk down here; that would put the fire out."

Jon wrapped his lips around the faucet again, as long as water ran through his mouth the fire was quelled. After several minutes of flushing, the pain did subside enough for Jon to return to weeding.

The hot pepper had temporarily taken his mind off the pain in his heart. But deep, down inside, there was no assuaging the ache of watching Betsy sink day by day back into psychosis.

SATURDAY, JULY 22

"Brothers Lester, Rob, Kip and Jonathan will meet Brother William after breakfast in the parking lot," announced Marie from the platform. She went on to list chores for some of the girls, but Jon's focus was on the table where Betsy and Agnes sat with other Main Trailer girls. Betsy glared at her food. Agnes coaxed her charge to eat something. Betsy had descended into full blown dementia in merely five days. Nightly "prayer" sessions had had no effect.

Jon contemplated whisking her away—but her condition was now too fragile. There was nothing he could do, especially since she loathed the sight of him. And how could he travel and take care of Betsy and little Jay at the same time? There was no one within a thousand miles that could render assistance. A sense of helplessness gripped him.

Jon had been installed in the bunkhouse with Marvin, Danny and Rob. Because Jon and Betsy's reunion had been delayed his bunkmates kept an embarrassed silence around Jon.

"Now don't you fret none, Brother Jonathan," said Bunny coming up behind Jon after breakfast. "We expected this manifestation. We knew they were hiding; now we have them where we can deal with them."

"Yeah, well, you're not having much success, are you?" Anger seethed in Jon; he no longer cared if they thought him rebellious, and might subject him to deliverance sessions.

Bunny ignored the challenge. "You just have faith, the breakthrough is coming any day now. In fact..." she lowered her voice so only Jon could hear, "... we are going to give Sister Betsy a placebo that she'll think is lithium. That way we'll fool the demons into hiding again. This is a secret that only a couple of elders know, and now you know; so, don't tell anyone."

Were they as crazy as Betsy? "When are you going to start?"

"Tomorrow. I'm sure you'll see a big difference right away."

"And if not?"

"You will, Brother Jonathan, have faith, you will." Bunny left to assign chores to some girls at a nearby table.

Jon stepped outside and saw William waiting for him in the parking lot, only then remembering that he was supposed to go somewhere with him. Gathered around the truck were Lester, Rob and Kip, along with elders Jack, William and Don. They were staring at a gunnysack on the ground.

"I took it away from the dogs," Don was explaining to Jack and William. "It must have wandered into camp. The dogs were tearing it to pieces. Poor thing!"

"What is it?" Jon asked.

"A 'possum," Don said, opening the gunnysack so Jon could see.

Jon looked at the bloody mass of flesh, bone and fur and remembered his dream. He looked up. Jack was studying him. Gone was Jack's perpetual smile; in its place was a slight frown.

"All here? Good. Up into the truck, men." William ordered. "Jonathan, you ride in the cab with me."

Jon lowered himself off the back wheel he'd been climbing to get into the truck bed, came around and slid into the passenger seat. As William drove out the gate Jon said, "Brother William, a couple of nights ago I dreamt about the dogs tearing that opossum apart. May I tell you another dream I had last night?"

"Sure."

"I dreamt I was attacked by a large black snake. The only weapon I had to defend myself with was a pitchfork. I couldn't hit his head; he kept dodging and striking at me."

"Hmmm... did he bite you?"

"I don't think so. I wasn't scared, but I felt an urgency to kill the snake because he might attack others."

"I'll pray about it. It's a good report, though." William fixed his eyes on the road ahead and quietly hummed a worship tune.

Was the black snake dream symbolic? If so, he had a pretty good guess as to what it meant. But... what if it was like the opossum dream and was about an actual event? He looked through the rear window to see how Rob, Kip and Lester were faring in the open truck bed.

An hour later they turned off the blacktop and pulled across a field; at the far end of the field was a barn. A local farmer, William explained, had donated a load of hay to the farm and even loaned the stake-bed truck with which to fetch it. William backed the vehicle to the barn door and shut off the engine. "The bales are inside. Let's get to it."

They organized an assembly line: Jon pulled bales from the stack and tossed them to William who in turn handed them to Lester, who passed them to Rob and Kip who stacked them on the truck. It was hot, dusty work. The men went to it with gusto, working up a sweat and a thirst. Half an hour later William called a rest.

"Y'all will have to stack them higher," William said examining the load, "… if we're gonna get all this hay in one trip." He pulled out a jug of ice water and passed it around. Each man took a hearty swig. William watched Jon take a long, satisfying drink and said, "We'll make a farmhand out of you yet, Brother Jon."

Jon was in no mood for left-handed compliments; his hay-dust irritated sinuses dripped like an icicle in July, his back ached and his arms had turned rubbery. But all this did little to distract from his heart's ache. While the others took their turn at the Coleman jug he sat on a bale, staring out at the woodlands.

"Okay, men, back at it," William eventually said when everyone had had time to cool down.

They all reassumed their places. Jon hefted a bale and tossed it towards William. Suddenly a large black snake from under the bale struck at Jon's ankle, just missing. Jon jumped back with a yelp, searching for some implement to fend off the serpent. He grabbed the first tool he could find from a nearby column —a pitchfork. William and Lester were at Jon's side in seconds; William seized a hoe and counterattacked. The snake tried to retreat into the stacked hay, but a second and third hit from William's hoe caught the snake in the middle; it writhed and bit the hoe handle. With a couple more swift chops its head was severed.

He then looked curiously at Jon, much like Jack had done earlier.

They finished loading the truck without further incident. William and Kip crisscrossed a rope several times across the load, securing it.

"Isn't that stacked awful high?" Jon asked.

"We can only make one trip," William said, "God will make sure we get it all safely tucked away in our barn." He shook his head slightly at Jon's lack of faith as he tied the rope off and tested it with a final tug.

Rob and Kip had made a niche for themselves in the hay; Lester joined Jon and William in the cab. The over-loaded truck swayed as they traversed the irregular field and then onto twisty, narrow country lanes. But soon they were driving near the speed limit. William encouraged singing praise songs as they went. There was a sudden loud snap, followed by Rob and Kip shouting. William pulled over. Several of the topmost bales had caught an overhanging tree bough and now lay strewn over the road behind.

THURSDAY, JULY 27

"I don't think it'll work, Marvin," Jon said as he dangled his feet from the top bunk.

"Sure it will, Brother Jonathan. The elders received a word about canning chickens in mason jars. The Move will learn a new method of preserving food for the Tribulation. Once we slaughter and can the chickens, we'll store them in the root cellar where they'll be kept cool until we need them."

"Ever hear of botulism? If it's not done properly, we could all die."

"God's not going to let that happen," Marvin said. "Doubt affects you too much. Look on the positive side. You can't let what's happening to Betsy color your thinking about everything."

Rob and Danny entered the bunkhouse, deposited their Bibles on their bunks then retreated back outside. Danny called over his shoulder, "Better hurry, lunch call is about to sound."

Jon and Marvin were alone again. Jon said, "I know it appears that way, but there are genuine risks. The Lord won't protect us from foolishness. Remember what happened to the hay."

"That was only a dozen or so bales. The rest is in our barn. It seems to me that you're just looking for things to gripe about."

"Well, if anyone has cause, I do."

"I bind that spirit of doubt and rebellion in Jesus' name!" Marvin said.

"Knock it off, Marvin. I don't have demons of doubt and rebellion. Look, you're my best friend, and you've given me wise counsel and helped me through some bitter disappointments. But, you aren't always right. The elders aren't always right. Who knows what they'll try next? Lithium works—it was an answer to my prayer. But they twisted it around to suit their philosophy. I'm at my wit's end. I don't know what to believe any more. And when you tell me they're going to try a new way of canning chickens … I never heard of such foolishness."

"It's chicken parts. The Babylonish world system cans chicken soup, so what's the difference?"

"I dunno. Maybe you're right. Maybe I am too cynical. It's just that Betsy and I have been through so much…"

"Praise the Lord! See, those demons of doubt and rebellion were bound, just like I prayed."

"A word with you, Brother Jon, if I may," William said as he pulled Jon out of the lunch line.

Now what? Jon winced. Was his doubting the eldership known? Marvin stared after them for a moment, then went inside to lunch. William led Jon to the fire ring, indicating for Jon to sit beside him.

"Your wife has not been fighting the demons like we expected. Have you said anything to her about the placebo?"

"Of course not; that would defeat the whole plan."

William scanned the meadow. "Have you said anything to someone who might have had contact with her? We believe the demons got wind of our plan."

"I've said nothing to anyone except in my prayers to the Lord."

William sighed. "Well…" he began, then paused as he watched his aged mother emerge from his trailer with little Jay in her arms.

Tears welled in Jon's eyes and a lump formed in his throat at the sight of his son in the elderly woman's arms.

"We're putting Betsy back on lithium—but a limited dosage," William continued.

A tear rolled down Jon's cheek.

"Just enough for her to get back in the fight. She's so used to the medicine doing her job that she doesn't realize she needs to fight."

"How much dosage are you going to give her?"

"We're seeking a word on that now. We'll start this evening and see how things go." William rose abruptly and crossed the commons to the Main Trailer.

That afternoon Jon worked in a lower cornfield with a crew of elder brothers. Mickey was nearby using a scoop on the farm's tractor to dig out a hollow for the proposed root cellar. A rough-hewn plank structure was to be built in the hole, then covered with several feet of dirt. The subterranean earth's temperature was expected to keep the root cellar cool enough for food storage.

Mickey hit bedrock at about three feet and was unable dig deeper. In the following days a frame was constructed, roofed and planked in, then covered with two feet of topsoil. Bill Thompson had overseen the final touches and hung the door. The root cellar project took three days from start to finish; the end product reminded Jon of the "soddies" built by American settlers. "There," Bill proclaimed to the workers, "… now we have a root cellar to store mason jars. The earth will keep the interior a cool fifty degrees. If it will work in Mississippi, it'll work anywhere."

Jon's back ached from shoveling dirt around the structure; his hands had grown new blisters in the effort. He looked dubiously at the final product, wondering if this too would be a fiasco like the way they handled Betsy. As of yet Betsy had not responded to the combination of placebo and lithium.

CHAPTER THIRTY-SEVEN

Cease... to hear the instruction that causeth to err... Proverbs 19:27

WEDNESDAY, AUGUST 16

"...For I'm part of the family, the family of God," the entire dining room finished singing the grace before supper.

"Amen," Jack said loudly enough for all to hear. Scraping of chairs filled the hall as diners sat and the chattering hubbub of mealtime began.

Jon sat at Chester's table. A stream of serving girls bearing food platters and pitchers of milk issued from behind the kitchen partition. Jon glanced at Jack's table; Betsy sat beside Agnes, glaring about angrily, ignoring both food and conversation. Her eyes met Jon's. He flashed a quick smile; she started, then abruptly turned away. It had been three weeks since the "half-placebo treatment" had been started and Betsy showed no improvement.

"Wow! Oh wow! That sauce is hot!" Kip said, quickly slurping some milk. "Be careful not to use too much hot sauce, brothers. That's the hottest sauce I've ever had."

"Made from peppers grown here on our farm," Chester said. "I believe Brother Jonathan can attest to its potency."

Jon came back to his immediate surroundings. "Yeah, if it was made from our peppers, it's hot, alright."

Mick O'Shea took up the challenge. "Y'all don't know what hot sauce is 'til ya et South American food. Pass that down he-yah; I doubt I'll even feel a tingle."

Kip withheld the squeeze bottle. "I don't believe I ought to, Brother Mick, as your brother in the Lord, it wouldn't be right to let you be tortured like that. I mean it's really hot. Too hot for consumption."

"Yeah, yeah! You made yore point, Kip. Now pass that bottle ovah he-yah an' let a Texan show y'all how to et hot sauce." Mick impatiently held out his hand.

"No. I'm serious, Mick. This sauce is really, really hot. You'll not like it. I know you like spicy food and all, but this is way beyond spicy."

Mick's eye twitched as he repeated, "Pass that bottle ovah he-yah. The hot sauce ain't been made thet kin burn my mouth. C'mon, now, pass it ovah."

Kip yielded. "It's against my better judgment," he said with mock concern. "Here you go. I warn you, it's really hot."

Mick seized the sauce and liberally doused his meal. He then took a bite; the entire table watched. He chewed and swallowed. Within seconds beads of sweat broke out on his brow and his cheeks turned bright red. He half rose from his seat gasping for air as he sputtered, "Milk! Gimme milk!"

Even the somber Chester couldn't stifle his laughter.

Kip controlled his merriment long enough to say, "I tried to tell you."

Mick put the drained glass of milk down and glared. "You didn't tell me it was that hot!"

"What's your assignment this afternoon, Brother Jon?" Don, the elder asked.

Jon was headed for the Noble's trailer to see his son. "I've been told to report to the chicken house. Something about slaughtering chickens."

"Oh, that's right," Don said. "Aren't they going to try that new method of de-feathering?"

"Somebody said something about 'skinning' chickens? I've never heard of skinning a chicken, but…." Jon shrugged his shoulders. "If it doesn't work, I guess we'll singe and pluck them the old-fashioned way. They're going to can them, too."

Don nodded, then said, "They—uh, the elders—asked me to talk to you… about Betsy."

He had Jon's full attention. Why had they sent the rookie elder?

"It, uh, seems that she isn't responding. Dr. Black has seen her and recommends a full dosage of lithium. How, uh, how do you feel about that?"

Jon felt like screaming, "Why didn't you believe God answered my prayer the first time?" Instead, he calmly replied, "I think that's probably best."

Don's jaw relaxed and his eyebrows descended. He spoke a few words of encouragement and then left... presumably to report to Jack.

Despite the elders' blunders, Jon still trusted the Move as the truest manifestation of Christianity on the planet. If only Betsy was herself, life would be so good. If it took medication to bring Betsy back, so be it. It seemed to Jon as if the sun had suddenly started shining again as he crossed the yard to visit his son.

Skinning chickens was a fool's errand. The skinners finally gave up and resorted to the old-fashioned scalding, plucking and singeing. Several sisters were canning chicken parts in mason jars on the other side of the shed. The team, intent upon slaughtering and canning a hundred pullets, ignored the dinner call. Chester, overseeing the operation, assured the work crew that food would be set aside for them.

When they were finally done, Jon, along with Danny and Kip, jounced over the field in the back of the farm pick-up to store the result of the afternoon's work—153 mason jars of chicken legs, thighs, breasts and wings.—in the root cellar.

FRIDAY, AUGUST 25

"When will we be together?" Betsy asked.

Jon took her hands in his. Betsy had been herself for several days, so much so that the couple was encouraged to sit together during meals and meetings. They spent their free time visiting their baby. "You know I want to, Betts, but the elders don't think you're—we're not ready just yet."

"I know." The pair sat at a patio table in front of the Main Trailer. Jon could almost feel Bunny's watchful eyes. Betsy looked across the field at children playing kick ball with the pack of farm dogs frolicking at their heels. "It's just that we've been apart so long... and now that I'm doing better... we sit together in meals and meetings... I think it's time we were together as a family. But, I get so confused; I hardly know what month it is... everything is so jumbled in my mind. I miss living with you and Jay. When will we be together as man and wife?"

"Soon, very soon. That little trailer where Marvin and I bunked will be our little home, as soon as the elders approve."

"I'm ready now. What more do they want from us?"

"Now Betts, you know how easily you wear out from just an hour with Jay. Even time with me tires you. Imagine 24 hours a day, every day. The spirit is willing, but the flesh is weak. You're getting stronger, but don't take on too much too soon. We need time to be a family again."

"I want to leave. I don't want to live in a dingy little trailer fit only to be a storage shed. I want to go back to Pennsylvania."

Betsy remained adamant that the Move was a cult. But then, Betsy hadn't lived among the troubled youths who'd benefited from being on the farm. Sure, there had been mistakes and abuses—but they were well intentioned.

"I think Brother Jack knows I'm called to be an apostle, and wants to start teaching me things I'll need to know." Jon clung to the belief that their trial was apostolic training. What sense would it make to pay such a high price but walk away before graduating? "You do want me to be an apostle, don't you?"

A smile flitted across Betsy's lips. "Yes, of course."

SATURDAY, AUGUST 26

"That's you Brother Jon," Marvin called across the garden plot as they weeded. "Didn't you hear?"

Jonathan stopped hoeing as the announcement repeated, "Brother Jonathan McComb, report to the Main Trailer."

Jon stretched his back. "Now what?"

"You go, I'll put your hoe away," Marvin said.

Jon dashed off, leaping the gate, running full tilt around the bend and up the hill.

David was just coming down the hill at a leisurely pace. "Y'all been called to the Main Trailer, Brother Jonathan," he called after Jon.

"I know," Jon panted, slowing. "Do you know what it's about?"

"Y'all got visitors."

"Visitors?" Jon slowed. "Who would visit me?"

David shrugged and proceeded downhill.

In the parking lot was a dark blue Chrysler with Pennsylvania tags.

"It can't be—!"

But it was. Jon stepped inside the addition. Betsy sat cuddling Jay on the sofa between her mom and Jon's mom. Jon's and Betsy's dads stood off to one side, eyeing him. "M—m—mom, Dad, Mr. and Mrs. Rutlidge, wh—what a surprise."

"Yeah, boss, we figured you'd be surprised," Charles Rutlidge said.

"Your folks have come from way up north to see y'all, isn't that ni—ce?" said Jack from the hallway. He stepped into the room, his bright smile beaming like a lighthouse. "Sister Marie, would you be so kind as to get some chairs for our guests?"

Marie ducked behind the curtain and reappeared moments later with folding chairs. The girls then made themselves scarce. Ron McComb and Charles Rutlidge sat, as did Jonathan. Brother Jack remained on his feet. "How was all y'all's trip?"

"Fine, fine, we made good time," Betsy's Dad said. Jon recognized that cool, appraising look Charles Rutlidge was giving Jack. He then turned his steely, blue eyes on Jon and said, "I see Betsy's been getting her lithium. Good, good! I told you the day you married her that if she got her lithium regular you'd have no problems."

"Well, as I tried to explain, Betsy's problems aren't only medical—."

"Brother Jonathan," Jack interrupted, "...why don't you take your family and show them the farm? Will y'all be staying for lunch? We'd love to have you."

"Actually," Jon's Dad spoke up, "... we thought to do a little sightseeing with Jon and Betsy. Can you suggest any tourist locations?"

"As a matter of fact," Jack said, "... I recently visited the historic Waverly Mansion and plantation. It's not far. I can get directions..."

"That'll do," Charles Rutlidge said. "We'll eat somewhere out along the highway."

Jon searched his parents' faces. Was this a kidnap attempt? Betsy would welcome such an event.

Jon volunteered, "How about if I drive. My car could use a good run, it's been sitting in the field since—."

"No," Betsy's dad said. "We'll go in the Chrysler, it's roomier than that old BelAir. I'm glad to see you still have it, though." All rose to their feet. Betsy handed Jay to her mother who cuddled her grandson, smiling and talking baby talk. Jon's mom and dad followed silently.

"Y'all have a good time," Jack said with a wink at Jon.

"And remember who you are and what you're called to," Bunny added, coming up behind her husband.

"Sit up front with us, Jonathan, and let the ladies have the back," ordered Mr. Rutlidge. Jon sat sandwiched between father and father-in-law. Both mothers likewise hemmed Betsy in. Jon twisted around to see if Betsy was all right. She smiled wanly.

The car proceeded out the mailbox entrance. Charles asked, "We saw where Betsy lives—in a tiny cubbyhole; and where your baby lives with that old woman, but where do you live, Jon?"

Jon pointed at the whitewashed bunkhouse as they drove past, reluctantly admitting, "There. Four of us share it."

"I never thought I'd see the day when my son-in-law would live in a doghouse," Charles said. "Ron, did you ever think your son would come to this?"

"No, I never did," Jon's dad said.

"Now you two cut it out," Minnie Rutlidge said from the back seat. "We're here to have a nice time, not to pick on these kids. We can talk about these things later; but now, I'm hungry, let's find someplace to eat."

The car turned toward Eupora, not the Natchez Trace and parts north. Jon exhaled a long, relieved breath.

After eating at a restaurant, conversation in the car was kept to polite, non-personal topics. They toured Waverly Mansion and its grounds; the grandparents doted on little Jay who gladly absorbed all their attention. Frosty relationships thawed as the afternoon wore on; even Jon's dad lost his reserve and acted more himself, cracking puns that made everyone groan. Both grandmothers jostled Jay and advised Betsy on everything from diaper rash to burping.

"Son," Ron McComb said as they ended their outing and headed back to the farm, "… I want you to know I came with the intention of dragging you home; and we would have if Betsy wasn't doing well. But your father-in-law refuses to interfere. He says he gave his daughter away, and as long as she's doing all right, he'll leave well enough alone."

"That's right, sonny boy," Charles said, "… you make sure she gets her lithium, and I don't care what religion you got. You was raised right, and the Bible says, 'train up a child in the way he should go, and when he is old he will not depart from it.' I know you'll come to your senses some day and leave this bunch of nuts. Ain't no sense making hard feelings by dragging you back to Pennsylvania if'n you ain't ready. Right, Ron?"

"There's something else," Jon's dad said. "I've got a growth… my doctor thinks it may be… serious. I'm seeing a specialist next week. If anything happens… I want to know you'll do what's right."

"Of course I will, Dad," Jon said, wondering if his father's haggard features were from more than just travel. "But… you don't know for sure that it's serious, right?"

"Well, considering that I've smoked most of my life…."

"I'm sure it's nothing," Jon said with more confidence than he felt.

Upon arrival back at the farm, the McComb's and Rutlidge's declined an offer of accommodations, choosing to travel homeward before nightfall.

"Jonathan, when you come to your senses, come home," Charles Rutlidge said. Ron McComb's grim expression had returned—or was it a grimace of pain? Jon's mom was in tears; Betsy's mom put on a brave smile but said nothing as they drove out the lane.

CHAPTER THIRTY-EIGHT

... I will also command the clouds that they rain no rain upon it. Isaiah 5:6

WEDNESDAY, SEPTEMBER 13

Jon leaned on his hoe and looked over the withering cornstalks. Despite the flooding spring rains, the summer hadn't produced enough rain to do more than dampen the dust. No silky tassels or plump ears appeared on the stalks; there was no hope of canning any corn this year.

In the distance a small but determined cloud skirted the farm's border, dropping its load of moisture on a neighbor. A faint rumble of thunder reached Jon's ears. William had heard on the radio that the entire region suffered drought. The garden produced limited yields only because it was watered regularly, but the fields were sere.

So was Jon. Meetings were pumped up emotional sessions, declaring that they were going to set Creation free, yet no one was ever set free enough to move out of the Main Trailer; only a few of the boys showed improvement in their walk with the Lord. And Betsy, though she sat with Jon at meals and meetings, still resided in the Main Trailer.

Jack and Bunny were pleased at the way Jon and Betsy had handled their folks—yet nothing changed. Jon still worked the fields all day and spent nights in the bunkhouse with three other guys; Betsy did chores in the kitchen and washhouse and roomed with Agnes.

Whenever Jon dropped by Bunny encouraged, "Soon, Brother Jonathan, very soon, y'all will be a happy family again," but nothing ever came of it. Betsy urged Jonathan to demand use of the Michael's trailer. Jon broached the subject with Jack once and was told, "When the time is right, we'll know." Pressing him further would only be counterproductive.

And Betsy still insisted that the Move was a cult.

"But Betts," Jon said, "… they know the Bible better than either of our church backgrounds. God brought us here. I can't deny the miraculous events that guided my decisions."

That had been days ago. Jon sighed and resumed hacking at the weeds around unproductive corn stalks.

He looked up to see Mickey driving the tractor toward the root cellar, hauling a few canned goods for storage. No one had been near the root cellar since the canned chickens had been stored weeks prior. Grateful for a break in hoeing, Jon dropped his hoe and trotted over to assist unloading the wagon. "Hey, Lester, take a break, let's give Mickey a hand," Jon called.

Lester dropped his hoe and jogged toward the root cellar. Mickey dismounted and disappeared inside with an armload of mason jars. Just as Jon and Les arrived, Mickey burst out the door and yanked it shut, still hugging the mason jars. "Yuck! Phah!"

Jon's eyes watered at the foul reek permeating the area. Mickey took a fresh breath and said, "Exploded! The chicken jars exploded! Must be 120 degrees in there. There's broken glass and rotten chicken everywhere. I've got to tell Brother William. You two stay here; keep everyone else out—especially the farm dogs. If they get a whiff of this they'll be rolling in it." With that Mickey took off on foot across the fields.

Minutes later William's pickup barreled around the corner and across the cornfield, leaving a trail of broken stalks in his wake. Jack was also in the pickup, along with Mick O'Shea and others. They jumped out of the vehicle and were momentarily engulfed in a dust cloud. Mickey led inside, holding a bandanna over his nose. William entered next, followed by Jack. Jonathan gazed into the dark, littered interior from the doorway. Waves of stench flowed out. Jon, fighting nausea, stepped back, allowing others to see.

"Ruined! All ruined," lamented Mick O'Shea. "All them chickens that gave their lives for us…"

"And everything else," William said, emerging from the root cellar. "All the herbs we'd hung up, potatoes, canned tomatoes… it never cooled down… We've lost our foodstore."

Jack was the last one out, pulling the door tight. "Well, praise the Lord," he said. "The Lord gives and the Lord takes away, blessed be the name of the Lord." Then to Mickey, "Knock it down. Cover it deep."

Mickey spent the rest of the afternoon scraping dirt from the cornfield to bury the root cellar.

THURSDAY, SEPTEMBER 21

Dear Mom, Dad and Danny,

It was good to get your letter. No I am not angry with you, nor have I stopped loving you. I have been very busy with farm chores etc. We are through with the first part of harvest, with the second part to begin soon.

Betsy and Jay are doing well. Jay is so—o big! Betsy is really getting stronger; soon she'll be able to take care of Jay. Then we, all three of us, can live together. The Lord is working patience in us, it seems that the Lord must work patience in those that would serve Him.

Meanwhile a fellow was brought into the camp, who I am, at various times during the day, helping overcome the demons who have tried to destroy him. He got messed up when he used drugs (LSD etc.) and listened to rock'n'roll music. I can remember when you both—Mom & Dad—warned Sonya and me against it. Sonya listened to you, but I didn't, however I was fortunate. Rock'n'roll is satanic. It does nothing but destroy and bring death spiritually. He came here really messed up and deceived but through love and truth he realized he was being tricked by Satan and he called upon Jesus to deliver him from his torment. And the Lord came in the power of the Anointing and several demon spirits left. A few of the stronger ones came back but most of them also, have left permanently. It's like what the LORD said when He told Joshua that He would not drive out all the enemies at once because the people of Israel could not fill the land that quickly and the wild beasts would take over the land.

I tell you this because demons are real and they do attack God's servants— God allows it to make His people stronger. If you would like, I could send you some scriptural proof of demons.

Well, let me talk about life instead of death. God has bountifully blessed me in showing me many areas of my life where my reactions are very displeasing to God and one by one, line upon line, precept upon precept God is bringing me to the measure of the stature of the fullness of Christ—that is, to fulfill my part in the body of Christ (Eph. 4:13) Well, glory to God!

I appreciate your concerns abut my schooling, I think you might be interested in knowing that many elders and members of this Move of God have attended such noteworthy institutions as Houghton, Nyack, Wheaton, Baptist Theological Seminary, Southern Baptist Seminary, Covenant and many more—Moody, Kings, etc. are some more. They have found out that there is a difference in knowing about God, and knowing or having union with Him. After all, Jesus Christ lives right inside of us—indwelling our soul—He is closer to us than our next breath, so to speak. Everyone who God has called into this Move had felt empty and unful-filled in the old order church system, just like me. I used to read the Bible and see where it said "Be ye perfect even as your Father in heaven is perfect" (Matt. 5:48), and "That they may be perfect in one that the world may know Thou hast sent me..." (John 17:23)—and wondered what was meant because everybody knows that Christians are just sinners saved by faith. But I Jn. 3 says that a holy, perfect, incorruptible seed has been placed within me, and that cannot sin!! Now I begin to understand that those perfection verses mean for me to yield to the Holy Ghost within me—to let that Christ nature flow out of my spirit and flow through my soul, through my body (I Thes. 5:23) and finally when all the members of the body of Christ have done this (and it will happen at once—in the twinkling of an eye) we will be fitly joined together (Eph. 4:16).

Another example that I used to wonder about was where is all the persecu-tion the Bible speaks of that Christians would have to endure? I dismissed it with thinking that perhaps the Caesars and Spanish Inquisition was what was meant, or maybe the Christians in Russia & China were to do the suffering in our age. But Jesus said to take up our cross daily and follow Him (Luke 9:23) when we as sons of God (I Jn. 3:1&2) do take up our cross daily and walk as Jesus did (by yielding to that Holy seed within) people around us will hate us and eventually persecute us, but in our unjust sufferings we are perfected (Matt. 5:11) and (Heb. 5:8&9).

I pray for you all daily, especially Dad and the pain he is enduring. Do go see a doctor if you haven't yet, there is so little room for being stubborn in this walk. I hope to be sending you a tape soon. That's all for now,

Love in Christ, your son, Jon.

TUESDAY, OCTOBER 10

Jon and Betsy strolled hand in hand down over the field, past the wash house to the parking lot. Jon fumbled in his pocket for the car keys, opened the door and slid behind the driver's seat. "Let's see if the battery still has enough juice to turn the engine over," he said. The engine chugged a few minutes then roared to life. "Hey, hey," Jon shouted. "I can't believe it! It's been months…"

Betsy smiled, flashing her green eyes at Jon. "My Dad got us a good car. He knows how to pick 'em." Then she said, "Jon, I think you should ask the elders if we can go home to visit our folks on Thanksgiving."

Letting the car idle, Jon said, "Oh Betts, we aren't even living together yet. I'm positive they won't allow that. Why, we'd have little Jay with us, and all that that entails… No, I'm sure they'd never give permission."

Betsy straightened up; a look of determination crossed her face. "I think they will. After all, I'm doing fine, now. I spend most of the day with Jay, and every spare minute with you. I'm recovered from my breakdown. I don't know why they don't let us live together. Thanksgiving is a month away, and I'm sure by then I'll be even stronger. I'm sure they'll give permission."

"Okay," Jon said, "… if you're so sure, you ask Brother Jack. If the elders say we can go, we'll go." Jon decided to not risk angering Betsy by direct confrontation; let the elders deal with it.

"All right, I will."

Jon nodded, sure nothing else would come of it.

Jon hustled to the Golden Tabernacle, Bible in hand, eager to join Betsy in the meeting. She waited just outside the doorway, all fancied-up in a pretty dress, her hair coifed. A bright smile lit her face as Jon rounded the corner. "Hi, Hon," she said.

Others passing through the portal gave the pair a knowing smile.

Jon kissed her lightly and took her hand. She resisted following, staying rooted to the spot. He looked back at her, eyebrows arched.

"I have news," she said quietly.

"News? From home?"

"No… news about home." Betsy smiled. "We're going home for Thanksgiving and Christmas!"

"Wha—at?"

Smiling demurely and lifting her fingers to toy with Jon's shirt button, she repeated, "I said, 'we're going home for Thanksgiving and Christmas.' I asked Brother Jack."

"And he said yes? I can't believe it. I'm going to ask him, myself."

"Go right ahead."

All through the praises and teaching Jon thought Betsy must have misunderstood. Neither Jack nor Bunny attended the meeting; their hands were full with a new girl recently come to the Main Trailer—the unmarried, pregnant daughter of an apostle.

FRIDAY, OCTOBER 13

"Brother Jack, may I see you a minute?" Jon said as three elders were headed into the Golden Tabernacle. William and Chester gave Jonathan a quick glance, then continued on inside without Jack.

"Y'all know how I like my coffee," Jack called after his companions. I'll be right along." Then turning to Jonathan, he said, "What's on your mind, Brother Jonathan?" Looking at his watch, he added, "Where were you going just now?"

"Down to the farmside to help replace some posts in Solomon's pen. We just finished Bible study. I, uh, I'd like to ask you a question. Did you tell Betsy that we could go home and visit our folks for the holidays?"

"I did."

Jon blinked, sure that there must be more. Finally he asked, "Do you mean we can go to Pennsylvania, Betsy, Jay and me?"

"I don't see any reason why not. Sister Betsy seems to be doing pretty well. By the time Thanksgiving comes around, she'll be able to handle the trip and the emotions of visiting y'all's folks. You do want to go, don't you?"

A ray of hope broke over Jon's soul. "Uh, sure, sure, I'd—we'd like to go—for a visit."

"Is that all you wanted to know?"

Dazed, Jon nodded. He numbly walked down the meadow toward the farmside. Going home? They were going home! Joy welled up within and he skipped the rest of the way to the farm side. They were going home!

Dear Dad,

I trust that you are being patient in your present distress. I also trust that you are making the job of the nurses and doctors around you much easier than is your custom to do, by not complaining and teasing too much. The Lord is doing a work of patience and being contented in any circumstance in you. Once you realize God let this situation happen to you to do a work of glory for His honor in you, this unpleasant circumstance will be more tolerable. As Paul said: "… and we glory in

tribulations also, knowing that tribulation worketh patience; and patience expe-
rience, and experience, hope; and hope maketh not ashamed because the love of
God is shed abroad in our hearts by the Holy Ghost who is given unto us..."

Well, I don't want to get to preaching, so I'll tell you some good news. Betsy,
Jay and I are coming up for a visit at Thanksgiving. Are you glad? I knew you
would be. We'll leave Mississippi on November 20 and get to Betsy's house in time
for Thanksgiving. We'll stay there a week or two then come on out to the Poconos
for over Christmas. After that we'll probably come back down to Mississippi. So
that will give you and us time to fellowship with each other. Also you can become
better acquainted with your grandson.

Well, I hope this letter has fed you some life and lifted your spirit to rejoicing.
We'll see you soon. Give Mom & Danny our love,

In the redeeming love of Christ Jesus,
Your son, Jonathan

Jon reread the letter. It was preachy… Oh well, his folks needed to hear the truth sooner or later. And… he wanted them to understand that their trip was just a visit.

MONDAY, OCTOBER 30

Jon stood eagerly outside the Main Trailer holding a box containing some of Betsy's belongings. Within minutes the door opened and Betsy tripped lightly down the stairs carrying her suitcases. Jack Halstead had chosen the interval between supper and the evening meeting to inform Jon that he and Betsy could move into the Michael's trailer. It was dusky by the time Betsy emerged with her things, but her smile lit up the twilight for Jon.

"Well, praise the Lord!" someone called after the couple as they walked the pebble pathway. "Hallelujah!" called another, then someone else shouted, "Glory be!" Jon's face flushed. Their reunification was no secret, even though he and Betsy had only known for the last half-hour. Another girl had come to the farm with severe problems, and Betsy's bed was needed. Jon hurried to stow Betsy's things in the tiny trailer. He'd gather his things from the bunkhouse after the meeting.

The elders felt that the timing wasn't quite right for their baby to be with them yet. Jon and Betsy needed to get accustomed to each other first. Jack cautioned them that this was on a trial basis, to see how things went.

"I'll just put my stuff on—there's two beds!" Betsy said with dismay.

"I know, I know, but at least we'll be together. We can make do for a little while."

"But… I've been dreaming about falling asleep snuggled in your arms. And… where's the light switch?"

"Uh, there's no electricity. Marvin and I used an oil lamp."

"I suppose there's no heat either?"

Jon smiled wanly. "We could think of it as getting prepared for the mission field," he suggested.

"It's not at all like I pictured it," Betsy said and sat on a bed.

Jon sat and draped his arm over her shoulders. "I'll talk to Brother Jack about improving these conditions. But anyway," he said taking her chin and drawing her face close, "…we're together, and alone." They kissed for a long, passionate moment.

"I will praise the name of God with a song, And will magnify Him with thanksgiving…" The song Jon had written resounded over the loudspeakers, calling the faithful to the meeting.

Jon and Betsy parted, staring into each other's eyes. "We mustn't be late for meeting," Jon said. "Where's your Bible?"

Betsy grabbed her Bible from the box. The two then headed across the darkened field guided by the glow of the streetlight from the Golden Tabernacle.

Though neither were able to concentrate on the teaching, they gave earnest praise during the worship, casting shy looks at each other as they lifted their hands and gustily sang, "Victory in Jesus" and "John Saw the Multitude…"

After the meeting Chester stepped up to the microphone and announced, "Brothers Jonathan McComb, Lester Ingles, Terry Soo and Fred Caliano will report to me in fifteen minutes."

"I can't believe it!" Jon groaned.

"Why did he call your name?" Betsy asked.

"Clean-up crew. Every two weeks he assigns a new clean-up crew to break down tables and sweep the building, then set up for breakfast. It takes an hour and a half… I can't believe he chose me, today of all days. In fact… this is the first time he's ever chosen me… as if he's been waiting for the night you and I would be together."

"You're not coming back to the trailer with me? I'm afraid to go through that dark field by myself. Tell them this isn't right."

"You're right, I won't let them… wait, wait a minute. This might be a test—or a trap. What if the elders planned it this way so they could say to you, 'If you're afraid to be out there alone, you're not ready to be with Jon yet?' Or what if they judge my refusal to do clean up as rebellion—proof that we're not ready to be together? They might even say we're not ready to visit home."

J.M. MACLEOD

"Would they do that?"

Jon cautiously surveyed the room. William and Chester were discretely watching them. "Maybe I'm paranoid, but if we comply, they'll have nothing to use against us."

"I'm scared to be out there all alone."

"I'll walk you out; you read the Bible till I come. You'll be okay. Marvin and Danny will be right next door."

"I really do want us to be together, and I really do want to go home and see my parents."

"Then you'll do it?"

"If you walk me out and come back as soon as you can."

Jon squeezed Betsy's hand. "Good girl. We're so close now, let's not let anything intervene."

Jon walked Betsy out to their tiny trailer, lit the oil lamp, said a brief prayer with her, and jogged back, arriving just in time to start clean up.

"Isn't this your first night back with your wife?" Terry Soo asked, his eyes steadily holding Jon's

Jon nodded and took the other end of a table Terry had broken down.

"This isn't right that they should do this to both of you. You've been through so much."

Jon shrugged. "I'm willing to serve my brothers and sisters, even at my own displeasure." It sounded trite even as he said it, nevertheless, if any elders or their spies were listening, it was the appropriate thing to say.

Terry shook his head. "I've seen too many things here that are not God's wisdom. There are other Christian groups with even more revelation and power than the Move, you know."

Jon stopped. "There are? Who? Where?"

Terry lifted one hand and waved off the questions. "That is not to say that Sam Fife is one whit behind any of them… he has so much revelation—it must be of God. Yet, all the elders in this Move are not of his caliber." He briefly turned his eyes toward Chester.

They grabbed another table. Terry asked, "Do you know what your calling is?"

Remembering Bunny's rebuke to David for revealing his calling, Jon cautiously said only, "Yes."

Terry waited, then discerning that no more was forthcoming, uttered, "Ahh," and smiled as he and Jon hefted another table. With a nod of his head he said, "I was praying and I asked the Lord about your calling… I could not believe what He told me. I said to Him, 'Lord, Jonathan? Are you sure?'"

They placed the last of the tables along the wall and began breaking down chairs.

Terry shrugged and said, "I don't see it possible; but the Lord can do anything."

An hour and twenty minutes later Jon set the last chair by a table and headed out the door.

Chester was waiting just outside. Looking past Jon into the night sky he said, "The Lord exhorts men to lay their lives down for their wives. I trust you know how to control…er… your needs for your wife's sake." With that he turned and walked away.

Betsy was asleep, an open Bible on her lap. Jon gently pulled a blanket over her.

Jon was on clean-up for the entire two weeks. Both he and Betsy eagerly looked forward to the end of his assignment so they could walk to their abode after meeting and stay together.

SUNDAY, NOVEMBER 13

"Brothers Jonathan McComb, Mitch Lukowski, Kip Harkins and Harold Michaels, report to me in fifteen minutes," Chester said from the podium.

Betsy's hand tightened on Jon's. "Not again!" she pouted as they queued for the evening snack.

"Shh-shh, it's all right. It's only a week till we go home. I don't know if he's making up for the time I wasn't assigned duty, or he's trying to keep us from being intimate or…"

"Well, if that's what he's trying to do, it didn't work did it?" Betsy giggled.

"Not so loud; others will hear."

Betsy squeezed Jon's hand again and gave him an impish grin.

SATURDAY, NOVEMBER 19

Betsy sheltered baby Jay against the raw wind. "You go have a look around if you want. I've seen enough of this place. She retreated from the frigid gusts, nuzzling their baby close to her all the way to the Michael's trailer. Jay had been with Jon and Betsy for the last week, and since there wasn't much farm work to do, they spent most of their time together as a family.

Jon watched Betsy walk along the pebble pathway, then turned his gaze across the sloping meadow to the runoff pond and sighed. He drank in every detail, wanting to remember the vistas, sheds, trailers, rutted roads… everything. He hiked down to the farmside, not missing any detail. This was where the Move hatched sons of God and grew them to maturity; he was one of those hatchlings. He had a calling. After their visit north, he and his family would return to grow deeper in revelation and service, eventually discovering where the Lord wanted them.

Betsy had threatened, "Once we get off this place, I'm never coming back!" Jon knew she meant it, but… she'd change her mind once she got back out in Babylon and saw how wicked the world really was. He smiled as he passed the cursed fire ant mound, the garden of hot peppers, the potato and corn fields where he'd spent hours under the hot sun, the leveled root cellar and the billy goat pen that again needed posts replaced.

SUNDAY, NOVEMBER 20, 8:00A.M.

The Chevy sat in the parking lot; its trunk and back seat jammed with belongings. Betsy slid into the passenger seat, their son on her lap. Jon closed her door and walked around to the driver side, pausing for one last look. He slid behind the wheel and noted that it was raining—just the opposite of the first moment they arrived to a burst of sunlight after that dismal trip nine months ago.

A lone figure hunching over against the rain rambled down the pathway toward the Golden Tabernacle. It was David, the seer—the first person that had greeted him that long ago day.

David looked up and smiled. "Remember who you are, and what you're called to." The very words Bunny said every time anyone left the farm for any reason.

Jon headed the BelAir past the mailbox with "Church at Sapa" scrawled on its side, turned right and headed for the Natchez Trace and parts north.

EPILOGUE

Let us hear the conclusion of the whole matter... Eccl.12:13

The McComb's spent the weeks before and after Thanksgiving with the Rutlidges in Sunbury, Pennsylvania, then drove east to be with Jon's family in the Poconos for Christmas.

They didn't contact the local Move body, nor did local body members contact them, though they were well aware that the McComb's were back home.

After being out from under the constant barrage of meetings every day (and twice on Sunday) Jonathan began to see the flaws in Move teachings—things that Betsy had perceived even through her confusion. Such flaws as:

Christians are not called to isolate themselves from the world, but to be salt and light in it.

The Gospel is to be proclaimed until Christ returns, not selfishly kept hidden so Move members can attain "perfection."

Trusting hyper-spiritual interpretations of scriptures that only elders could correctly grasp is a sure way to deception, especially when their interpretation of "the spirit of the word" opposes the plainly written letter of the word. The Holy Spirit will not ever contradict that which He has inspired.

The discipline administered by the elders in Sapa Mississippi was not only physically harmful and, at times, dangerous, but also humiliating. Instead of the love of Christ leading to repentance and resulting in true spiritual growth, those who came under their discipline were often hardened in their hearts; many of those young people later left not only the Move, but the Faith as well. Many still bear the hurt and bitterness caused by the callus attitudes and actions of those who were supposed to be gentle shepherds of the sheep.

The McComb's desired their story be shared with Body of Christ at large so others who have a hunger to know God better but are not well-versed in the scriptures could take a warning from their experiences and avoid suffering a similar fate. Though they survived the ordeal, they bear painful scars.

Jonathan and Betsy never returned to the Move's meetings nor the Mississippi farm. Instead Jon's parents had a finished basement which made an ideal place for Jon and Betsy to start anew.

Jon and Betsy became involved in a Baptist Church with Jon's parents and eventually became youth group leaders. Within a couple of years, Jon was elected to the deacon board. In time they bought a house, and Jon worked full time for a local school district while Betsy raised their four children at home. Jon and Betsy eventually became involved with a coffeehouse ministry, street evangelism and led home-based bible studies.

In spite of the false teaching and mistreatment that Jon and Betsy were subjected to while in the Move, they still believe in the Baptism and gifts of the Holy Spirit, as well as foundational Christian truths taught by the Move. But they also realize that many of the Move's doctrines are wrong; and the bizarre methods of correction and discipline utilized by the elders bordered on cruelty, not Christ's love.

In trying to come to grips with the seemingly contradictory events of miraculously answered prayers leading them to a group of self-deluded, controlling religious group, the McComb's have come to understand, For the gifts and calling of the Lord are without repentance (Romans 11:29) i.e., that a person (such as those in eldership in the Move) may receive spiritual gifts and leadership appointment at a certain stage in their life, but may later wander off the path of truth and as a result, stray from demonstrating Christ's love. Though such errant departure (whether in doctrine, ethics or morals) does not bar them from using God's gifts, nevertheless, it is all the more reason for believers to stay vigilant and compare everything against the standard of scripture.

Over the years they have wrestled with the question of demon possession versus bi-polar illness. To the best of their understanding, it seems that a physiological weakness of Betsy's was exploited by demons that overwhelmed her mind with false, religious feelings and experiences, especially in the intensely spiritual environment of the

Move. Medication helps her maintain a balance so she can recognize and repel any such spiritual attacks.

As to the "deep insights" of the Move…Sam Fife's method of interpreting an implicit "spirit of the word" that is contradictory to the explicit letter of the word is dangerous. If there are deeper insights to be gained from certain Bible passages, such insights will never contradict the plain, written meaning of the letter of the word. Holding to this method of exegesis helped Jon and Betsy get deprogrammed from the Move's heretical teachings.

Many months after Jon and Betsy returned to East Stroudsburg they were visited by Doug, a young Move member from Mississippi, who was passing through on his way to a farm in Canada. Doug updated them on farm activities.

Seeing the dramatic effect that lithium had had on Betsy, the elders tried giving lithium to every person in the Main Trailer with behavioral problems. Doug also informed them that one of Agnes' children, the older boy—Fred—had been tragically killed in a farming accident in Canada. Doug also said that because the McComb's had never returned, everyone on the farm was forbidden to sing any of the songs Jon had penned.

Some years later the McComb's learned that Sam Fife had received a revelation that he was to put his wife aside for a year and co-habit with a certain woman elder in order to conceive one of the end-time prophets of Revelation 11. After a year passed and no conception occurred, Fife confessed his error at a Move convention. This false prophecy and subsequent immoral actions made no difference to his leadership role.

Fife then began preaching that the Lord had shown him that he wasn't going to physically die, but would be alive when the Lord returned.

Fife's airplane crashed into a Central American mountainside in 1979, ending his life.

THE END